Behind
the
Forbidden Door

Behind the Forbidden Door

TRAVELS IN UNKNOWN CHINA

Tiziano Terzani

HENRY HOLT AND COMPANY · NEW YORK

Library of Congress Cataloging-in-Publication Data
Terzani, Tiziano.
Behind the forbidden door.
Translation of: Fremder unter Chinesen.
Includes index.
1. China—Description and travel—1976–
2. Terzani, Tiziano—Journeys—China.   1. Title.
DS712.T4213 1986   951.05'7   86–3093
ISBN 0-03-008508-X

First published as *Fremder unter Chinesen*
by Rowohlt, Hamburg, in 1984.

First published in English as *The Forbidden Door*
by Asia 2000 Ltd, Hong Kong, in 1985.

First published in Great Britain by Allen & Unwin in 1986

Printed in the United States of America
1 3 5 7 9 10 8 6 4 2

ISBN 0-03-008508-X

To Folco and Saskia

On whom I imposed my love for China

THE PEOPLE'S REPUBLIC OF CHINA

USSR

MONGOLIA

Urumqi

Kashgar

XINJIANG

GANSU

QINGHAI

TIBET

Lhasa

SICHUAN

Chengdu

NEPAL

BHUTAN

INDIA

BANGLADESH

Kunming

YUNNAN

BURMA

VIET

LAOS

CAMBODIA

Contents

Preface

I became Deng Tiannuo in 1968. At that time China was in
the middle of the Cultural Revolution and Mao, from
Peking, was the spark that lit the prairie fire of western youth,
inspired by his anti-authoritarian message. Seen from afar,
China seemed the most creative, innovative place on earth and
Mao a genius attempting the greatest experiment of social
engineering in the history of mankind. His goal was a more
just, more humane society.

Since time immemorial, young generations have been
fascinated by new ideas and have often been oblivious of the
consequences new theories entail in practice. My generation
was no different, and many were caught in the illusion pro-
jected by Mao's China. If our world was old and imperfect,
if past hopes had turned into great delusions, here was a new
chance. China was not going to be another Soviet Union or
another Cuba. China was different, and thus China became
a myth, the myth of "the other."

I wanted to see it for myself and prepared by studying the
Chinese language and Chinese politics and by giving myself
a Chinese name — Deng Tiannuo — so I would be less foreign
when my time came to live among the Chinese. It took me years
of waiting because only a few selected and trusted ones were
called to "paradise."

I had to wait for Mao's death and for Deng Xiaoping to
open China's doors before I could set my sails and leave with
my family for Peking. I arrived in January, 1980, and it was
immediately obvious that reality was less attractive than
dreams.

Looking for the unique form of socialism that had allegedly
been built there, I found only the ruins of an utterly failed
experiment. Looking for the new culture that had supposedly
sprung out of the revolution, I came across only the stumps
of the old culture that had been methodically, systematically
destroyed in the process.

Among the many doors Deng Xiaoping had opened were
those of the concentration camps and re-education schools to

which some 20 million intellectuals had been sent. Meeting some of the people who had been victims of Mao's folly, I quickly realized that Deng Tiannuo's dream had been China's nightmare.

It had been inspiring, within the protected atmosphere of Columbia University in New York, to read Mao's slogans, such as "Do not cut off people's heads for, unlike cabbages, they do not grow again." But it was a different matter to discover that, behind the facade of propaganda, heads had rolled, people had been tortured, and that, at the end of the Great Proletarian Cultural Revolution, China was like a barren desert full of dispirited, disorientated people.

Deng Xiaoping's China, unlike Mao's, was willing to be seen and studied. People spoke almost freely and for a while even the walls told stories of what really had happened — Democracy Wall being one of the best sources. This period was a unique opportunity and I could not miss it.

I traveled wherever I could, from western Xinjiang to eastern Shandong, from the southernmost island of Hainan to the far north of Manchuria, trying to talk to as many people as possible. Not without some difficulties, for the attitude of today's Chinese officials toward outsiders is not much different from that of the nineteenth century mandarin who, for the first time facing a foreigner able to speak Chinese, turned to his aides and asked them, "Who is the traitor who taught him our language?"

I wanted to live in a normal Chinese house in a Chinese neighborhood, but that was impossible. Foreigners had to stay behind the walls of the diplomatic compound, whose gates were guarded at first by armed soldiers and later by policemen. I wanted to mix with Chinese but that, too, turned out to be difficult because all unofficial contacts between a foreigner and a citizen of the People's Republic are illegal, even though nobody seems to remember the law that says so.

An old gentleman I had met a couple of times soon after my arrival in Peking let me know through a common acquaintance that I should not contact him again. He had been visited by the Public Security Bureau and told that he could see me, but only on the condition that each time he wrote a report on what we did and what we discussed. That he considered too much of a humiliation, and we never saw each other again.

In today's China, a foreign journalist who wants to interview a government official or simply meet with a writer, a painter or a university professor has to write an application. If permission is granted, the encounter takes place in the usual reception room, with armchairs fitted with white antimacassars, in the presence of a Party secretary and with somebody taking notes of all the questions and answers. This procedure frustrated me and I soon looked for my own way into China.

I started traveling by train, not in the special compartments for foreigners, but on "hard seats." I started bicycling through the provinces, talking to normal people and listening to peasants telling simple stories about their villages and their families. I got interested in Peking's old pastimes and games and started to raise crickets and pigeons and to meet, at the free markets of the capital, old men who taught me the ancient art of making concerts with these creatures.

Thus, I slowly came across a magnificent, human China, a China I had never dreamed about, a China much more real than the one the officials want to present to the western public. In this way I made my little discoveries, like this one in Tibet. While the group I was traveling with went to see the usual red flag factory and the usual school, with a borrowed bicycle I managed to reach a secluded place north of Lhasa and watch a sky burial. Local tour guides say this ceremony, where human corpses are cut into pieces and fed to the vultures, no longer exists.

Yet, by doing these things, I gradually left the path set for me.

As in the fable in which the guest of an enchanted castle is told he can do whatever he likes except look behind a certain closed door, for otherwise he would release some evil spirits, I too could not resist that forbidden door. And punctually the evil spirits caught up with me.

After four years in China, I was arrested, interrogated and re-educated for a whole month, as if I were a Chinese. Yet, just by being treated like a Chinese, I was given a unique chance to take the ultimate trip into China's heart of darkness.

11

Suddenly I was swallowed into the belly of the whale and experienced the power of the police which, in spite of the recent immense changes in the country, remains the dread of one billion Chinese.

Finally I was expelled, accused of a crime I had not committed.

Lu Xun, the celebrated modern Chinese writer, explained it decades ago. "When you want to drown a dog, charge him with rabies."

My "rabies" had been the attempt to break the wall that separated me from the realities of the country. My crime had been to search for an unrehearsed China; to look for a way out of the maze of prohibitions and taboos designed to keep me away from the people. I could not have done otherwise.

I went to China as to a second home, and what I saw there meant more to me than just a "good story" which one reports. When I realized, for instance, to what extent the communists had destroyed Peking, I felt about it as I would feel if I were to discover that Florence, my hometown, had been devastated by a man-made earthquake.

It was in friendship that I approached the Chinese, and it was not long before I became immersed in their predicament, in their quandary — a great people and civilization torn between the nostalgia for a golden past and the realities of a gray present.

I did not pretend to know what was good or bad for China and certainly could not read into her future. I could, however, look into her past and examine what thirty years of communism had done to the country.

If Mao's policies had brought China great miseries, what Deng Xiaoping was doing in order to half-reverse those policies left me equally skeptical.

Undoubtedly, Deng's reforms have brought advantages and some material progress, but they have been accompanied by new injustices, new privileges and corruption. Above all, though, they are making the Chinese dangerously insecure about their own culture, their own values and ways.

Deng's slogans, such as "To get rich is glorious," instinctively made me worry about the new course. How can it be glorious to be rich in a country that is doomed to be poor for a long time to come? How can becoming rich be an ideal for rebuilding a nation and educating a new generation?

Though poor and underdeveloped, China is not simply another country of the third world. China has an immense tradition and civilization of its own. Why then, does this great country forgo, even renounce, its own path to development and happiness and borrow instead ideas and values born under completely different skies?

By adopting western standards in its economy, culture and even, clumsily, in fashion, is China not renouncing its uniqueness, thus giving the Chinese a new inferiority complex which could, in turn, cause an explosion and yet another backlash?

These and other questions I asked aloud. I asked them publicly at press conferences, I asked them privately at home while Chinese friends pointed worriedly at the ceiling to remind me of the microphones that the Public Security Bureau is said to have installed in every foreigner's flat. I never thought it necessary to hide my feelings or opinions for they had a quality the Chinese usually respect: sincerity.

Having planned to spend a few more years in China, I had no intention of postponing the transcribing of my thoughts until after my departure, to when I would be "safely" abroad.

The pages that follow may give the impression that I wrote them because I was expelled. The opposite is true. I was expelled because I wrote them.

They were never written in hatred, but sometimes in anger and, more often, in sorrow.

Hong Kong, April 1985.

1

Free to Fly but Only in a Cage

China under Deng Xiaoping

At the center of the center of China lies a corpse that nobody dares remove. Wrapped in the red flag of the Communist Party, protected in a glass coffin, inside a huge, dreary mausoleum, in the middle of the Square of Heavenly Peace, the embalmed body of Mao Zedong is a symbolic link between today's China and her recent past. It is also an ominous point of reference for her future.

Deng Xiaoping, the man who has taken Mao's place at the helm of the country, has "put heaven on earth and earth on heaven," as the Chinese say about the immense changes brought about under his leadership. But he stopped in front of this awesome monument of marble and granite into which China's ideological guidelines have been cemented for posterity.

Unlike Mao, Deng does not write poetry and his philosophy is simple common sense. There are no statues of him around the country, no portraits in public places or homes, yet in only seven years in power Deng has proved himself to be one of the greatest revolutionaries this country has known. He has undone whatever Mao did, he has hailed whatever Mao condemned, he has tried to reconstruct whatever Mao, in his folly, destroyed.

Mao's folly had a logic: he thought the revolution had unleashed immense forces, he thought that China had the strength to take a path never explored before by human societies in search of justice and happiness. Thus he closed China to outside influences and tried to build a completely new society, where people would be equal and where each would work to the best of his ability for the common good. His plan failed and engulfed the country in a civil war which brought it to the verge of collapse.

Deng Xiaoping inherited a dramatic situation: the peasants

were unhappy, the minorities along the borders rebellious, the intellectuals disaffected, the youth uneducated, the economy in a shambles, the Army weak, the country isolated on the world scene. It took great courage to pick up the pieces of that disaster and take stock of a utopia that had scarred, but also inspired, millions of people. Deng Xiaoping had that courage.

Mao had put politics before economics, thus condemning China to underdevelopment. Deng reversed this priority and launched the Four Modernizations. In order to build his new society, Mao had pursued, like other revolutionaries of his kind from Stalin to Pol Pot, the sacrilegious goal of creating a "new man." Deng, having witnessed the miseries that goal had provoked, gave man back to nature and let his instincts loose. Mao had stressed moral over material incentives. Deng spoke of "raising the standard of living of the people."

Under his rule, hardly a single aspect of Chinese life has remained untouched and Deng's China looks completely different from Mao's. Today's China is like any other country: people dress colorfully and talk to each other; lovers go hand in hand; children, when asked what they want to be as grown-ups, answer "pilot," "doctor," "train conductor" and not, as in the past, "whatever the Party wants me to be." The skyline of Chinese cities has changed with the mushrooming of tall residential buildings ordered by Deng Xiaoping. The fields in the countryside are green expanses, now that they have been divided into small plots with each peasant growing his own crop.

The propaganda image of Mao's China used to be a picture of a group of smiling peasants sitting in a circle and reading the latest editorial of the *People's Daily*. The propaganda image of Deng's China appeared recently in all Chinese newspapers: a photo of a peasant family standing proudly in front of a Japanese car they had bought.

Deng has reversed, contradicted, reshaped almost everything that was characteristic of Mao's China. One thing he has not touched, however, is the ideological framework in which the country moves. Marxism–Leninism and Mao Zedong-thought remain the guiding principles of the country and the Chinese Communist Party, the monopolistic center of power. Thus,

15

daring as they are, Deng's reforms are withdrawn every time those principles are challenged, and newly granted freedoms are curbed every time the Party's indisputable legitimacy to rule is threatened.

One of Mao's most resolute steps toward his utopia was the establishment of the People's Communes in 1958. One of the most courageous and, for its implications, most significant moves by Deng Xiaoping has been to dismantle the communes, thus freeing the peasants from the unproductive constraints of collectivism and unleashing the repressed entrepreneurial energy of millions of people.

The results have been impressive: agricultural production has increased at a rate double that of the past 20 years; the redundant labor force has turned to various private activities, and free markets have sprung up all over the country; and the reintroduction of money among peasants has turned the Chinese countryside into a huge market for consumer goods.

"Mao gave us liberation, Deng gives us prosperity," reads a recurrent slogan in the countryside. "Thirty years ago we lived with a cow. Now we live in a two-storey house," the peasants write on their newly constructed homes.

How long will this responsibility system last? The private plots given to the peasants on the basis of yearly contracts are already exploited to the maximum. To keep up with the present growth rate some investment is needed, but the peasants are not ready to put money into land which does not belong to them.

Deng is therefore facing a simple dilemma: either to let the market forces play freely and allow the successful peasants to acquire more land at the cost of the unsuccessful ones; or let the state nationalize agriculture by combining small plots into bigger ones, thus starting anew the process of cooperatives and collectives introduced in the fifties, something which is feared by the peasants.

The same is true of the private sector of the economy. Mao had abolished it. Deng allowed it and now he encourages it. All over China there are private restaurants, cafes, hotels, private tailors, hairdressers, doctors, traders; there are private construction companies and factories, private transport companies and private schools engaging millions of unemployed youths and semi-employed peasants. The internal logic of these enterprises is to grow and to expand, but there are no rules fixing their limits and no legal guarantees for their survival.

Basically, the economy must remain socialist while the private sector is permitted to move within the framework of the national plan. "It is like a bird free to fly, but only in a cage," says a leading Peking economist.

Mao had a vision of a new China. Deng Xiaoping has none, and many of his reforms look like experiments tried out in order to solve this or that problem but without any commitment to accept their ultimate consequences. Deng sees the necessity of importing western technology, but he does not intend to import the ideology that comes with it. That is why he gave his approval to the campaign against "spiritual pollution."

In order to pacify the minorities and gain respectability with international public opinion, he proclaims the principle of freedom of religion. However, he wants it to be limited to Islam, Lamaism, and Christianity, the religions of some of China's minorities. He does not want to have a revival of Buddhism and Taoism, which are the more traditional and thus the more dangerous religions of the Chinese masses.

Deng wants to build up industry, but he does not want to leave all decisions to managers and technicians: Party secretaries still have the last word. He sees clearly that there cannot be modernization without the participation of intellectuals, but he does not want to give them the freedom to think and to express their thoughts. Whenever they try to question politics and power they are immediately silenced.

Deng is intrigued by capitalism and its successes and has given orders to experiment with it and learn from it. But in the newly opened management schools of Shanghai and Dalian, where young Chinese are studying the capitalist science, pupils must attend courses in Marxism–Leninism and Mao Zedong-thought as well. What Deng wants is to refine the socialist system, to make it more efficient with whatever means are available. What he does not want to do is to change it, let alone turn China into a capitalist country.

In the enthusiam of having rediscovered China as an immense market and as a potential ally against the Soviet Union, the west often forgets a highly important point: China is and wants to remain a communist country. As such the Chinese system in the long run is bound to have more affinity with Soviet communism than with any western system. Much as in the past when the European and American left were enchanted by Maoism, the right on both sides of the Atlantic Ocean is now fascinated by Dengism. The Chinese remain the greatest illusionists of the world. Only the illusion changes.

Mao died on September 9, 1976. A month later, in the course of a well-planned and well-executed putsch staged by the old guard within the Army and the Party, Mao's widow and closest followers were arrested. The Chinese, and now everybody else parroting them, call this group the Gang of Four. Here one point has to be made absolutely clear: the Gang of Four never existed. It was invented by Deng Xiaoping and his henchmen in order to blame the disasters and the crimes of the Cultural Revolution on a limited number of people (indeed four) and not on the real culprit, the multi-million-member Communist Party of China.

At that time it seemed that China was at the dawn of a new era. The removal of Mao's portraits from around the country, the announcement that the "criminals" of the past would be brought to trial, the open discussion of the mistakes of the Cultural Revolution, the free expression at Democracy Wall, gave people both outside and inside China the impression that Deng Xiaoping really wanted to turn a page and write a completely new chapter of Chinese history. A few people even thought that the monopoly of power by the Communist Party was over and a young dissident, Wei Jingsheng, publicly called for "the fifth modernization," democracy. Without this, he said, the other four would never be achieved.

Deng Xiaoping, who had opened up Democracy Wall, suddenly closed it down again and had Wei Jingsheng sentenced to 15 years' imprisonment. The Peking Spring, as the shortlived period of freedom of expression came to be known, was quickly over and the literary and artistic production that had blossomed between 1978 and 1980 sank back into obtuseness and orthodoxy.

The privatization of the economy and the breakdown of the collective mode of social organization, in which everybody is his neighbor's policeman, has loosened the control over the population and has indeed forced Deng Xiaoping to proceed to a fifth modernization (but not the one wanted by Wei Jingsheng): the modernization of the police apparatus. Deng has divided the old Ministry for Public Security into two separate bodies: one in charge of the surveillance of the internal population; the other to take care of espionage, counter-espionage and surveillance of foreigners in China.

Units of the People's Liberation Army have been transferred, under new command, to the two new police bodies; large funds have been put at their disposal and sophisticated electronic equipment has been bought for them from West Germany and Japan. The ideological, structural model for these organs is the Soviet KGB. The methods used in their work are also the same. As China opens up to the world and more and more Chinese come into contact with foreigners and foreign ideas, social controls and repression must become more strict and severe. This explains the increased power of the police and the recent wave of executions throughout China.

Many of the hopes of 1978-1980 have turned out to be illusions. Yet Deng Xiaoping's regime remains a popular one, especially because people know that the only possible alternatives would be either a return to the radical ideology of Maoism (possibly in the form of a military/police dictatorship) or, even worse, chaos. This is why people stand behind Deng and why his only real opposition is in the ranks of the Army, the police, and the Party, from which Deng has not yet been able to remove all the remnants of the radical past.

In today's China there are still plenty of people nostalgic for the Maoist days, and most of them are in precisely those institutions upon which any communist regime has to rely. For the time being these military men, policemen and apparatchiki disguise themselves, pretending allegiance to the new line. But in keeping a low profile, they are only waiting for an opportunity to strike back and settle accounts with their old enemies who are now in power.

19

Thanks to his prestige, Deng has so far been able to keep all these dark forces within his own regime at bay. Whether after Deng's death his designated successors, Zhao Ziyang at the head of the government, and Hu Yaobang at the head of the Party, will manage to do the same, remains an open question. Time plays an important role and the more time that goes by the better are their chances. "If only Deng Xiaoping could live another 100 years...," one hears said again and again from the man in the street, who contemplates with fear Deng's mortality.

When that day comes, Deng will bequeath to his successors a China that is in much better condition than the China he inherited. Yet it will be a China without faith or ideals. With his utopia, Mao, at least at the beginning, had inspired the people. He had made them dream. The young thought they were the vanguard of a revolutionary movement that would sweep the world. No longer. "For the revolution we could die," says a former Red Guard. "How could we die for a refrigerator?"

Old China was a universe to itself, and believed in the fiction of being the center of the world. By keeping away all external influences, while trying to build up a new but completely Chinese society, Mao continued that fiction. Deng Xiaoping, by opening the doors of the country, has broken the spell and China must now painfully come to grips with the fact that she is just an underdeveloped country — the biggest of them all.

Old China is dead, Mao's new China was never born and Deng's China, having renounced the claim of being a universe to itself, is now struggling to become, at best, a copy of the rest of the world. The Chinese deserve better, for as a people they are far from dead. When the portraits of Marx, Engels, Lenin and Stalin adorn China's main square on great socialist occasions, it is sad to think that this great country, with its long history and immense culture, had to resort to the ideas of those four extremely alien, western gentlemen in trying to find a cure for her illnesses. Even more sad is to see how the Chinese, with their enormous cultural energies, are still today not given the opportunity to use them in search of new ways.

20

That glass coffin in the center of Peking not only contains the remains of Mao and of his shattered utopia. It contains as well a symbolic commitment to an ideology that has brought China her liberation, but has also restrained her material and spiritual development. That ideology, communism, is no longer creative. It has lost the ability to inspire and to move and has only preserved the power to keep the country together in fear and repression.

While that corpse remains at the center of the center of China, the Chinese will not have the freedom to set their own course, or the fantasy to invent their own future.

2

Death by a Thousand Cuts

The destruction of old Peking

Once upon a time, in a faraway land, there was a wonderful city. It had rich palaces, stupendous temples, colorful triumphal arches, magnificent gardens and thousands of harmonious, gray houses. Each was built around a peaceful courtyard, all aligned with the regular chessboard scheme of streets and lanes.

All around, the city had 26 kilometers of huge, imposing walls. These walls had gorgeous gates, guarded by stone lions. It was a sacred city, constructed at the edge of a desert, according to plans that had come directly from heaven.

It had a magic spell. It had a bewildering charm. "Pékin est le dernier refuge de l'inconnu et du merveilleux sur terre" (Peking is the only remaining refuge of the unknown and the marvelous in the world), Pierre Loti wrote in 1900. "Awe-inspiring," Arnold Toynbee called it in 1930.

In 1949, when the communists took it over, Peking was still unique. It was a supreme example of architectural magnificence, a city of lingering splendor that seemed meant to live for ever.

No more. Peking is dying. The walls are gone, the gates are gone, the arches are gone. Gone are most of the temples, the palaces, the gardens, and more and more of centuries-old Peking vanishes every day under the blows of hammers and the crushing of bulldozers.

The city has lost its inner order that once reflected the geometry of the universe. Where there was harmony and perfection, chaos and confusion are now taking over.

"If Venice sinks, the whole world cries and protests. If Peking disappears, nobody even notices it," says Philippe Jonathan, French planner working at Qinghua University and so far a lonely campaigner for a "Save Peking" movement.

"The fate of this city ought to concern us all, because the greatness of Peking belongs to the culture of mankind."

The destruction goes on. While the central government declares its determination to protect and restore what is left of the old Chinese capital, the Ministry of Culture proceeds to pull down an eighteenth century princely residence in the northeast corner of the city, in order to build dormitories for its own employees. While a group of architects work out a project meant to preserve one of Peking's most classic quarters, the area around the Drum Tower, old houses and shops in the area, their fronts carved in wood, their roofs made of colored tiles, are hastily being replaced by new cubicles made of bricks and cement. While the thirteenth century observatory at the southeast corner of the old Imperial City, with its bronze instruments forged by the European Jesuits, is being rebuilt to become a museum, right next to it a tall, ugly block of flats is being completed, thus obstructing the view and dwarfing into ridicule the once-imposing dimensions of the historical monument.

"Yes, we should not have built that house there," says Liu Keli of the Peking Bureau for the Protection of Cultural Relics. "It has been a mistake."

Mistake. Mistakes. Ten years of Cultural Revolution, which sent millions of young Red Guards to burn, smash and destroy everything that was old, are now acknowledged as a mistake. The Great Leap Forward, which forced people to throw anything made of metal into backyard furnaces, including ancient statues and vases, to melt them into pots and pans, has also been recognized as a "mistake". It was a "mistake" to dismantle Peking's walls, a "mistake" to take down the gates, the arches, the temples.

Since 1949, an almost uninterrupted series of mistakes has transformed once-splendid Peking into a shapeless slum, a charmless conglomerate of ancient structures left to rot and new hideous construction purporting to be modern. "The destruction of Peking is the worst crime the communists have committed," says an American scholar of Chinese origin. After 33 years of absence he went back to visit his native town, only to find it "murdered and disfigured beyond recognition," as he put it.

For over 2,000 years there has been a human settlement in the area of Peking, but the construction of the northern capital (which is what Peking means) started in 1409, when Emperor Yong Lo of the Ming dynasty moved the government to this location from the southern capital, Nanking.

The legend says that a mysterious Taoist priest, who had descended from the sky, gave the emperor a big parcel containing the detailed plans of the whole city. Indeed, there was something divine in what only human fantasy and work contrived to build in the featureless monotony of the north China plain.

Walls within walls, moats within moats, Peking was a reflection in stone of the cosmic order. Each building was in a calculated position: the Temple of the Sun to the east, that of the moon to the west, the Temple of Heaven in the south, balanced by that of earth in the north. And in the middle of it all was the purple Forbidden City, the Great Within as it was called, the heart of China, the center of the center of the world, the seat of the emperor from whom all power emanated.

For centuries the inhabitants of Peking knew they were living in an extraordinary place and feared two things. One was the dragon of the waters, who was said to live in the bowels of Peking and threatened to emerge out of a famous well next to Hatamen gate and flood the city. The second fear was of invaders who, envious of Peking's beauties and treasures, would try to attack and destroy it.

Against the dragon they placed a huge marble turtle over the well, and told her to stay on guard until she heard the sound of the gong, when somebody would come to relieve her (each gate had a gong that struck at midnight). Then they proceeded to take down the Hatamen gong and replace it with a bell. The turtle stood guard for centuries, until it was recently destroyed together with the well to make space for a new road.

Against the danger of invaders the inhabitants of Peking placed joss-sticks in front of a special god who bestowed upon the city walls a magic spell which protected Peking against all enemies from the outside.

Both systems worked. Peking was never flooded, and though

invaders came and went, though dynasties rose and fell, the magic spell of the walls held and the capital never suffered major destruction.

When, on October 1, 1949, Mao Zedong stood on the terrace of the Gate of Heavenly Peace, his back against the Forbidden City, his eyes toward the south, and declared the establishment of the People's Republic of China, the Peking he was looking upon had not changed much since the days of the emperors.

Even the Japanese, who had occupied it, had respected the grand design of the old city, had not touched the historic center and had gone into the western suburbs when they wanted to develop a new Peking. Not so the communists.

For them Peking, symbol of old China, was the quintessence of all they had fought against and wanted to change. "The very map of Peking was a reflection of the feudal society, it was meant to demonstrate the absolute power of the emperor," says Professor Ho Renzhi of Peking University. "We had to transform it, we had to make Peking into the capital of socialist China." In this they have not failed.

The communists started by taking down the pailos, the triumphal arches in marble and painted wood, which had been built across streets over the centuries to honor the memory of chaste widows, faithful mandarins and upright generals. Fifty-five splendid pailos had survived even the introduction of cars and tramways in Peking. In a matter of weeks they were all done away with. The authorities said that they were a great hindrance to traffic, but more likely they were eliminated because they were reminders of old virtues and values which the new regime did not want the people to treasure any more.

The communists then changed the very orientation of the city and, instead of the old imperial south–north axis, stressed a new, more political east–west boulevard. They did so by enlarging and extending the existing Avenue of Eternal Peace, Changan.

In the old days, one approached the city from the south along one straight kilometer of pailos, bridges and gates which, like a musical crescendo, prepared the traveler for the explosion of splendor of the yellow-roofed, purple Forbidden City

25

against the bluest sky.

Today, visitors coming from the airport are driven into the city from the east, along the flat, characterless Avenue of Eternal Peace. It is marked only by the tall apartment houses of the ghetto for foreign residents, the Peking Hotel, the gigantic emptiness of Tiananmen Square, the post office building, and further modern hotels.

Old Peking had no squares, for people had no need to gather in masses, or to express their opinions. Tiananmen Square, flanked by the Greco-Stalinist architecture of the Great Hall of the People and the Museum of the Revolution, has become the heart of new China. Here were held the major celebrations of the new regime, here started the Cultural Revolution, here China with millions of shouting people showed her support for Vietnam, her hate for America, her opposition to revisionism, and so on.

After Mao died and went to occupy the center of this square in his mausoleum, thus further breaking the remaining harmony of the square, Tiananmen has only been used by people flying kites and by out-of-town visitors who come to have their pictures taken under the last of the Mao portraits. Since the brief Peking Spring in 1978-79, when a few people used the square as a forum for voicing their grievances, new regulations have been posted at all corners. "Without the approval of the People's government it is prohibited to parade, to hold rallies, to make speeches, to write, to distribute, or to put up any kind of propaganda...."

In old China, the walls of a city were the greatest pride of a city's people, and the worst punishment that an emperor could inflict for some terrible crime, such as parricide, was their partial or complete destruction. Peking's walls were the greatest, the mightiest, the most legendary city walls in China. Not even the International Expedition, which in 1900 came to Peking to relieve the foreign legations from siege and punish China for the Boxer Rebellion, dared touch the capital's walls. The communists, however, had no such hesitation.

The destruction started in 1950. Fearing the anger of the people, who might feel distressed at losing the protective spell of their walls, gangs of workers were brought at night to perform their unpopular task. "It was as if my own flesh was being torn off, as if my skin was being peeled off," wrote China's top architect, Liang Sicheng. He was later accused of being a rightist, was forced to make self-criticism and to denounce his colleagues, and died in disgrace in 1973.

Pulling down the walls at first sparked a debate between those who wanted to preserve at least part of them as "a necklace around the neck of Peking," and those who wanted to destroy them as "a chain at Peking's feet" which would hinder the development of the city. In 1958, somebody proposed to turn what was left of the walls into a high-level promenade, with foodstalls and souvenir shops. It would have continued to provide a spectacular panorama of the city, as it had done since 1860, when a special imperial decree allowed foreigners, but not their females, to climb the bastion. The proposals were made to no avail.

The last parts of the walls and the last gates were taken down during the Cultural Revolution, this time by squads of intellectuals who, as political prisoners of the Red Guards, were forced to destroy those last vestiges of the "feudal" China in which they allegedly believed. "With every blow I knew we were committing a kind of cultural suicide," now says a professor of history. "But at that time, even if the Red Guards had ordered me to take down the Forbidden City, I would have done that too. What was the point of protecting one monument, when the whole country was being destroyed?"

Indeed, some people within the top leadership wanted to get rid of the whole of old Peking and Marshal Peng Dehuai, hero of the Korean War, victim of the Cultural Revolution and now again a hero after the fall of the Gang of Four, even proposed destroying the Forbidden City as the most significant symbol of the past. But he was overruled. Mao Zedong, and particularly Zhou Enlai, realized that they had to protect some of the old places as a showpiece of their national pride.

In 1958, the government ordered a survey of all monuments that had any historic, religious or artistic value in Peking: there were 8,000. It was decided to preserve 78; the rest could go. During the Cultural Revolution even the 78 were attacked and partly destroyed.

In 1982, a new survey was conducted to see what could still be saved and rebuilt. To the old 78 sites another 70 have been added. In some cases this means almost complete reconstruction. Deshenmen gate in the north of the city has just been rebuilt, largely in cement, since almost nothing was left of the original structure of brick and wood.

Where the outer walls stood, a highway now circles Peking. Where the inner wall stood, south of Tiananmen Square, there runs what the people now call the "Hua Guofeng wall," a long row of tall, gray, uniform blocks of flats built by Mao's successor to provide better housing for Party cadres. For months and months those flats remained empty, as a big struggle broke out about allocation (children of high cadres, for instance, managed to bypass senior middle cadres). When they were finally assigned, everybody was unhappy. Most of the glass windows were already broken, the water did not have enough pressure to reach the upper floors, and the elevators did not work. "We built those flats when we were still under the influence of the Gang of Four, when the workers decided everything and the architects were left aside," explains the deputy director of Peking's Planning Commission. What is being built now by the architects is not much different.

Due to the immense pressure of the population (Peking is growing by some 360,000 people every year), and the government's determination to improve the standard of living in the capital, row upon row of pre-fabricated blocks are going up everywhere in the city and...deteriorate soon after. Made of cheap materials, according to the most simplistic and banal blueprints, buildings are being put up without any coordination, without any care for details and environment, so that suddenly thousands of people find themselves in the labyrinth of new settlements that have no markets, no schools, no patches of green and — as many letters to the local papers complain — not even parking spaces for their bicycles.

The city of Peking does not yet have an urban development plan. There are no regulations for new buildings, except that they cannot be more than 40 meters high. The municipal government has no power to interfere with or stop any arbitrary construction. "Each unit is an independent kingdom; each

Party secretary is a local emperor," is a current saying among the people.

A unit is the working group to which each citizen belongs. A school is a unit; a factory, a hospital are units. A unit, or better, its political commissar, the Party secretary, has power over its members and absolute jurisdiction over the property and real estate the state has allocated to it. Each unit handles its property as it sees fit. "We had to destroy this place, we had no choice," says a responsible cadre of the Institute of History of the Academia Sinica, which last year leveled a beautiful mansion with many courtyards, a refined example of classic Qing dynasty architecture in the north of the Forbidden City, and replaced it with a pitiful high-rise building. "We needed space and we had no other place to go."

Almost half the surface of old Peking has thus been destroyed since 1949. Precisely the grandest, the most spacious, the most significant and the most precious buildings were the first to go.

When on January 31, 1949 the communist armies entered Peking, which a Kuomintang general had surrendered without a fight in order to save it from destruction, princely palaces, temples and mansions abandoned by the ruling class of the Nationalist regime fleeing to Taiwan were immediately requisitioned and given to thousands of peasant-soldiers who had poured into the capital. The best buildings of Peking became barracks. All other residences and properties of persons classified as "enemies of the people" were also confiscated and became administrative centers of the new regime. Each working unit, with its dependants, moved into the compound assigned to it during this division of the spoils.

Within the boundaries of the compound, each unit grew, expanded and modernized with no care whatsoever for the original purpose of the place and its historic or architectural value. Old structures were torn down to build dormitories, ancient furniture was thrown away and burned to make space for beds and desks, rock gardens were turned into volleyball fields.

The 12 most famous "wang fus" (princely palaces) of Peking were remodeled in order to house, among other units, the

29

Ministry of Health, the Central Conservatory of Music, the Ministry of Education, a publishing company and the cultural troupe of the Army. The largest of all Peking's residences, that of Prince Kong, with its dozens of pavilions, ponds, reception rooms and gardens, was divided up among various units, the most prominent of which was the Peking Air Conditioner Factory. This palace, known to all Chinese for having inspired the author of the popular novel *The Dream of the Red Chamber*, is now among those monuments the Municipality of Peking would like to restore. But the problem is that vast sections of it have already been irreparably damaged, while others have been destroyed completely. What is left is being used as a dormitory for policemen whose unit refuses to move out.

"Units of the People's Liberation Army must avoid as much as possible damaging ancient structures and famous scenic spots," ordered the general chief of staff in a recent letter to all regiments in Peking.

More than 35 years after Liberation, Peking still looks like a city under military occupation. The Army is still in control of some of the central areas of the capital, and still entrenched in some of the nicest buildings, now hidden behind anonymous, gray brick walls.

To walk around the Peking of today, searching, if not for the monuments of yesterday, at least for the sites where they used to stand, is a frustrating, depressing experience. The maps of the city before 1949 are "neibu" (for internal use only, confidential or secret). "The communists don't want people to realize how much they have destroyed," says an old intellectual. The maps of the city that can be freely bought in bookstores are transportation maps only, marking exclusively the main streets, the routes of buses and of the underground. These maps make no reference to the thousands of little lanes ("hutongs"), which are the texture of Peking, and give no indication of historical sites. Old people are still able to point out the location of a temple or a former palace, but young people have grown accustomed to having their way barred by walls without asking themselves what may be behind them.

On the dilapidated entrance to the Yellow Temple, outside

the former northern gates of the city, a sign says "no visitors." The Black Temple, nearby, is inaccessible, for it is in the middle of a restricted military area. The old Christian cemetery of Chala in the western suburbs of Peking, where Matteo Ricci and other European Jesuits were buried in the seventeenth century, can only be visited with special permission: the compound is now the Communist Party cadre school.

The seventeenth century tombstones of the Jesuits Matteo Ricci, Adam von Schaal and Ferdinand Verbiest have recently been salvaged and put together again. All other tombstones are lying about in pieces and are being used as picnic tables by the Party students.

Sometimes it is only by chance that one learns which unit occupies which famous site. Some time ago, 20 fire engines rushed to the Temple of Ten Thousand Ages, four kilometers west of the Forbidden City, to deal with a devastating fire that had broken out. The temple had always been one of the best preserved temples in the capital, for it was the preferred resting place of emperors on their way to the Summer Palace. A small article in the *Peking Evening News* reported the fire, the second in a few months, saying that it had caused extensive damage and that it had been lit by children exploding firecrackers. The temple, the paper said, is now occupied by the Army propaganda unit. Hundreds of military men and their families have lived in it since 1949.

Peking was a city of many temples. Maybe too many. Apart from those that had remained centers of devotion, there were those that had started to function as schools, as hospitals with quack doctors, or as market places. A few, like the Lama Temple with its dubious monks, had become the hide-out of bandits, draft-dodgers and hooligans dedicated mainly to the extortion of money from occasional visitors. The communists put all the temples to good use.

"Transform Peking from a consumer city into a producer city!" was their slogan. In order to produce, Peking needed factories. Factories needed space and the temples, with their many open courtyards, were ready-made areas for industrial development. This policy, intended to increase production and at the same time to destroy religion, was called the "ji" (push

31

out) policy, as a neibu book on old religion in China reveals. Its tactics were simple: a unit would move discreetly into a temple compound and start work with a few machines. The Party cadre of the unit would explain to the monks how much more important production was for the country than their prayers. More and more machines would move in, taking more and more space from the monks, until the latter would all be pushed out.

Thus above the colored tiles of the temple roofs, next to the bell towers, rose at first dozens, then hundreds of chimneys spouting black smoke, and temple after temple was turned into a factory. During the Great Leap Forward alone, 1,400 factories were opened in the center of the city. They are still there. The Temple of the Great Buddha produces molds for iron furnaces; the Temple of Cultivated Wisdom produces electric wire; the Temple of the God of Fire produces electric bulbs; the Temple of White Clouds, center of Taoist studies in China, was turned into a huge warehouse with various mechanical workshops.

Peking, whose serene blue skies were legendary, thus became one of the worst-polluted capitals in the world. Eleven thousand coal-burning boilers pour clouds of suffocating coal dust into the air. "Air and water pollution are serious in Peking," warns a front-page story in the Chinese magazine *Health*. During last winter, the coal dust precipitated from heating fires over the city was calculated at four tons per square kilometer per month.

Peking, which for its dry climate was considered one of the healthiest places in China, now produces what foreign residents call "Peking lung," a form of chronic bronchitis.

In winter, millions of Chinese take to the streets with white cloth masks over their mouths and noses, looking like an army of doctors and nurses ready for the operating room.

An American scientist, who brought a small instrument known as an air quality monitor to Peking to measure the particles in the air, registered 120 in the Chinese capital. Thirty is considered the safety level. "To jog here in the morning is like smoking a pack of cigarettes a day," says a foreign doctor. Local authorities are well aware of the problem, and continue to announce plans to move factories away from the central areas and to impose pollution control measures.

In 1978, the Peking Municipality solemnly promised "to turn Peking into a clean city in which someone standing on the White Pagoda in the North Sea Park can have a clear view of the Western Hills." This was one of the common views from Peking before Liberation. Now it is an extremely rare sight. A yellowish, murky blanket of smoke hovers over Peking on windless days. The factories are still there. The measures to control pollution have not been applied.

Again, at the beginning of 1982, Peking announced a plan to make the capital "a first-rate modern city, a model for the rest of China." The spokesman of the Academy of Sciences declared, "The eco-system research project is the first in the 3,000-year-old history of Peking." The idea is to study what to do. The study will last until the end of 1985. Meanwhile, Peking papers will continue to publish letters from readers complaining that fruit trees do not bear fruit anymore, and that the smoke, stench and noise coming out of the neighborhood temple-factory makes life unbearable for the people.

Not all the temples became factories. Some were simply destroyed to make space for roads, such as the Abundant Tranquility Temple and the Sleeping Buddha Temple outside the former Hatamen gate; or to make space for new buildings, such as the Temple of the Law Pagoda, eliminated in order to make room for the Peking Workers Stadium; or the famous Longfu Si (Temple of Flourishing Happiness), sacrificed to put up a department store. The two huge marble turtles of this temple were thrown among the ruins of the old Summer Palace and are still there upside down.

In order to maintain the fiction of freedom of religion, which every Chinese constitution has asserted ever since 1949, a couple of token temples were at first left open.

The Dongyue Miao (Temple of the Eastern Peak) lasted until 1959, with thousands of worshippers milling around the 105 buildings of the compound and praying in front of the over 1,000 deities which it housed. It was here that the souls of the dead were supposed to present themselves to the evil gods presiding over the underworld prisons, in order to be told what punishment and torture they would have to undergo if in life they had not behaved well. This temple, the biggest Taoist shrine in northern China, was therefore most popular among Peking's inhabitants, who came here to pray for their deceased relatives and to intercede on their behalf.

When the temple was closed, it was given to the dreaded Public Security Bureau which supervises the lives of all Chinese.

Now, with all the statues gone, many of the buildings torn down, and a new red-brick building coming up in the middle of its courtyard, the temple is a school for security policemen. "Here at least the communists have respected the spirit of the place," says an old Peking intellectual who lives nearby. "The temple dealt with prisoners in the past, and so it does today."

The temple is just behind the Qijia Yuan compound, one of the special neighborhoods where foreigners are made to live, and it is said that from inside the old temple the secret police listen to all their telephone conversations, and read all their mail.

Today, in the whole of Peking there is not a single real temple, a temple as a temple ought to be, as temples are wherever there are Chinese. There is not one place where people come and go as they please, without paying an entrance fee; a place where they can pray, offer incense to the gods, sit in meditation.

The three temples now reopened in the Western Hills, as well as the Five Pagodas Temple, which was recently reopened after being used as a breeding center for police dogs for 15 years, are used as amusement grounds for Sunday outings. It is for this reason that all of these temples have been put under the supervision of the same unit which, within the Peking municipal administration, is in charge of public parks and the zoo.

In Peking itself, the Confucius Temple has been turned into the Capital Museum (at the moment, it houses a collection of bronze statues recovered from the Peking Garbage and Waste Company). The Fayuan Si (the Temple of the Source of the Law) houses the reborn Buddhist Institute and, like the Huangji Si (Monastery for Broad Assistance), is used to entertain visiting Buddhist associations from abroad.

The Lama Temple, in the north of the city, caters mainly to common foreign tourists. The few old monks walking through its courtyards, in order to provide good snapshots for curious tourists, have been imported from Inner Mongolia. The young ones, who guard the various halls while reading unholy books such as *Today's Cinema* or *Sports Daily*, look more like young policemen in disguise than novices in training. Here, one does see the occasional tourist from Hong Kong putting joss sticks in front of a statue, many of which are imitations of the old ones which have disappeared. No Peking Chinese would do that, not least because the entrance ticket costs 50 cents, which for most Chinese is half a day's pay.

At the beginning of the sixties, the communist regime had already managed to transform old Peking into a city quite attuned to their vision of a socialist capital. The new communist power had its symbols in the tall buildings constructed around Tiananmen Square, the workers had a huge stadium, the peasants a great exposition hall, the minorities their big palace and the railways a new Peking station. All these new buildings had their own grandeur, and the joke of the time among the people was, "I thought the communists did not like temples, yet they build new ones themselves." What the new regime had not yet touched was the intimate structure of the capital.

Peking used to be a town of privacy, where each family lived in a house around a courtyard, within high walls screening it against the rest of the world.

One beside the other, these courtyard houses, in Chinese "sihe yuan" (courtyard uniting four buildings), were lined up along the chessboard scheme of Peking's hutongs (lanes) which form the texture of the city. There were hundreds of major hutongs, and the smaller ones, as Peking's inhabitants used to say, were "as many as the hairs of an ox."

Of courtyard houses, a typical feature of northern Chinese architecture since the twelfth century, there were tens of thousands. On the outside was a small ornate gate, flanked by two stone carvings, in the gray wall of the hutong. Inside, after a spirit wall meant to push back evil influences, the delicate harmony of four, single-storey rooms, their fronts painted in red and green, their roofs gray and curved, their windows of white paper against the geometry of wooden lattice work, surrounded a quadrilateral court shaded by a huge tree. It often led into another similar court, and yet into another one, depending on the wealth of the family.

The courtyard house was the last hide-out of privacy, the last refuge of individualism which the new regime had to conquer.

In 1966, Mao Zedong unleashed the Red Guards to do the job. "This house is too big for you. One room is enough for your family. The others must serve the people!" was the common refrain. Gangs of youngsters with red armbands (only the children of workers, peasants and soldiers had that honor) invaded the courtyards, followed by masses of people, and held "people's trials" of the owners and their families.

The houses were stripped, all property was confiscated. Trucks were loaded with furniture, paintings, vases, porcelain, dresses and jewels and were driven off. What was left was thrown into the courtyards, smashed, and burned. Courtyards became battle grounds, with people beaten, sometimes to death. Trials lasted for days and many people, fearing what might happen to them, committed suicide, destroyed their own belongings, or sold their own libraries by the kilo as wrapping paper.

When the trials were over, new people from outside the city and from the crammed dormitories of factories moved into the courtyard houses and lived side by side with their original owners, now poor and destitute like everybody else. Where one family used to live, 10, 20 and sometimes more families moved in, gradually occupying all available space, cutting down the trees, and building shacks in the courtyards for kitchens and storerooms.

The work of the Red Guards was methodical. Through courtyard house after courtyard house, hutong after hutong, the new regime entered the heart of Peking. Today there is not a single lane that recalls the refined, modest elegance of old Peking, with its long gray walls interrupted here and there by a small red door and the branches of trees waving over a curved roof, under which people of infinite strength had for centuries kept alive the traditions of a great civilization. There is not a single courtyard with the rarefied atmosphere in which a scholar and his friends could view the blossoming of the chrysanthemum and spend a night writing poems to the moon.

"Temples and palaces were the extraordinary aspect of this city, and their destruction was obviously a great loss," says a Chinese historian. "But it was the destruction of the ordinary, of the courtyard houses, that really killed old Peking."

Hutongs are now miserable, dirty, haphazard. Courtyard houses, once examples of quiet harmony, are dilapidated, chaotic camping sites, filled with a confusion of hovels, barracks, of stoves, bicycles, piles of coal and bricks over which people dry their laundry. On the pavement of the courtyards, inhabitants squat to cook, to wash, to work, to play with children. Above their unpainted doors, for which now nobody cares, many courtyard houses still carry the old slogan, "A socialist courtyard is happiness." Many have put up a more recent and more realistic sign that reads, "Lock your bicycle and look out for thieves."

Aware of the problems arising from such massive cohabitation, the *People's Daily* dedicated one front page to a model situation the whole country should emulate. "Nine households like one family" was the headline. The story told of 39 people, who for 20 years have been sharing a little place with one kitchen (with nine stoves and two tubs of water) without quarreling. "Their living space is very small, but their spiritual place very vast," concluded the Party daily.

Actually, relationships among families in one courtyard are very difficult. The Cultural Revolution was nearly two decades ago, but old inhabitants still regard the newcomers as intruders, and the latter still think of the former as "class enemies." People still suspect each other and lower their voices when speaking within the family to avoid being reported by the neighbors. Recently when a foreigner offered a chicken to a sick Chinese friend, the friend refused it, fearing that his neighbors might smell it while roasting and denounce him for "illegal relationships."

"Since the Cultural Revolution, we have lived under the level of decency," says an old intellectual who still lives in his old courtyard, but with the addition of 23 families plus a small factory. Every morning he has to line up in front of the street's public toilet, 50 meters away from home, while the bits and pieces of what used to be his old bathroom lie in a corner of the courtyard, smashed by Red Guards as a symbol of "bourgeois individualism."

The story of Peking's toilets is another despairing example of the absurdity of past policies. Though the courtyard houses were built originally without sewerage (most of Peking still has none), many Chinese families under foreign influence had installed toilets, some even bathrooms, during the thirties and forties. They were all methodically destroyed between 1966 and 1968, when an innovation came to life that still plagues Peking: the neighborhood toilet. This is a small block of gray bricks protruding in the hutongs every two or three hundred meters, one entrance for women, one for men. Inside is one long, dirty, suffocating ditch with no individual partitions.

A common sight in the center of Peking today is lines of people waiting in front of the public toilet for their turn, some to empty the night pots of the family. The local papers carry frequent letters by people complaining about the fact that their neighborhood toilet has not been emptied for months, that the stench emanating from it makes eating revolting, and that the stolen electric bulbs have not been replaced, causing people to fall at night on the slippery floors. Recently, a special sanitation unit of 750 men was created by the Peking Municipality. Among its duties is to watch out for people stealing doors, windows and hooks from public toilets.

It will take a long time before living conditions in Peking can improve, because the population has increased dramatically since 1949, and because for the past two decades no major resettlement project has been started, the exception being a few "simplified houses" as they were called ("simplified" meaning that the flats have neither a toilet nor a kitchen). Only in the last four years has the municipality resumed building public housing.

In 1949, there were 1.2 million people living in Peking. Today there are 9.2 million. When taking over the capital, the communists brought in their armies and their cadres, but chose to build a few imposing, huge administrative and representative buildings instead of housing developments to lodge these people.

The disproportion between the unutilized public buildings and private space is still apparent. The Industrial Exposition Hall, the Agricultural Exposition Palace and the Museum of Military History, for example, are most of the time not put to use, while many people still live crammed in dormitories, away from their families. All ministries and other public offices have huge conference and ping-pong rooms, while the employees still live in crammed quarters.

In 1949, the average living space in Peking was 11.2 square meters per person. Today, it is 3.5 square meters per person, hardly enough for a double bed.

While Peking needed massive restoration and construction work above ground, immense investment of energy and capital was put under the ground. The story of Peking's tunnels, like that of the tunnels of all other cities in China, tells the story of a folly that drove a nation into misery.

Mao launched the tunnels with a slogan: "Dig tunnels deep. Store grain everywhere. Be ready for natural disaster and war!" Work started in 1969. "We did not have machines, so we worked with our hands. Everybody was a volunteer," says Dai Jinshang, responsible cadre of the Peking Anti-aircraft Tunnel Office. "We had no experience, but still we carried on."

Every day, after working hours, millions of people with shovels and picks dug into the ground under their factories, their shops, their schools. Tons and tons of earth were carried away in small wheelbarrows. Millions and millions of bricks, thousands of sacks of cement, tons of iron rods were swallowed by a staggering labyrinth of tunnels stretching in all directions under the surface of Peking.

The underlying idea was that China was about to be attacked by the Soviet Union and that the people had to find refuge in the tunnels, and through them a means of escape into the countryside. Entrances to the underground were everywhere: under the sliding floor of a big department store, in the playground of a school, in the cellar of a factory, a university, a housing estate.

For months and months, people did nothing but dig and dig. The earth under Peking was heaped up like an immense anthill, and costly and scarce materials, which could have built a whole new town above ground, were wasted to construct a huge network of tunnels. Even in the case of war, the tunnels would have been virtually useless against today's biggest conventional bombs, let alone the nuclear ones.

While work was still continuing, it became clear that the project was a mistake. The problem of the authorities was now to put the immense monster to a different use. Parts of the tunnel were therefore turned into a tourist attraction, with souvenir shops and briefings by responsible cadres. "Please don't take pictures," tourists are told to increase the thrill. Other parts of the tunnels are being used as warehouses by shops above ground; as dormitories for workers or employees; as small factories and canteens. In the humid and badly ventilated air, a working unit of the western district of the city has started to grow 250,000 kilograms of mushrooms a year.

All information about the tunnel system is still secret. But one has to assume that the whole network extends over some 30 square kilometers. For the time being, the most apparent result of the tunneling under Peking is that the capital now suffers from a serious water shortage. The vast construction has completely disrupted the natural underground water network, and has increased water pollution by lowering the water table.

Peking used to be a city of many pleasures. In 1949, around the Pearl Market crossroads, outside Qianmen gate, there were 237 brothels with some 1,000 prostitutes. The new communist government made it clear that this was intolerable, but the business continued. Not for long.

One evening in early 1950, communist troops surrounded the whole area, arrested hundreds of people, shot a few who resisted, and took the prostitutes to labor camps. The girls reappeared later in a play portraying the horrors of their lives under the old regime and telling the world how well they had been re-educated by the new one.

In today's Peking there are no brothels, and probably not too many people regret the loss of them. But many people regret the loss of many other things that were easily available and made life pleasant in the old days. In 1949, there were 10,000 restaurants within the city. Now, there are only 1,700 of them catering to a population that has meanwhile grown seven times as large.

Peking was known for its famous cooks. Now, good cooking is done exclusively in restaurants for foreigners. The foreigners return from their China tour believing that the whole country eats like they have eaten. But food in places open to Chinese just fills the stomach and nothing else. Hygienic conditions are appalling in the "masses restaurants," where foreign tourists hardly ever go. The floors are a mish-mash of leftovers and spit. Tables are covered with sticky plastic cloths that get wiped only once in a while with dirty, greasy towels. People eat in a hurry, pressed by those standing by ready to take over their seats, while others stuff themselves squatting on the floor and an occasional beggar waits to empty the remnants of a dish into his plastic bag.

There are not many beggars in Peking today (people say that a sanitary cordon around the city prevents poor peasants from getting in to beg), but one notices them. They are seen around the Yongdingmen railway station, in the overcrowded streets south of Qianmen, or at night searching through the piles of garbage in the small hutongs.

Peking was a city of festivals and temple fairs. There was a festival to greet the spring, one to pay homage to the stars, one for the moon, one to light lanterns and one to hang winter clothes in the sun. The streets, with their daily happenings of funerals, marriages and ceremonies upon ceremonies, their shops with signs and banners, were a continuous, colorful show for the people.

Now, with no more ceremonies, no more festivals or shop signs, the streets of Peking have lost their character. People no longer gather in response to the sound of gongs or trumpets. Now they gather to watch the occasional street fight, usually resulting from a bicycle accident.

For a short while after Liberation, the communist regime had its own display of festivals: there were festivals to greet its new leaders and to celebrate various anniversaries. By and

41

by even those were abolished, with the result that the life of ordinary people in this city, which used to be one of the most spectacular and fun-loving in the world, today dully flows away, one day like another.

For millions of Peking people, who still have no running water at home, the day starts with a mug in one hand and a toothbrush in the other, rinsing their mouths on the sidewalks.

Then follows lining up for breakfast, lining up for the bus to go to work, lining up for fish, for vegetables, for beancurd, for milk and again lining up for the bus to return home.

Peking's nights have no enticements. The city goes to bed with the sun. Restaurants close at 8:00 p.m., but many start throwing their customers out at 7:30, when waiters begin to splash the floors with water.

Private dancing parties, which young people were briefly allowed to organize for themselves between 1978 and 1980, are now prohibited because "they disturb the normal life of the masses," and because the music they played is now considered "pornographic." Cinema houses and theaters are few (69 in the whole of Peking) and offer a choice of only five or six films. Tickets must be bought days in advance or through one's working unit. For those who don't want to go to bed early, the one thing left is to play cards or chess under the dim neon light of the lampposts along the streets.

In old Peking, even in the worst years of civil war and Japanese aggression, there was always a place where a man in misery and despair could look for distraction. The district of Tian Qiao (the Heavenly Bridge), west of the Temple of Heaven, was a neighborhood full of theaters, teahouses, opium dens, restaurants and "chicken-feather inns," as the cheap mass hotels for coolies and beggars were called.

It was to the Tian Qiao that Rickshaw Boy, the protagonist of Lao She's best novel, went when, desperate from the death of his wife, sick and unable to work, he wanted to distract himself through the night. Among foodstalls, acrobats, musicians and storytellers, he felt human warmth while among other human trash like himself. Today, the completely cleaned up Tian Qiao neighborhood looks as somber as any other, with all traces of its former life gone, except for a renovated theater that gives performances mostly for foreign visitors.

Until the Cultural Revolution, there were still a few teahouses in Peking which had storytellers to attract customers to sip tea, while listening to endless accounts of heroic stories of the past. They were all closed, but recently two have again begun their fascinating business, one in a shack where the old Peking execution ground used to be, the other inside the Drum Tower.

Peking opera, the most famous and most popular entertainment in northern China, which was also abolished during the Cultural Revolution, has reopened. But it is no longer the same, nor is it meant to be.

Peking opera, with its vast repertoire (over 2,000 different plays), had been for over a thousand years one of the chains of transmission of Chinese culture. It was in front of the stage of itinerant troupes, at dozens of theaters, at market fairs, that people learned about their history, their literature, customs and poetry. Popular wisdom was passed on, from generation to generation, through the famous lines of famous characters of the Peking opera.

Obviously this form of art reflected the old feudal system, and since as such it molded the people's outlook on life the communists took control of it immediately after 1949. First of all, they reduced the repertoire to a few dozen plays. Operas where landlords were positive characters could not be played at a time when landlords were being put in front of people's courts, accused of all kinds of crimes and often executed.

The final attack on Peking opera came with the Cultural Revolution, when actors were thrown into jail or sent to labor camps.

Over the last two years, Peking opera has been revived. But, with the excuse that young people don't like it anymore, it is being modernized and by that "killed as Peking opera," as a foreign scholar of this particular form of art says. Traditional stories are changed to suit the policies of the times. Ghosts are eliminated from the plot, for "they are not real, but just a product of superstition." Emperors and mandarins are given only one wife, for polygamy is now illegal, and the young man, who in the classical text used to sing "at 20 a man should have a wife," is made to sing "at 30 a man should have a wife," for this is the line of the family planning program.

Peking was a city of tailors, barbers, carpenters, famous for their excellent and prompt work. No more.

A common Chinese has to wait an average of seven months to have his suit or her dress made, and frequent letters from readers to the *Peking Daily* and the *Peking Evening Post* report horror stories of people who, after long sacrifices and lines, find themselves with garments that do not fit and can in no way be altered.

In front of the Lan Tian tailor shop in Wangfujing Street, one of those thought to be more careful, people line up at 5:00 a.m., waiting to get a number which will allow them to enter when the shop opens eventually at 9:00. The shop takes only 25 customers a day.

In 1949, there were hundreds of small and medium-sized private tailors, each one competing against the other for fame and customers. Now, there are only 165 collective tailor shops and they don't give a damn, one way or the other. The only one that pretends to pay some individual attention is Hung Du (Red Capital) in the main street of the old legation quarter, but it only caters for foreigners, Party cadres and Chinese delegations going abroad. Its work is not impressive. This is the shop that used to provide Mao with his famous jackets; their sleeves covered half his hands. "He wanted them that way," says the man who used to sew for the Chairman, but also counted among his most refined customers the late Premier Zhou Enlai.

Peking had thousands of different shops. During the first 20 years after the revolution they were abolished or reduced for ideological reasons, in order to pursue the reforms meant to change the former capitalist economy into a socialist one.

In pre-Liberation days, Peking had 300 secondhand and antiquarian bookstores. Now only one is left. The old, beautiful Liu Li Chang Street, where most of them were, side by side with dozens of curio shops, was completely destroyed in 1980 and is now being rebuilt as a fake old city.

In 1949, there were 72,303 commercial services employing 115,000 people. Now with a population seven times bigger, the shops in Peking number fewer than 10,000, and employ 120,000 people.

In the old commercial city, there were entire hutongs specializing in one product, or in one form of trade that gave the name to the whole street. There was a hutong for jade, one for lanterns, one for bird cages, for flowers, for furs, for hats, for furniture.... All these are gone.

The little shops, where each morning one man, or all his family, got up and thought about the business of the day, have been turned into collective factories, transferred elsewhere and made into impersonal places where everybody putters along indifferently.

If an ordinary Chinese needs to repair a table or a chair, he won't be able to find, in the whole of Peking, a single carpenter to do the job. If he wants to make a table by himself it is equally impossible. In a city of 9 million people, an individual cannot buy a piece of wood, a piece of iron, a tube of plastic or a sheet of rubber. To buy a piece of window glass he is well advised to present a letter from his working unit, introducing him and his needs. That is why roofs are leaking, windows are patched up with cardboard and even new flats are soon dilapidated: nobody has the means to keep them up, even if he wants to.

"Bricks are not for sale, so I had to steal them," says a man who, with water and mud (cement is also unobtainable for individuals) is building a shack outside his house to store coal for the winter.

Common furniture, like a bed or a cupboard, can only be bought in special state shops by couples who show their marriage certificate. That is why peasants, who have easy access to wood, come from as far as 200-300 kilometers away, balancing on their bicycles cheap armchairs and sofas to sell in Peking on the free market.

Sometimes it happens that a shop has something that has been missing on the market for months. Because of this it has become a habit for Peking people always to carry their savings in case they come across what they have been looking for for a long time.

Department stores have large quantities of common use

consumer goods, such as soap, pots and pans, standard blue or green trousers, sweaters, shawls. It is to buy food, which is still rationed (each person is entitled to 15 kilograms of grain, half a kilogram of cooking oil and a certain number of eggs, according to season, per month), that one has to stand in line to get what one is given.

What is displayed in the window is not always for sale. A man who had seen some fresh and cheap vegetables in a shop near the Soviet embassy realized that they were there only to trick "the revisionists" into believing that such was the standard of supplies all over Peking. A group of customers, who recently saw some beautiful lean pork in a shop in the Jing Shang district and had gone happily inside to buy it, were told, "This is not for sale. This is just for the inspection committee." They went back in the afternoon after the inspection committee had passed, and this time they were told, "The meat is not for sale. It is reserved for the back door." Whereupon they wrote a bitter letter to the Party daily.

"Back door" is the common expression to describe the way one can obtain things which are unobtainable for the normal citizen. "To go through the back door" means to have a friend in a unit or to know a cadre who is ready to do a special favor, obviously in exchange for a present. In today's Peking there is a "back door" to everything: to a good doctor or to a good school, to a good job or even to a passport.

The vast extent of this form of corruption, spread all over China, is partly due to the enormous population increase since 1949 and to the failure of the authorities to cope with it.

Only half of the children in Peking can go to a kindergarten. Schools are so crowded that they must have morning and afternoon shifts. Hospitals are so overbooked that patients have to wait weeks for an operation. Hence the need to find a different way to get what one needs.

In the whole of Peking there are only 32,000 hospital beds for the whole population, while there are as many as 10,000 beds in special clinics reserved for Party cadres and Army personnel. An ordinary sick person has to be taken to a hospital in a three-wheel cart, for the few ambulances are reserved for top people.

One could explain all this by saying that China is still a poor country, but other deficiencies are clearly due to absurd ideological considerations. Certain public services, for instance, were abolished because they were "humiliating" symbols of the old society. Thus the travelers who arrive every day by the thousands at the Peking railway station find no help for carrying their luggage, in spite of the fact that Peking today has a great number of young unemployed. But it is considered inappropriate for a man to carry the bags of somebody else.

Public buses are irregular and are constantly packed, so that quarrels and fights are a common occurrence among nervous commuters. In 1957, there were still 11,000 rickshaws in Peking which, for a reasonable price, would take one anywhere in the city. During the Cultural Revolution they were abolished as "bourgeois leftovers." In October 1980, pedicabs were reintroduced, with some embarrassment, but to this day there are only 750 of them.

Young unemployed people have been encouraged to take up all sorts of small private enterprises, such as pedaling rickshaws, running small foodshops, or taking photographs along the streets. Basically, of these liberal reforms, the only one that has really made an impact has been the opening of the neighborhood free markets, where peasants from nearby communes bring the produce of their free plots. This has relieved Peking of recurrent shortages and eased the distribution of vegetables and eggs among the population of the capital. Employees of state offices and workers have formed the habit of using the 15-minute break allotted for morning exercises to jump on their bicycles and run to the nearest free market, where they buy their supplies of onions and cabbages. "This is also exercise," people like to say.

Peking was an immense treasure house, to which centuries had brought gifts of beauty and extravagance from all parts of the empire. The Forbidden City was an immense museum. The princely palaces were museums, and many of the courtyard houses where normal people lived were small museums.

Chiang Kai-shek, when he escaped to Taiwan, ordered the great collections of the Forbidden City to be taken along. They are now in the National Museum of Taipei. "For China it is

47

a loss equivalent to the loss of the Louvre for Europe," says a foreign art historian.

However, much of what was left in the palaces, the temples and the common houses was destroyed during the political campaigns of the last 20 years. What suffered most were religious images. Now that a few temples, half destroyed and stripped of all their statues and paintings, bells and bronzes, have been reopened, the major problem has been finding objects to refurnish them with.

The 18 bronze hermits now in the Guangji Si, a temple which during the Cultural Revolution was turned into a prison for Buddhist monks of the Peking area, came from a temple outside of Peking that was destroyed. The temple museum consists of bric-a-brac presents and souvenirs brought to Peking by various visiting Buddhist associations and displayed behind glass windows.

The huge bronze Buddha in the Fayuan Si monastery came from a countryside temple that had been protected by the peasants from Red Guard violence. Being too tall for its new home, the Buddha had to be lowered into the ground to make space for his head under the roof. A beautiful, 7-meter-long reclining wooden Buddha, on which the temple now prides itself, was found in a garage. It had been put there after the temple in which it had been lying since the Ming dynasty was destroyed to make room for a road. In order to make the statue fit into the garage, the huge arm sustaining the Buddha's head had been sawn off.

In the private houses of people, nothing, absolutely nothing is left of the old days. Not a table, not a chair, not porcelain, clocks, or books. "The government is selling to the foreigners the antiques it requisitioned," says a man whose whole property and collections were taken away or destroyed by the Red Guards.

A so-called theater shop off Changan Avenue, a shop in Wangfujing Street, and another one at the Temple of Heaven, are selling antiques to foreign residents and tourists. From time to time old Peking residents recognize, among the objects displayed, some of their own pieces that were taken away by the Red Guards.

48

Some people are given back some of their old belongings, if they can be traced. But nowadays there is little use for them. People have no space, they cannot sell them privately, and end up selling them back to the state for one-tenth or one-hundredth of the price at which such things will then be sold to foreigners in the state shops.

Moreover, China's need of foreign exchange is now preventing people in a city like Peking from enjoying some of the little pleasures that were normal until the recent past, such as a Yixing teapot of red earthenware, or a Hunan pottery brush-holder. Until a few years ago, anyone could buy these easily for a few cents, whereas now, like many other products, they are reserved for export and do not show up on the local market anymore.

Among the small pleasures of daily life in old Peking was the raising of animals: dogs, pigeons, birds, crickets filled the leisure time of both young and old men. Even that has passed. The first to disappear were the dogs. The order came in 1950. Mrs Peter Lum, wife of a British diplomat, witnessed the massacre and related it in her book of memoirs, *Peking 1950-1953*. "The dogs were taken away to be hanged or to be clubbed in small carts, like garbage carts, closed tight and packed solid. If you passed one you could hear them thrashing inside and see blood on the sides of the carts."

People in Peking reacted badly and the communist authorities said that the instructions had been carried out too radically. Yet the killing continued and soon there were no more dogs. The official reason at that time was that dogs were rabid. In 1953, on the contrary, the Minister of Health explained to visiting foreign journalists that dogs had to be killed because the United States had started bacteriological warfare in Korea and dogs had been found to be carriers of terrible diseases.

More simply, people in Peking thought that dogs were eliminated because the secret police did not want to be bothered by their barking while going around at night to arrest spies, landlords and counter-revolutionaries.

Other people insist to this day on explaining the whole affair by the story that, when still a young man, Mao Zedong was once arrested and put in jail. When trying to escape, he

49

was stopped at a surrounding wall by a barking dog. "I shall destroy all walls and dogs, if ever I become emperor of China!" the young revolutionary is said to have promised himself. And he kept his word: Peking's walls and dogs were soon destroyed.

Foreigners, in their ghetto-like compounds, have continued to keep a few dogs and this has been tolerated. Yet not without problems. At the beginning of 1982, an east European ambassador was called in by the police and confronted with a list of "crimes" his dog had allegedly committed on its outings outside the compound. A sentence had been passed. The dog had to be executed. After long hours of negotiations, the dog was saved by the fact that the ambassador pleaded guilty on behalf of the animal and begged for clemency, since according to the Chinese calendar, that was the Year of the Dog.

During the brief spell of liberalization following the arrest of the Gang of Four in 1976, even dogs started to reappear here and there and it was a pleasant surprise, while going for a walk among the ruins of the old Summer Palace, to hear the long-forgotten sound of a bark. It was not a lasting one.

In 1983, the Peking Municipality reissued its old regulation about dogs, and policemen with electric rods went around Peking electrocuting all those they could find. Peasants were left with the skins and put them up to dry in order to make warm gloves for the winter.

After the dogs, in 1956 came the turn of the sparrows. Their crime was that they ate too much grain. During the Cultural Revolution it was the turn of goldfish, cats, pigeons and crickets. The small pleasures that these pets gave to people were considered "bourgeois."

Pigeons had already been prohibited once, during the days of the Empire. Police had discovered that people living near the state granaries had trained their birds to fill their beak and fly back home with the loot. A man with 100 pigeons could take up to 25 kilograms of grain a day.

In 1982, pigeons, prohibited during the Cultural Revolution and resurrected after it, were again declared undesirable because they made too much noise, disturbed public order and dirtied laundry hung out to dry in the courtyards. A huge pigeon market, which had come to life spontaneously in the

Long Tang Hu (Dragon's Pond) Park in southern Peking, where thousands of young people gathered mainly on Sunday mornings to buy and sell and discuss business, was closed by the police because "people trampled and destroyed the grass in the area."

Half a dozen little free markets have popped up in Peking and are still open, providing birds, goldfish and again a few crickets for the lovers of the old "small games," as the people called their hobbies.

Peking used to be a city of scholars, artisans, intellectuals, artists and government officials coming from a young bourgeois class. The arrival of Mao's armies into the Chinese capital saw, like all communist victories, the beginning of a profound social revolution that has turned Peking into a city of peasants, workers, soldiers and Party cadres.

Society was turned upside down: the old ruling class was deprived of its homes, its properties, its privileges, and a whole new race of people has taken over the power apparatus. Over the last 35 years the men in command of Peking, from the zoo to the transport companies, from the power station to the industrial bureau, have been — and still are — men whose prime quality was to have joined the revolution in the early days and to be trusted by the Party. This has brought great changes to all aspects of life.

The very language of Peking has changed. Many former expressions have been eliminated and military terminology, used by the guerrillas during the civil war, has crept into today's way of speaking. Habits reflecting the communist obsession with security and secrecy of the underground days were introduced to Peking in 1949, and still survive 35 years later. When answering a telephone call, the receiver does not disclose his name, the name of his unit or even his telephone number. The other side behaves in exactly the same way, so that telephone calls go on this way:

"Wei....(Hello)"
"Wei....Wei...."
"Wei....Who are you?"
"Wei....Who are you?"
"Which unit are you?"

"Which unit are you?"

This can go on for quite a while before one of the two gives away the secret of his identity.

The listing of telephone numbers was an equally well-kept secret until two years ago when the communist authorities decided to print the first Peking telephone book since 1949.

When the communists took over Peking, there were 29,000 telephones in the capital, that is 2.1 telephones for every hundred persons. Now, there are 115,000 telephones, which, considering the sevenfold increase of the population, amounts to only 1.3 telephones per hundred persons. In 1949, more than half of Peking's telephones belonged to private people. Now, all telephones belong to units or are public telephones. For security reasons, the communist authorities disconnected all telephones in private homes and they have made it impossible ever since for an individual to acquire a new one: the installation of a new phone costs one year's salary, the monthly rent amounts to one-third of a month's pay, and anyway the problem is a theoretical one, since no private person without a high government job is allowed a phone at home.

Common people can use the public phone...if it works. Recently, the *Youth Daily* told the story of a man who, having tried in vain to use various phones in his neighborhood, wrote to the paper about his experience and concluded with a parody of one of Mao's famous stories, that of the old man who removed mountains. "What does it matter if it is difficult for me to make a telephone call. When I shall die, my son will try. When he shall die, my grandsons will continue to try."

Public telephones are installed in the rooms of the street committee, so that every conversation can be listened to and immediately reported to security officials by those whom the Peking people call "the policemen with small feet."

These "policemen with small feet" were introduced into Chinese life after 1949 and still dominate the daily existence of all families.

Each street is divided into sectors. Each sector has a street committee, whose members are usually old retired ladies, born when feet binding for girls was still a custom. Many of them came from the countryside into Peking with the communist armies. The duties of the street committee vary with the political pressures put upon the people from the top, but even in normal times they range from checking unplanned pregnancies, to reporting the presence of outsiders visiting a family, to checking what a family acquires. Often these "policemen with small feet" can neither read nor write, yet their approval is the essential first step for a person wishing to change his residence, or to send his child to the neighborhood kindergarten.

The "policemen with small feet" can at any time enter people's homes, inquire about what's cooking in the pot, and look under the bed, allegedly to check whether the family abides by the rules laid down by the hygiene campaign, but actually to check whether anything or anybody is hiding underneath.

Through the unit where he works, through the street committee where he lives, every Chinese is constantly under scrutiny, under the control of the one organization, the Public Security Bureau, that presides over his whole life and sets the range of the path within which he can move. If he leaves it, other checks intervene.

A Chinese who enters a hotel in order to pay a visit to a foreigner, or even a relative coming from abroad, has to register with the policemen at the door, has to give his name, his address and the name of his unit. Both the street committee and the security bureau in his working unit will be immediately informed of his visit, and he will have to give reasons for it.

Defiance of these rules lands people in trouble and can lead to re-education camps.

Many places in Peking, usually the best (hotels, restaurants and shops), are out of bounds for common Chinese. "Before, it was prohibited to dogs and Chinese, now it's prohibited only to Chinese," screams an American of Chinese origin. Dressed in a blue jacket and blue trousers, she is mistaken for a local resident and therefore chased away rudely from the Marco Polo shop which occupies the former Hall of Fasting in the park of the Temple of Heaven.

53

This hall, where in the old days the emperor used to rest and prepare himself for the annual sacrifices, has been transformed into a shopping center for carpets, cloisonné, furniture and handicrafts. But common Chinese can only glue their noses against the glass window, under a sign that says "for foreign guests only."

The life of the communist leaders is quite different from that of common people and the difference became apparent immediately in 1949. Some of the best residences in Peking were assigned to generals and political commissars, and more and more sections of the Western Hills became restricted as luxury homes were built for Party bosses.

Next to the Forbidden City, one-third of which remained open as a museum, the communists established a new Forbidden City, Zhongnanhai, surrounded by the same oxblood red imperial walls that for centuries kept the Son of Heaven in unseen and unapproachable seclusion. Mao Zedong, Zhou Enlai, Liu Shaoqi and other top communists lived and worked there, controlling one another, suspecting one another, staging putsch and counter-putsch against one another, until the last one in 1976, when Mao's widow and her followers were toppled and arrested.

Communist leaders lived remote from the people. They were rarely seen in public and moved from their residences to their working places, to the Great Hall of the People or the Party headquarters, through a network of secret underground tunnels. Lin Biao barricaded himself in a huge compound, protected by a 10-meter-high wall in the western district of the city. Jiang Qing had her own private residence in the former palace of Prince Tuan, the leader of the Boxer Rebellion in 1900. From her walled compound, an underground road provided her with an emergency escape to a military airfield some 10 kilometers away.

Kang Sheng, head of the secret service, took over a large courtyard house north of the Drum Tower. In the garden he dug a nuclear shelter, which is now one of the thrilling attractions for foreign visitors. After his death, Kang Sheng was posthumously purged and expelled from the Party, as if membership of it were carried on by the soul. His house was turned into an exclusive hotel and restaurant, Bamboo Garden, for foreign guests only.

At first there was some resentment against the privileges the leaders granted themselves. But it was explained that these were rewards for the many sacrifices they had made for the revolution, and soon people stopped questioning the inequalities.

Now it is an accepted fact of life that even low-ranking Party cadres should be carried around unseen through the city, pretty much as in the old days, when palanquins with drawn curtains transported the mandarins of the empire.

It is an accepted fact of life that in the center of Peking, in hutongs where the majority of people still live miserably, there should be different compounds protected by barbed wire, with well-maintained rooftops, that there should be tall chimneys showing that those houses have central heating, and that the door, though modest from the outside, should be locked. "Open door means courtyard of the people; closed door means courtyard of a leader," say Peking residents mockingly.

Party cadres of higher levels have access to all kinds of goods and amenities which for common people are only a dream. They have special shops where their servants buy fresh meat, fresh fish and vegetables (one of these special shops, just outside the eastern gate of the Forbidden City, sells vegetables that are not treated with chemical fertilizers). They have special hospitals where they can be treated with drugs which are elsewhere not available. They have cars at their private disposal. In trains they travel in the best compartments, at the theater they sit in the front rows, at the cinema in the back ones. The cloth of their garments is of better quality; so is education for their children.

"China is still a poor country. If we had to live like everybody else, we wouldn't be able to work properly," says a high-level cadre confronted with the subject of privileges.

In a way, this is true. As it is probably true that Chinese society as it is today is not the society the communists envisioned when they took over the country 35 years ago. This is part of China's tragedy.

The communists had a moral right to win the civil war against Chiang Kai-shek. The Nationalists were corrupt, inefficient and increasingly unpopular. For almost a century China had been a declining, some thought of it as a dying, civilization, a civilization that could no longer resist the direct attacks, or even the peaceful competition, of the rest of the world. China was "the sick man of Asia," and the major powers of the time were ready to share its spoils.

The communists presented themselves as its saviors, as the only force that could stand up against foreign aggression and represent a new hope for China. They represented a new beginning, and that is why thousands and thousands of people sacrificed their lives to the communist cause and why many intellectuals, though not communists themselves, joined forces with the Revolution.

Now, 35 years later, new China is far from what the communists hoped for and promised. They have stopped China's decline, they have put the country on the road to development; but what they have achieved has cost the people a high price, and the mistakes they have committed in the process have caused immense confusion and misery.

Due to their ideology, the communists looked on anything connected with the past as being responsible for China's evils and backwardness. But they did not realize that to destroy is much easier than to rebuild. Thirty-five years later, the communists find that the old world is dead and that the new one is still unborn, that the old civilization is gone, and the new one they dreamed about is still to come. The temptation to blame others for the loss is always present.

On October 18, 1982, a ceremony took place in the Forbidden City to commemorate the 122nd anniversary of the destruction of Peking's old Summer Palace, the Yuan Ming Yuan (Palace of Great Brightness). It was looted and then burned by French and British troops during the second Opium War, in 1860. "Imperialism wants to destroy Chinese civilization and the Yuan Ming Yuan is but an example of this," said Lian Guan, a member of the central government, in his speech announcing a plan for the reconstruction of the palace. "So as to let posterity know who destroyed it and how," added Liao Mosha, vice-chairman of Peking's Consultative Committee.

The destruction of that palace, of which today not even the foundations are to be found, was one of the appalling episodes of foreign aggression against China during the last century. Yet, it is highly confusing to say now that imperialism wants to destroy China's civilization. The destruction of old Peking, which with its walls, temples, palaces and gardens was one of the highest symbols of Chinese civilization, is a tragedy the Chinese have imposed upon themselves, without any foreign help.

In 1949, Peking was still a splendid shell in which a weakened, corrupt, dying society waited for change and for rebirth. The communists, in order to bring about those changes, chose to get rid of everything that was old and promised to turn old Peking into a new capital, symbol of socialist China.

Thirty-five years of upheavals, suffering and great efforts have turned Peking into an anonymous conglomerate of roads, buildings and squares that one can hardly call a city. Thirty-five years of conflicting policies have turned Peking into a capital which is neither Chinese nor socialist, unless socialism must mean monotony, desolation, lack of fantasy and of vitality.

This happened because the communists have discouraged any independent thinking, have pushed aside the intellectuals, have not used the "experts," and have left the "reds" to make all decisions.

In the fifties, in intellectual circles, there were still discussions on how Peking ought to be changed. A man like Liang Sicheng, head of the architectural department of Qinghua University, proposed a form of architecture, a "national style," that would integrate Chinese tradition with modern experiences. He was criticized and purged; his plan was damned.

Each unit continued to build as it pleased. All debate was muffled, and soon nobody spoke out anymore, or dared to criticize what had been done. Thousands of intellectuals, accused of having rightist ideas, were deported from Peking in the course of various campaigns precisely aimed against them.

The communists, who had taken down the walls of Peking in order to free the capital from her feudal chains, built another, even more enslaving wall within the heads of people: a wall of fear and ideological prejudices.

Behind the Peking of today, there is no grand design, there is no scheme, no thought. One can wander for hours and hours through the city without encountering a single building of the last two decades that strikes one as an architectural statement, that can be taken as a model of what new China has been able to contribute.

The only impressive example of something new and original is the Fragrant Hills Hotel, designed by I.M. Pei, the American architect of Chinese origin. He has provided the best architectural lecture in decades on how to mediate between China's tradition and modernity. After two years of effort and care, down to the last detail, architect Pei left Peking the day after he had turned "his baby," as he called it, over to the bureaucracy of Party cadres and security officials who now manage it.

China's top leaders now realize that, for the much-desired modernization of the country, the role of intellectuals is essential. Thus, intellectuals are now called in again, are given privileges and offered Party membership. It is not without deep significance that, on Changan Avenue, across the road from the ancient observatory, a huge, multi-storey concrete building to house the Academy of Social Sciences is rising exactly on the plot of land where the Imperial Examination Hall used to stand. There, for centuries the candidates aspiring to officialdom, locked in its thousands of tiny cells, wrote down their memorized knowledge in order to be accepted as mandarins.

On the site of the institution that passed down a culture keeping China immobile for 2,000 years, soon there will be standing China's school of modern thinking, the think-tank which ought to provide the country with plans and ideas for its future. For Peking it might be too late.

Hastily seeking remedies for the appalling conditions in which most of the capital's 9 million people still live, the local authorities have embarked on a massive construction effort, yet without a general plan, without a comprehensive layout. Huge, faceless highrises are shooting up here and there. At the end of this year, 55 million square meters of new flats will be completed, eating up more and more of the little that is left of the old city.

Old Peking continues to die. An ancient prophecy says that the city at the edge of the desert will one day be taken back by it.

When sandstorms hit Peking, and the sun becomes surprisingly blue in the yellow sky, and sand covers everything, enters every door, every window, every mouth, it really looks as if the old sand demons are out to take back their treasured city.

But sandstorms last only a few hours. Bulldozers and hammers work every day, relentlessly sending old Peking into the bottomless abyss of oblivion.

3

The Sky Is High and the Emperor Far Away

Xinjiang: the province at the Soviet border

Flat. Dry. Awesome. Under a cloudless sky, pulsating with heat, the endless surface of sand and gravel reaches beyond the horizon and human fantasy. At times it is gray like dead ashes, at times brown or violet, black like soot or rose-red like an impossible peach blossom. A man could walk for days in any direction and meet nothing but his death in an utterly empty moonscape of dust of changing colors blown relentlessly by the wind.

The Uighurs call it Takla Makan, "you go inside and you never come back," but the Mongols call it simply Gobi, "the desert." Millions of years ago it was the bottom of a sea. Now it is an immense corridor cutting through Xinjiang, China's most western province. For centuries this desert has been on the path of history, with great battles and kingdoms won and lost over these sands.

Through here went the camel caravans on the Silk Road to exchange goods between the west and the Celestial Empire. Through here came Christianity with the first Nestorian missionaries; through here came Islam with the Turkish conquerors. Through here went the Chinese monk Xuan Zang in search of Indian Buddhist scriptures and Marco Polo in search of the riches of Cathay.

Through here, in the case of a confrontation between the two communist giants, would come the Russian tanks heading for the heart of China or for the country's nuclear installations at Lop Nor, hidden in the southeastern edge of the desert. But for the time being they will not come, or at least the Chinese do not seem to expect them.

The barrels of the heavy anti-aircraft guns sticking out of clay hills are covered with canvas, and the trenches, hastily dug six years ago along the main roads leading from the border

60

to the capital Urumqi, are now unmanned and reclaimed by fresh grass.

In February 1979, when Peking's troops invaded Vietnam and a "punitive" action by Hanoi's ally, the Soviet Union, was considered possible against Xinjiang, hundreds of thousands of people were evacuated from Chinese border towns like Altay, Tacheng and Ining. Now they have all gone back to their homes. Tension has disappeared and the atmosphere is extremely relaxed. Any impression of being at a likely front line is completely lacking.

Only a few years ago the rare visitor was treated to violent anti-Soviet propaganda, with theater performances of "heroic" Xinjiang people capturing "Soviet spies" and young militia girls doing target practice with live bullets in the courtyard of the Kunlun Hotel. Local authorities wanted to impress visitors with the war-preparedness of Xinjiang.

Now they seem to be concerned not to scare tourists away. "Since 1972 there has not been any major problem with the Soviets," says Abdulla Rahim, deputy director of the foreign affairs department of the Xinjiang provincial government, who even now denies border incidents (with casualties) that had been previously reported by both Peking and Moscow. The only episode he could mention was one about a lonely spy who "some time ago" put a microphone under somebody's sofa with a wire leading directly over the border.

Following an intense exchange of letters between Moscow and Peking, the two countries have now agreed to meet to discuss the "normalization" of their relations. Xinjiang, which over the last 20 years has been one of the major bones of contention between China and the Soviet Union, and therefore a likely battleground of opposing communist armies, might soon become the ground of a renewed, though cautious, Sino-Soviet cooperation.

Signs of detente are already noticeable. At the six border posts, once tightly sealed, along the 1,935 kilometers that Xinjiang shares with the Soviet Union, Russian and Chinese postmen meet six days a week to exchange bags of mail addressed to each other's territory. Military officers of the two sides meet to discuss and organize the "repatriation" of cows

61

and goats that have gone across the mine fields and the dividing lines. The radio war between Xinjiang and Soviet Turkestan has scaled down recently, and so has the internal propaganda about "enemies."

The loudspeakers which every morning wake the 800,000 inhabitants of Urumqi at 6 a.m. no longer obsessively remind people to be "vigilant," no longer tell stories about "treacherous Soviets," but rather broadcast stories about foreign countries and the need to learn from them. "When you are in Malaysia do not miss visiting..." says the soft voice of the woman speaker resounding over the muddy streets and squares becoming animated with people, donkeys, camels and goats. The irony of such an absurd recommendation in a country like China, from which people cannot travel as tourists, is easily missed because the radio broadcasts in Chinese, a language which for large numbers of people here is foreign and not understood.

For centuries Xinjiang has been inhabited by non-Chinese, and their descendants are still the majority of the population. To walk through the Urumqi central market, the bazaar that has recently been reopened after having been shut down during the Cultural Revolution, is like going through a museum of mankind. Except for Blacks, all other races seem to be represented.

In the heavy smell of the spices on sale and the smoke of shish kekab being prepared on charcoal fires by bearded Muslims, one mingles among Kazakh men with aquiline noses, who wear fur hats and leather boots; moon-faced, stocky Uighur women in multicolored dresses over dark stockings and wearing golden earrings; almost blond Uzbeki boys with bright, wide eyes; high-cheeked Mongols; and the odd White Russian who came here in search of refuge from the Soviet revolution of 1917 and unwillingly stayed on after the Chinese one in 1949.

Of all the people history brought to Xinjiang, the Han (the Chinese), though militarily present since the second century before Christ, are the most recent settlers, and as such they are not liked. The western visitor who wanders alone through the back streets of Urumqi is looked upon as a sort of distant relative by the local Mediterranean, Balkan Turkish kinds of people. They often, with amused laughter, point at the similarities of their noses and facial features that distinguish them and the westerners from the Han Chinese. But the control of Xinjiang, a natural invasion route toward China, has been traditionally considered vital by the various rulers of the Middle Kingdom and the Chinese have been persistent in their attempts to control the province.

"If Xinjiang is lost, Mongolia is indefensible and Peking is vulnerable" was the common Chinese saying for centuries. Apart from its strategic value, Xinjiang (new dominion) was for the Han what the far west was for the Americans: a new frontier to be explored and extended, a new territory to be developed. It still is.

With a land mass as large as Germany, France and Italy put together, with immense, almost untapped reserves of oil, uranium, coal and copper, Xinjiang is still a virgin land. The province, which represents one-sixth of the whole territory of China, has only one-hundredth of her total population (11 million people). Throughout the ages the Chinese control of Xinjiang has been contested by strings of invaders. During the last century, the tzarist empire and various western powers tried, with some success (Russia acquired with the "unequal treaties" vast areas of land), to cut the links between Peking and her faraway province, particularly working on the deep resentment of the Kazakh, Uighur and other minorities against the repressive, "foreign" rule of the Qing dynasty.

The Chinese held on, but even today they are very sensitive about the accusation (mainly coming from the Soviet Union) that they have no right to be in Xinjiang, that they are here as foreign colonialists and that they oppress the local populations. The Urumqi Provincial Museum, where Uighur girl attendants wait silently while a Chinese guide gives ritual explanations, seems to be open just to rebuff these charges.

In the two main halls, introduced by the usual Mao quote, "Make the past serve the present," there is not a single item related to the history of the 12 different minority peoples living in Xinjiang. The collection is made of exhibits recording the over 2,000-year-old presence of the Hans in the region: silk brocades of the Han dynasty, tricolor clay figures of horses

63

and soldiers of the Tang period and stone tablets recalling deeds of Chinese emperors and generals.

In case he might have missed the point, the visitor is given a small brochure in which it is said that all this material, unearthed since Liberation, "shows that Xinjiang has been an inalienable part of our great motherland since ancient times." The same message is delivered to those who visit the splendid ruins of Kaoshang, 180 kilometers southeast of Urumqi in the desert depression of Turfan, 155 meters below sea level. In the summer it is so hot there that one can literally cook an egg by burying it in the burning sand, while in winter it is the coldest spot in the whole of China.

In the middle of nowhere, in a landscape of rose-red clay that seems as old as time, stand the remnants of ramparts, towers, temples and houses the Chinese built with mud and straw in the first century B.C. to accommodate troops extending the boundaries of the Han empire. It is said that at the same location, at the time of Alexander the Great, Greek traders built a city called Ephesus. Some recent discoveries of ancient Greek coins support this point.

The Chinese abandoned Kaoshang in the fourteenth century and again at the beginning of this century. The ruins, half buried in the sand, were rediscovered by German travelers like von Le Coq and Grunwedel. The visit ends under the blinding sun with the Chinese guide saying, "The long history of Kaoshang proves that Xinjiang has been an inalienable part of China since ancient times."

Though their military presence in Xinjiang certainly dates back over 2,000 years, the Chinese rarely had complete control over the region, especially in times of weak dynasties. "Heaven is high and the emperor far away," the local people used to say, and anti-Han rebellions attempting to make Xinjiang a political unit independent from Peking were recurrent. The last one was in 1945 when, with Soviet help intended to turn the new state into a Soviet satellite like Mongolia, the local minority people set up an Eastern Turkestan Republic.

Since the end of the Qing empire in 1911, Xinjiang had been in effect a Russian protectorate, so the whole region was economically much more integrated with the Soviet economy than with that of the rest of China. To please the Chinese and the Americans at Yalta, Stalin himself worked to mediate the abolition of the independent republic and Xinjiang was officially described as part of China in 1946.

Even after the communists, who had worked underground among the local Han and the minority people (Mao Zedong's brother was murdered by the pro-nationalist warlord of Xinjiang), took over the province in 1949, an anti-Chinese independence movement survived. It was swiftly crushed.

Today nobody questions the sovereignty of the People's Republic of China over Xinjiang. Roughly 1 million soldiers are defending its border and its society has been through the same upheavals and transformations as the rest of the country.

Much more than in any other province one sees quotations from Mao's works inscribed on posters along the streets and huge, white plaster of Paris statues of the late chairman are in the halls of factories, schools, theaters and public buildings all over Xinjiang, clearly here more than anywhere else a symbol of unity and of the ideological glue that keeps this immense country of different people together.

Anti-Chinese sentiments among the non-Han, if still existent, are latent and certainly very much under control because the Chinese now feel rather confident in Xinjiang. In 1979, they opened the province to selected visitors, and since 1980 it has been added to the destinations of regular tourists.

"The minority people welcome us here," explains Zhang Pingsheng, a minor Chinese official in Urumqi. "We have brought railways, roads, factories and development." This is true. In 1949, there were only 3,000 kilometers of primitive roads, and now 24,000 kilometers of paved roads connect the main cities of Xinjiang. Before Liberation the train from Peking reached only Lanzhou, the capital of Gansu Province. Now the railway is open up to Urumqi, and a new track which will end in Tibet has already reached Kurla. The Karamai oilfields in the north have been extended and dozens of small and medium-sized textile and chemical factories have been put into operation, but this industrial progress has not particularly touched the two largest minority groups: the Uighurs who are by and large oasis dwellers and farmers, and the semi-nomadic Kazakhs who are mainly herdsmen in the mountains. Of the 200,000 industrial workers of Urumqi, the majority are Han.

In the tractor factory at the foothill of Yaomo Shan (The Devil's Mountain) on the outskirts of the provincial capital, out of the 2,100 workers who produce less than 1,000 Dong Fang Hong (The East is Red) tractors a year, only 13 percent are non-Chinese.

Minority people, all of them faithful Muslims until Liberation, were on the contrary deeply affected by the atheist policies of the communists, and later by the establishment of the People's Communes that forced the Uighurs to collectivize their land and the Kazakhs to renounce their nomadic customs in order to settle in fixed areas. The effects of these two shocks, which in different ways were felt in the whole of China, have been almost completely absorbed.

Though the average Chinese still looks upon minority people as "barbarians" (in much the same way as he looks upon any other non-Han, or any other foreigner for that matter), Peking's official policy toward the minorities cannot be described as one of discrimination. Particularly since the Sino-Soviet split, the Chinese have been very aware that any deep-rooted discontent among the minorities could be exploited by the Soviets with subversive aims. A constant comparison between the ways in which the same ethnic groups are treated on the two sides of the border (vast numbers of Uighurs, Kazakhs, Mongols, Kirghiz, Tadjiks and others live in the Soviet Union) is the final test of the allegiance of these minorities.

The Xinjiang provincial administration, which constitutionally (like Tibet and Inner Mongolia) enjoys a higher degree of autonomy than other provinces in China, has given ample opportunities of advancement to minority people in the fields of education and public administration. This is, however, not so in the Army, where few minority people are recruited and very, very few minority people become officers.

In the University of Xinjiang in Urumqi, out of the 2,380 students, 1,360 come from minority groups, and 43 percent of the teaching staff is non-Han. "Minority students are actually favored over the Chinese ones," explains the university vice president Anwar Hanbaba, himself a Uighur. "To pass the newly introduced entrance examination, a Chinese student needs to reach 260 points, a minority student only 90 points." This system of "favoritism" continues throughout the university. The reason is that the language of instruction is Chinese and the minority people do not know it.

Uighurs, Kazakhs and other minorities have been left free to maintain most of their customs; the Han language has not been imposed on them, and minority families have the option of sending their children either to a Chinese school or to a school of their ethnic group. In the urban areas the tendency is toward the first option, in the rural areas toward the second. The result is obviously that those who learn Chinese and let themselves be assimilated by the Chinese have better opportunities of advancement; the others are cut off from the mainstream of life which is and will become more and more Chinese.

Since 1949, thousands of demobilized PLA soldiers have been settled in state farms in various parts of Xinjiang, but mainly along the borders. Thousands of college graduates from eastern China have been sent together with thousands of cadres purged and ordered to "xia fang" (go to the countryside) during the various anti-rightist, anti-revisionist campaigns. The result is in the statistics.

In 1949, the population of Xinjiang was 4.9 million people. The Han numbered only 300,000. Today the population is 11 million, and the Han number almost 5 million. Before Liberation the Uighurs, the Kazakhs, and the others were in effect the largest majority in Xinjiang. Today they are what the Chinese call "ethnic minorities." With overpopulated areas along the basins of the two main Chinese rivers, the Yellow and the Yangtze, with overcrowded cities along the eastern coast of the country, this policy of internal migration toward the open and rich land of Xinjiang was natural and logical. As such it will continue. Though recently a few thousand former "rusticated youth" have tried to go back to their original cities, the vast majority of those who were forced here in the fifties and sixties have adapted themselves and stay, while

67

thousands of new workers and cadres from the eastern cities move to Xinjiang. The incentives are not negligible. A teacher who earns 60 yuan (approximately US$30) a month in Shanghai gets 79 a month when he comes to Urumqi.

A worker of the second category (there are eight categories for workers) goes from 35 yuan to 50. A cadre of the eighteenth class (cadres are divided into 25 classes) who earns 90 yuan in Peking, gets 124 if he works in Xinjiang. Outside the main cities Han and minority people live completely separated lives, given the nature of their work.

In the East Wind People's Commune in the Bai Yang Go (the Valley of the White Poplars), in the Tian Shan chain (the Heavenly Mountains) that rims the northern side of the desert with imposing peaks covered by eternal snow, all of the 7,600 inhabitants are Kazakhs. There are 700,000 of them in the whole of Xinjiang and, like their ancestors for centuries, they are semi-nomad and herdsmen. In the Five Star Commune in the Turfan depression there are 35,000 people. They are all peasant Uighurs.

There are over 5 million of them in today's Xinjiang and they thus constitute the largest minority group in the province (100,000 Uighurs live across the border in the Soviet Union). The Chinese communist authorities have on three occasions run into great trouble with these minorities: once when they tried to give permanent residences to the nomad Kazakhs and a second time when they tried to take away some of their pasture land to turn into fields for growing grain. The result was that, in 1962, 60,000 Kazakhs crossed the border and went to the Soviet Union. The third occasion was during the Cultural Revolution, when Red Guards closed all the mosques of Urumqi and ended up fighting bloody street battles with local Muslim Uighurs.

The 1962 episode was a turning point in the recent history of Xinjiang and in Sino-Soviet relations in the region. Accusing Moscow of having lured the Kazakhs to escape and above all fearing the old Soviet influence over Xinjiang, the Chinese closed the five consulates the Soviets had in the province, expelled all Soviet advisers and sealed the border.

Moreover, they started a long-term process intended to cut

forever the ties between the minorities living in China and their friends and relatives in the Soviet Union. They abolished the Arabic and Cyrillic scripts in which both the Uighur and Kazakh languages were written, and introduced a romanized transcription similar to that used to transcribe the Chinese language. On August 1, 1976, the Chinese news agency Xinhua announced that the script reform had been completed and that the new romanized Uighur and Kazakh languages had replaced the old ones. Officially it is certainly so. Minority schools teach reading and writing in the new form, Mao's quotations along the roads are transcribed in the same way, and local papers for the minorities now use the same script. But signs outside shops, small personal notices that people plaster at bus stops advertising a bicycle for sale or looking for a flat to swap, are still written in Arabic. So is the only copy of the Koran left in Nanliang Mosque, the most important mosque in Urumqi.

"We save it, hiding it away," says the Imam, showing an ancient handwritten collection of colored cardboard pages bound together with an old rope, kept like an irreplaceable treasure in a newly made wooden box with a big lock.

Nanliang Mosque is in the main thoroughfare of Xinjiang's capital. Before Liberation, when the road was called Foreign Lane because the British and Russian consulates were here (the new name is Unity Street), there was a mosque every 300 meters. The buildings, cracked and rotting, are still there and the broken pinnacles of the towers from which the faithful were called to prayer still stick up over the roofs of shabby old houses. But most of them are no longer used for worship. One has been turned into a warehouse, one into a school, another is a depot for construction material. The rather free practice of Islam, which had survived in Xinjiang until 1966, was put to an end by the Cultural Revolution. Red Guards occupied the mosques, burned the holy books they found, smashed the old Arabic inscriptions over the entrances and "beat and beat us to get the faith out of us," recalls a 67-year-old Uighur.

Four years ago, Nanliang Mosque, together with half a dozen others, was reopened, and every day some 500 people come to kneel on the worn-out red carpets and pray in the dim light filtering through the broken windows and the leaking roof. Most are old men with long white beards and embarrassed, sad looks when one asks them how many of them have gone to Mecca ("none" is the answer). But there are some young people too who proudly explain that after prayers they stay on to copy the Koran in order to learn "to read and write."

The study of Arabic, which the Chinese authorities have abolished as an official language, seems to be for some young Uighurs part of an effort to preserve their identity, just as for many others it may be an expression of independence to keep their watches on Xinjiang time and not on Peking time (two hours ahead) as officially prescribed for the whole of China.

Nobody gets into trouble for this now. Uighur girls sing their national songs in the people's theater of Urumqi in their own language and are no longer forced, as was the case earlier, to sing in Chinese the usual "We Are Determined to Liberate Our Blood Brothers and Sisters on Taiwan." Nor is a cadre in the city of Turfan afraid of showing a handwritten copy (in Arabic) of the history of Turfan and the Uighurs. "You cannot buy anything like this," he says.

During the reign of the Gang of Four, even a collection of Uighur proverbs was banned as "foreign propaganda." In the Xinhua bookstore of Urumqi, the biggest in the whole of Xinjiang, the sections reserved for Uighur and Kazakh literature are still rather empty with only a few translations of Chinese authors, mainly Mao Zedong. But more recently, a few new books have been printed, and were sold out as soon as they reached the store.

The liberalization which has reopened the bazaars and some mosques of Xinjiang has also increased the number of private cattle the Kazakhs can keep and the area of the private plots the Uighurs can till, and reasserted as an official policy respect for the traditions and habits of the minorities. All this has greatly relaxed the relationships between Han and non-Han in the region.

The Chinese seem to be more secure about the allegiance of the minorities and no longer obsessed with fears of subversive plots and separatist movements. Against this background, Xinjiang seems to have all the ingredients for the leap forward

which the modernization process promises to the whole country: resources, underpopulated land and firm control over the
social situation.

The Chinese have since 1949 invested heavily in Xinjiang.
Xinjiang not only keeps all local revenue for its own use, but
also receives subsidies from the central government amount-
ing roughly to half the annual budget. More is needed but
modernization requires above all some basic choices.

"My factory is very old. We should change almost all our
machines to increase production," says a cadre of the July
First Textile Mill on the outskirts of Urumqi. Indeed the
factory was built by the Soviets in 1951.

It was also Soviet aid that built most of the other 12 textile
mills, the 16 large and small iron and steel plants, and the 100
large and small coal mines in Xinjiang. One sees Soviet traces
everywhere. Even many of the old black limousines carrying
high cadres around Xinjiang are still of Soviet vintage. In a
1950s treaty of friendship and mutual aid, Peking and Moscow
agreed on joint exploitation of oil and nonferrous metals in
Xinjiang, on improving the road connection between Xinjiang
and the Soviet Union, and on the extension of the railway
system to connect the Peking–Lanzhou–Xinjiang railway with
the Turkestan railway.

The Sino-Soviet split stalled all these projects. The Russians
had already brought their trains from Aktogay up to the bridge
on the Chinese border, but the Chinese stopped laying down
the rails far from it. "We did not want to give them a rope
to strangle us," has been said since.

Xinjiang had to rely exclusively on its links with eastern
China. Communication has improved since the time of the
Empire when, according to legend, camels carrying the famed
Hami melon to the emperor left with two jars of Xinjiang earth
in which the seeds of the melon were planted, and the melons
were ripe on arrival. But the more than 3,000 kilometers
between Urumqi and Peking are still a long distance to cover
even on roads and rails. Cut off from the Soviet Union, the
tractor factory of Urumqi had to get tractor engines from
Shenyang in former Manchuria, and there were production
delays of weeks and weeks before the factory decided to build

its own engines.

The situation has not changed much in this respect over the last 20 years, and, if the border between Xinjiang and the Soviet Union could be completely reopened, Xinjiang could only gain from it. In the new climate of economic readjustment such an option is not to be excluded. If some form of normalization can be reached between Moscow and Peking and the six Chinese paved roads leading to the Soviet border are reopened, not only local Xinjiang trade would improve, but the Chinese could consider the economic advantages of a renewed cooperation to improve the industrial base of the province.

As in other parts of China, certain plants in Xinjiang have become obsolete and unprofitable. The Chinese have the choice of "throwing everything away and buying expensive, modern equipment from the west," as some experts advise, or of buying from the Soviet Union, at lower prices, advanced machinery which can fit into the existing Soviet-built facilities to modernize step by step. "One thing is certain," a Soviet diplomat told me in Peking, "a Japanese nut does not go with a Russian bolt."

It is not unlikely that in the future, instead of the feared tanks, the Chinese will see Soviet trucks coming through the Dzungaria Gates and rolling down the dusty roads of the Xinjiang desert.

The language institute of the University of Urumqi has for the first time reopened a course in Russian. Sixty-three students have just enrolled in it.

4

The Kingdom of the Rats

Manchuria: China's industrial base

Land, land. Gray, flat, monotonous, frozen land as far as the eye can see. For days and days in its panting voyage into the wilderness, the train crosses huge frozen rivers shining like mirrors under the cold sun, cuts through gray, transparent forests without a leaf, passes groups of gray mud houses clustered around isolated factories vomiting spouts of black smoke into the milky white of the winter sky.

The grassland never ends and the train seems doomed never to reach the flat horizon from where blows relentlessly the paralyzing wind that whips and freezes this inhospitable land which the world used to call Manchuria.

The Chinese today refer to it as Dongbei, the northeast, the richest part of the country, the industrial base of the People's Republic.

One-third of China's heavy machines are produced here, half of China's timber, half of her coal, half of her oil come from here. China's tanks, her guns, her planes are made in factories hidden somewhere in the desolate vastness of this region.

If an enemy were to cripple China, he would have to strike here, for this region is economically the most important and strategically the most vulnerable. Dongbei has 4,000 kilometers of common border with Soviet Siberia, and it is here that Moscow deploys some of her best armored divisions. It was indeed at this border that communism fought its first bloody battle within its own ranks when in 1969 Chinese and Soviet soldiers killed each other by the hundreds for the control of an insignificant Manchurian island in the middle of the Ussuri River.

Forgotten for centuries beyond the Great Wall, which the Chinese had built over 2,000 years ago to protect themselves

73

against the nomads, Manchuria was a wasteland.

"Although it is uncertain where God placed paradise, we can be sure that he chose some other place than this," wrote French priest Huc traveling here in 1846. Soon after, all of a sudden, Manchuria became "the promised land of Asia." Some adventurers had come here to search for gold, silver and coal, and they found them all.

"Manchuria is a treasure house, and all great powers are eager to get the key to it," wrote a British man at the turn of the century. That key was the train. In 1896, the tzar of Russia obtained from the dying Chinese Empire the concession to cut a railroad through Manchuria, from China to Vladivostock. Japan went to war with Russia (1904) to share in her concessions. This gray, empty expanse of land that hardens like a rock at temperatures of 30 or 40 degrees below zero, became the *Cockpit of International Ambitions*, according to a book of the time, and hundreds of thousands of foreign troops died for it in battles that shook the world (Mukden, Tsushima etc...). Yet the railroad construction went on and the train, advancing through the grassland, brought to Manchuria conquerors and exploiters, misery and progress alike.

Building from scratch in the middle of the deserted region, the Russians created splendid Harbin, a miniature replica of imperial Moscow; in the south they opened the harbor of Dairen (still one of the most important in China).

The Japanese turned old Shenyang of the Manchus into a prosperous industrial center and, where the north–south and east–west Manchurian railroads met, they built New Changchun, epitome of a modern city with vast boulevards, imposing public buildings of granite, and expansive parks.

Manchuria attracted adventurers and businessmen from all over the world. White Russians flocked here by the thousands, followed by European Jews. Foreign capitalists opened factories, shops, mines and developed islands of welfare around which grew the shanty towns of millions of Chinese migrants who had escaped famine and death in Shandong and beyond. They worked in conditions of semi-slavery in the foreign concessions, and toiled under the brutal rule of the shortlived empire of Manchukuo, established with Tokyo's blessing in 1932. Planning to use Manchuria as a stepping stone for their conquest of China and to sustain with its resources their entire war effort in Asia, the Japanese speeded up the industrialization of the region and invested massively in it.

When the Chinese communists inherited Manchuria at the end of World War II, by then known as the "Ruhr of the East," the region was by far the most advanced of the country and, with the help of the Soviets, Mao Zedong decided to make it the industrial base for the construction of New China. Since 1949, Peking's biggest investments have been made in Manchuria, the best technicians have been assembled, and thousands of young people and thousands of political prisoners have been forcibly dispatched to the region to help reclaim land and open new mines.

Today, 35 years after these great efforts and Peking's claims of great successes, old Manchuria is still the most advanced region in China. But, more than any other region, it is also the symbol of the confusion, the disarray, the mismanagement, the crisis of confidence that grips the whole country.

Natural resources have been overestimated and are now running short. Factories are old and work far under capacity. Industries are constantly crippled by shortages of energy and raw materials. There is no fresh capital to invest. After a short period of decentralization, Peking is quickly taking back control of everything. Here the new centrally imposed policy of "readjustment" means that all projects intended to expand old industries have been cancelled, that hundreds and hundreds of projects designed to open new factories have been suddenly stopped and indefinitely postponed.

In the cities there is vast unemployment and growing youth discontent. People realize that the great program of the Four Modernizations, announced after the fall of the Gang of Four, is nothing but a pipe dream, and that even if it could be carried out "it would only be enjoyed by the children of the children of my children," as one worker put it.

The Number One Automobile Factory in Changchun, former capital of Manchukuo, was one of the prides of New

China. Completely designed, built and equipped by the Soviets, the factory started in 1956 to produce the famous dark green Liberation truck one sees all over the country.

In 1958, with a staff of 23,000, it turned out 30,000 of them. American journalist and Mao's friend, Edgar Snow, was told by the factory managers in 1960 that the plant was scheduled to produce 150,000 trucks per year by the end of 1962. It never did, and the factory reached its peak only in 1979 with an output of 72,000 trucks.

Last year, with a staff of 40,000 people, only one-third of whom were engaged in production, the output fell to 60,000 trucks. And this year? "The plan is not to produce less than in 1980," says Deputy Factory Manager Wu with a ring of embarrassment. Then, as a justification, he adds, "the factory is part of the national economy. We can only produce according to the quantity of resources allocated to us."

The external appearance of the factory is still imposing, with its tall sturdy buildings of red brick, but inside the workshops are signs of age and depression. More than half the machines are still the original Soviet ones, slow and old-fashioned. Only one assembly line runs, and around the few workers who keep pace with it many others loiter, chat and read newspapers.

The color of the trucks lined up for the final test is now pale blue, but basically this is the only innovation on the old truck, designed by the 200 Soviet engineers who worked here 30 years ago. Technical delegations of various western countries have recently come to this factory to discuss proposals to modernize it, but the sudden freeze on foreign currency, badly needed to replace at least part of the old machinery, has left everything as it was.

The only trace to be found of the new models of trucks, buses and small cars which the factory planned to produce by 1985 is a big oil painting of them outside the plant's main entrance.

Unlike Chinese factories of the past, this one does not show on its walls colorful boards with climbing arrows of targets and achievements. Instead, in the workshops hang the results of the exams of the various workers who, since the factory has nothing for them to do, have been assigned to study. Due to reduced production, almost every unit has people under this special regime called "half study–half work."

"We cannot fire anyone. So this is a good opportunity to retrain and requalify our people," says Deputy Manager Wu. Many more workers of the Number One Automobile Factory of Changchun may soon follow on this path of paid semi-employment.

Since 1958, this factory has also produced the Red Flag car, the black limousine that has been the status symbol of the powerful in People's China. How many of these very special cars are already in circulation or how many are now being produced is a well-kept secret ("it is a state matter," says Deputy Manager Wu). But the rumor that Peking might decide to stop its production altogether has been circulating for some time.

The Red Flag, it is said, costs too much, uses too much gasoline and, with its luxurious interior of wood and its plutocratic black mass that calls for absolute precedence on all roads and at all crossings, is a source of easily aroused popular resentment in a country where the great majority of the population still move about in carts drawn by horses and mules.

The shutting of the Red Flag line would be another bad blow for the 150,000 people who live off the automobile factory. Last year the plant offered no new jobs to the thousands of young people entering the labor market and nobody will be hired this year either.

The average salary at the factory, 55 yuan plus 8 yuan of collective bonuses, has not gone up over the last two years and has fallen far lower than the average salary of smaller factories in the same city. Young girls at the Changchun optical instrument factory, for instance, make up to 90 yuan per month, thanks to a system of individual bonuses which the auto factory has not been able to or has not wanted to introduce.

The economic reforms introduced in China after the fall of the Gang of Four, seen in the west as a good omen of quasi-capitalism (free play of market forces, competition among enterprises, more local decision-making power in management, planning and marketing) have in effect created wage differentials among workers and have disrupted the previously tightly controlled supply system of raw materials. No longer forced to hand over to the state all of their products, factories and other enterprises have been looking for the most profitable way to buy and sell goods, and have thus affected the production of other units.

Big cigarette factories suddenly found themselves without tobacco. Producers now preferred to sell it to smaller communal manufacturers. Other plants, on the contrary, could not sell goods they had over-produced, hoping for bigger profits. The Gemotang Commune factory not far from Changchun, for instance, had to ask its workers to sell among their friends at a 40% discount the bed springs nobody else wanted.

Steel plants manufactured more heavy iron sheets than needed, while the Harbin turbine factory had to reduce working hours for lack of a fine alloy required for its production. Canned food factories in Jilin Province remained idle for lack of material to make their tins. "A few capitalist measures within a socialist system combine the defects of both worlds without producing their advantages," says a foreign economist now studying this experiment in mixed economy.

While most factories in the Chinese northeast suffer from shortages of raw materials, all of them are crippled by the shortage of energy. In the tractor factory of Shenyang, which in 1958 started to produce the famous East Wind tractor, two of the three assembly lines are now idle and entire workshops are closed, their turning lathes covered with old newspapers. At 3 p.m., after a single shift of only six hours, the whole plant closes.

A recent accident in a power station in northern Dongbei, at the border with the Soviet Union, has further reduced the already insufficient amount of electricity at the disposal of the factory.

"The problem is not only ours. We all depend on the weather and in winter there is not enough water in the basins," says Deputy Manager Li Changfu. "The shortage usually starts in November and lasts until April."

The whole of former Manchuria depends on a single electricity power system that for almost half the year cannot feed the industrial network of the region. Manchuria has oil and coal, but all projects to use these resources on a big scale in order to solve the local energy problem have been shelved. Therefore it is for the state to decide which plants are going to use how much of the rationed supplies of energy. The choice is made on the basis of a priority list and the tractor factory of Shenyang, like many other plants that are now working only four days a week, is not at the top of the list.

The factory, built in 1953 by the Chinese around an old complex started by the Japanese, now employs 5,300 workers. It could produce up to 8,000 tractors a year, but the quota assigned to it by the central plan for 1981 calls only for 3,700. "Peking has a general idea of the national necessities. We are told that peasants don't need many tractors anymore and so we follow orders," says Deputy Manager Li.

In the past, tractors were the symbol of the modernization of agriculture and they were profitably used over large plots in the collective system of farming. Since the fall of the Gang of Four, and with the progressive dismantling of the people's communes, more and more land has been allocated throughout the country to private plots and a new accounting and wage system has been introduced. Peasants no longer share the general income of the commune or the brigade, but rather are paid for what their family produces. The result has been that people tend to concentrate their work on the specific plot assigned to them and, since these are not big, they can no longer make use of tractors.

Production of these and similar machines is therefore discouraged. "Can we come to visit your factory?" I asked over the phone to a plant which in the past was known to produce cultivators and other agricultural implements. "Sorry," was the reply, "we don't produce those things anymore. We now make sewing machines."

It would have been interesting to see how this conversion had been possible and how it was working, but the visit was ruled out as "inconvenient."

"Readjustment means switching emphasis from heavy to

light industry to produce what the people need," explains Jiang Wanjo, of the production control office of Liaoning Province, one of the three that form Dongbei (the other two being Heilongjiang in the north and Jilin in the center).

Throughout the region, heavy industries which used to produce equipment that was the symbol of the country's progress are now asked to contribute to the production of the long-desired new symbols of individual welfare: TV sets, radios, bicycles, sewing machines, tape recorders and watches.

For many plants the conversion is painful and at times impossible. In any case it means closing down workshops, leaving people without jobs (though still on the payrolls) and in general abandoning all previous plans to expand existing production.

If old plants now cannot grow, new ones cannot be born. In the middle of the Manchurian plain are the oil fields of Daqing, the biggest in China. Along the road that from the Daqing refinery cuts straight through the marshland, now completely frozen, runs a newly painted orange pipeline. It goes on for a few kilometers. Then, all of a sudden, in the middle of nowhere it stops. Further down the road, out of the flat steppe rises a cluster of new, big, empty oil tanks. They may have to wait years for their supplies. The huge plastics factory which was supposed to be built here and be fed by that pipeline and those tanks, has been sacrificed in the name of readjustment. In the distance one sees the stumps of the concrete pillars the factory should have rested on, one sees the black skeletons of tall modern buildings that should have housed the 4,500 people already hired to work in the factory.

The whole complex would have cost 2.5 billion renminbi ("people's currency" — 2 yuan being worth approximately US$1) and construction was to last five years. The German machines bought for the plant have already arrived and lie idle, wrapped in plastic in a hangar. The 120 foreign experts who were to help with the project have been sent home. Of the workers, some have been assigned to other jobs, some sent to study, and some watch over the empty, desolate buildings through which the wind of the grassland now howls.

"For the people in Peking this might be a small matter, but

for us it was a big project and not all the workers here understand why it had to be stopped,'' says a member of the Daqing administration.

Peking says that the construction of this plastics factory, like many other projects throughout China, had to be suspended for shortage of foreign currency needed to pay for the imported machinery. But the real reason might be an even more serious one: Daqing does not produce enough oil to feed this factory, or other projects conceived in the ambitious and illusory heyday of optimism that followed the overthrow of the Gang of Four from power.

''Daqing's crude oil output has increased at an average annual rate of 28 percent,'' announces an official Chinese brochure of 1978. That was not true and, based on that and other fudged figures, it was then estimated that by 1985 Daqing would contribute around 100 million tons of crude to the program of the Four Modernizations.

In effect Daqing reached the 50 million tons target in 1976 and never went beyond it. ''We now produce the same amount, and if we can keep it stable until 1985 it will be quite a world record,'' says Li Wenhai, a Party official at the Daqing oil fields. That quantity would amount to just about half of what was hoped for, and not even this now seems possible. Daqing's production of crude oil is expected to fall progressively over the next years. The story of Daqing is typical of China's political ups and downs.

At the turn of the century, while building the railroad through the steppe, the Russians opened a tiny station called Sartu. The Japanese, 30 years later, believed there was oil nearby, but they never found it. In 1959, a group of Chinese technicians, after months of trials, struck it. It was a few days before the tenth anniversary of the foundation of the People's Republic and the name Sartu was changed into Daqing, ''great celebration.''

The first winter was terrible. ''We had no place to live. At night the temperature was 40 degrees below zero. We dug trenches, we covered them with plastic sheets and there we slept,'' recalls a worker who has been here since the beginning. That was the time when the Soviets withdrew all their assistance from China, including their experts. The discovery of Daqing oil was used to boost China's morale.

Daqing became the test of the country's ability to do things by itself, the symbol of China's self-reliance. Workers flocked here from all over the country and this barren, savage plain became animated with thousands of people fighting against nature, drilling and drilling.

They succeeded and production rose steadily. In 1963, the Daqing refinery, completely built by the Chinese, stood up like a cathedral of steel in the emptiness of the grassland. Later followed the fertilizer plant and the synthetic cloth factory.

In 1964, Mao visited the oil fields and wrote the famous slogan, "In industry learn from Daqing." Daqing became a myth. Cadres from all parts of China came here on pilgrimage. Stories of Daqing's deeds filled the textbooks of the country, and model workers like "Iron Man Wang," who later was named to the Party Central Committee, became heroes the nation was asked to imitate. An old Chinese poem describing what one sees when looking down from the moon was modernized and memorized by generations of children with the addition of the sight of the Daqing oil field.

The Cultural Revolution did not affect Daqing. On the contrary, it stressed the myth even more.

People lived in primitive mud houses, but the oil fields continued to expand. The slogan was, "production first, livelihood second." The fall of the Gang of Four did not involve Daqing. In 1977, a national conference to learn from the experience of these oil fields ended with the drafting of a plan "to open 10 more Daqings by the end of the century." Oil production and Daqing were to be the pillars of the Four Modernizations.

Children in schools still repeat by heart the glories of Daqing. The walls of China are still covered with four white characters on red background, "In industry learn from Daqing." The only place in the country where there are no slogans is Daqing itself. Even what Hua Guofeng wrote praising Daqing during his visit here in 1977 has been erased. The big board on which it was painted now stands empty, in plain red, at the end of the street that leads to the railway station.

Of the hundreds of slogans and of Mao's quotations that once colored the Daqing plain, only one, hailing "The great unity of the people of the world," remains — in the courtyard of the huge guesthouse where hundreds of rooms were completed last year for visitors who have ceased to come.

Daqing is no longer a model of anything. Its demise is the end of a whole historical era of New China. The values for which Daqing stood were in its motto, "Hard work and self-reliance." Now, the first thing a visitor notices are yellow buses imported from Rumania shuttling among the various factories. "We could use China-made buses, but the rules of international trade have imposed these on us," says the local guide with some embarrassment.

When the machines imported from the United States for the new fertilizer plant arrived, a whole team of electricians refused to install them. Now there is foreign equipment in various plants. Some resistance to it remains. People complain about the poor quality of some imported machines and about the excessive automation of others that reduces job opportunities for a labor force as redundant here as in the rest of China.

In the past, Daqing was a model for "peasant-worker villages," something that was boasted of as an ideal combination of industry and agriculture. Now these villages are being slowly dismantled and people are scheduled to move to 10 major urban conglomerations where rows of modern houses are being built.

Daqing heroes of the past are equally pushed aside. "Iron Man Wang," whose picture is still in the school books of China, is no longer mentioned in Daqing itself, and the exposition hall dedicated to him after his death in 1970 houses drilling and pumping equipment. A large panel shows the locations of the oil fields. The northern one was the last to be opened. An old brochure of the time describes the fight against sub-zero temperatures. "The workers were scarcely able to stand against the wind, their eyebrows frosty white and miniature icicles hanging from their eyelashes. 'What is snow,' the workers said, 'even if it is knives that fall we will go on working to open up the new oil zone.'" That was in 1973.

Since that time, three more areas have been taken into consideration and studied as prospective oil fields but "the results have not been encouraging," as Li Wenbai of the Daqing administration admits. "Do you have any drilling teams working at the moment?" one asks. "No. No. Now it is too cold to drill," is the reply.

In the evening, as the large red lantern of the sun dives from the violet sky into the black, flat line of the horizon, it sheds golden reflections on the rows of half-buried mud houses over which twinkle the small paper lanterns lit by people to greet the new lunar year. Lonely animal carts pass under the bulging towers of the factories in the numbing cold. It is especially then that the idea that "the blood of industry," as oil is called in China, might dry up and "heroic" Daqing become a dead city like those that grew and vanished in the goldrush of the Wild West is a sad and disheartening one.

Some critics say that Daqing was from the very beginning exploited in an amateurish way. Others say that the limited resources were deliberately inflated for political reasons, and that in order to increase production more and more wells were opened on the same deposits (there are now 6,000 of them in an area of 1,500 square kilometers). The fact remains that people here, as in many other parts of China, have worked hard, sacrificed their lives, and for years have never asked questions, for they honestly believed that they were toiling for the motherland. These people, now in their fifties and sixties, rugged, wrapped in their padded jackets and wearing their dog fur hats, had faith. Their children don't.

In the new urea factory bought from Holland, groups of yellowish, uninspired young workers, like workers in any other similar factory in the world, look bored handling the plastic sacks that move on an automatic transport belt imported from a Hamburg company. "They don't study, they don't make effort. What they want is just a job," the guide says. Many don't even get that.

Daqing has a population of 700,000 people and the number of young people out of work is higher than anywhere else. "In other parts of the country they pay them and have them doing something. Here, there is nothing else for them to do.

We cannot send them around selling boiled water...the distances are too far," says a member of the local administration. The 150,000 oil workers employed by the Daqing oil fields at the height of production in 1979 are now redundant. "If anybody wants them we are glad to send them anywhere. But nobody is asking and we cannot fire them," says Mr Li.

The Party has difficulties explaining the general situation in the country to the people, and giving reasons why Daqing, once such a glory, is now so forgotten. Somehow the Party does not even try. Until 1978, every unit in Daqing had two hours a day of political study and discussion. Now the rule is two hours a week. "But some units don't even do that," says a Party official.

Harbin

People cross the Sungari River riding bicycles on the frozen water. Children slide down steep slopes along the banks and race around on wooden sledges with sails pushed by the wind.

Seen from the middle of this clean universe of white and unfathomable ice, Harbin looks from afar what it used to be, little Moscow. The onion-shaped cathedral dome towers over spiked roofs, fin de siècle buildings, tea houses along the river and public parks with their winter attractions of ice statues. A thick cloud of yellowish suffocating smoke hovers overhead.

At the height of the Daqing oil boom, most factories in this area switched from coal boilers to oil. Now that Daqing's production has slackened, the coal boilers have been ordered back and they contribute to making Harbin one of China's worst-polluted cities. Lacking any specific regulation, small and big factories here and there discharge their fumes into the air, their foamy wastes into canals and rivers, mindless of the consequences.

When, for the Lunar New Year, a friend's family in Harbin sat down for the important dinner in front of a big fish that had cost 10 renminbi at the neighborhood private market, a small handwritten note appeared in the fish's throat. "I wanted your money, not your life. This fish died of poison," it read.

In 1964, Harbin launched a beautification campaign. "Cover the city with trees so that it smells nice the whole year long," was the slogan. Today Harbin is dirty, dilapidated and malodorous, a good example of what the Chinese revolution in Manchuria inherited from the past and managed to squander.

The great iron bridge that crosses the Sungari River is still the one that, together with the railway, was built by the Russians at the turn of this century. The other big bridge in the middle of town was built by the Japanese, and even the tramway that carries people around Harbin dates from pre-Liberation days.

At the height of its prosperity, "Harbin had a population of 100,000 foreigners, 15 consulates, 63 restaurants, 5 theaters, 11 buffets and opium dens," according to a 1920s' guidebook. Now, in each of the mansions where one rich family used to live in splendor, a dozen families live in squalor, the walls unpainted probably for 35 years, the glass windows broken, the pipes unrepaired, the floors rotten, the roofs leaking, and the toilets smashed during the Cultural Revolution as "bourgeois items."

"At night the society of rats takes over," says a middle-aged man who shares a 3-by-4-meter room with six other relatives. Of the old White Russian community, only 40 are left. They are old, terribly poor and discriminated against. Though the whole city is a souvenir of the past, the Chinese, especially during the Cultural Revolution, tried their best to erase all signs of it.

The center of Harbin was, and still is, a roundabout where all major boulevards meet and where the Russians left a splendid example of an Orthodox church, completely made of wood, without a single nail. In 1966, with the excuse that some "reactionaries" were hiding in the cellars, the Red Guards burned it to the ground.

Now, in the empty unkempt patch of land where the church used to stand, there is a small sign. "Please take care of the flowers and trees. Everybody likes them," it says. In contrast, nothing happened to the tall monument the Soviet Army built to its dead soldiers at the same location. It was protected by wooden scaffolding and preserved from the radicals' rage. Like similar monuments to Soviet heroes throughout Manchuria, it is still there. A plaque put up by the Soviet commander in 1945 says in Russian, "Eternal glory to the heroes fallen in the battle against Japanese imperialism for the honor and the victory of the Soviet Union." A second plaque put up later by the Chinese, with a typical diplomatic twist, says, "Eternal glory to the heroes of the Soviet Army who fell in battle against Japanese imperialism for the liberation of the northeast and for the freedom and independence of China."

The Soviets entered the war against Japan on August 6, 1945, two days after the Americans dropped the atomic bomb on Hiroshima, and one week before Tokyo's complete defeat. The Soviets did not have to fight any major battles here, and arrived just in time to take over Manchuria from the Japanese with their unconditional surrender. "They know I don't like that monument, but they keep putting me in a room overlooking it," says a Japanese businessman in the International Hotel. He used to live here before the war and now comes back to sell Japanese equipment. "This city has changed a lot, but for the worse."

The International Hotel, designed by a Polish architect for Japanese interests in 1927, is shabby and badly kept. Though the city has been recently opened to tourism, this hotel, like similar ones in the other major cities of old Manchuria, seems in no way to serve the functional purpose of caring for its guests. Rather, it seems to be a parking place for children of high cadres. They have easy jobs in a warm place and do it in dirty, once white, service jackets, though part of their salary is a monthly allowance of free soap. "They get it to wash their working jackets, but they prefer to use it for their personal clothes," is a local guide's explanation. "Working clothes can well be dirty."

In the oldest part of town survives the only Russian restaurant of Harbin, the Huamei. One-quarter of its old, once pleasantly decorated wood-panelled hall has been cut away as a lounge for waiters and cooks, while dozens of Chinese customers hover over greasy, dirty tables on a floor black with mud and leftovers.

Above the restaurant's entrance is a red sign that says, "This place has been chosen as a model for hygiene." Across the street, the old New Harbin Hotel, with its oil paintings of naked women and its vast ground floor rooms once used for tables of baccarat, is off limits to common people and reserved for the "red mandarins," as some people call high Party cadres.

When in 1949 the Chinese communists took over the whole of Manchuria, they inherited an industrial infrastructure, a transport network and a capital of know-how built up during 50 years of foreign presence here that had no parallel in the rest of the country. Due to one of history's ironies, the communists owe all this to the legacies of tzarist and Japanese imperialism: the railways, the harbors, the factories. Anshan, still today China's largest fully integrated steel mill, was built by the Japanese. So were the mines of Fushun, still called "the coal capital of China."

Before withdrawing from Manchuria, the Soviet Army compensated itself for war damage by dismantling and taking away the machinery from dozens of Japanese factories, seizing all kinds of rolling stock and modern equipment, besides the Manchukuo reserves of gold bullion. Yet, after the Stalin–Mao pact of 1950, the Soviets came back to Manchuria and, in exchange for the agricultural products of the region, proceeded to help the Chinese rebuild huge factories and model workshops.

Today these Soviet-built plants are still the best. The linen factory in Harbin, completed by the Soviets in 1951, elegant, sturdy and functional, was the first of that kind ever to function in China. Today, more than 30 years later, with its 6,000 workers, compared with the original 3,000, it is still the only linen factory in the country. The great majority of the machines are still the old Russian ones.

Throughout the northeast the situation is the same. The railway carriage factory in Changchun is Soviet built. The Number One Machine Tool Building Plant, started by the Japanese in Shenyang, was modernized with Soviet and Czech help. So were the crane and locomotive factories in Dairen. Whenever one sees a nice iron gate and a solid, orderly building behind it today, one can be sure it was constructed in the fifties. The only later addition might be a huge plaster of Paris statue of Mao in his long coat with his right hand in the air.

The fifties were Manchuria's best years. The region had everything going for it. Whatever regime had recovered that territory for China at the end of World War II would have been expected to make a success story out of it, with its natural resources, vast space, sparse population and the popular enthusiasm that a new Chinese government enjoyed after decades of rule by foreigners and warlords.

The boom did not last for long. "First we had to face the Soviet withdrawal, then natural catastrophes, then years of readjustment, then the Cultural Revolution, and now again a period of readjustment," says Mr Lo, political cadre of the Heilongjiang provincial organization. "How many factories have been built since 1960?" I asked. "A few...a few, but not many," he replied. In reality almost none.

"The quality of life is now worse than in the fifties," one hears people say. The workers' flats built in Harbin before 1959 had kitchens and bathrooms. The new ones the local administration built last year, after a stoppage of almost 10 years, have only a tiny toilet.

The revolution has so little to boast about from its last two decades that in Changchun, where by far the best buildings are still those of classic architecture constructed by the Japanese, the first place tourists are taken to visit is the old residence of the puppet Manchukuo emperor.

Since the city was reopened to foreign visitors, the local administration planned to expand the profitable tourist industry and started to build a modern, 500-bed hotel. Now a tall, nearly finished building of glass and cement stands, empty and abandoned, on a major central square. Even some of the red characters of the slogan, "Long live the thought of Mao Zedong," hanging from the scaffolding have fallen off. Construction was stopped five months ago when the 3 million renminbi needed to complete the building was cut by the new "readjustment" policy.

The hotel had already cost 9 million renminbi and the investment, which could have yielded profit by next summer, is for the time being lost. Tourists will continue to come in small numbers and be housed in the old, once elegant, but now stinking, Japanese built Yamato Hotel. There the beds, the bathrooms, the curtains, the carpets seem to be those left behind by some Japanese general, like the cigarette butts one finds in the ashtrays on arrival.

"The Chinese keep apologizing for their shortcomings and ask us for suggestions," says an American tourist annoyed by the unpleasant decay of his accommodation. "Why don't they simply clean and repair what they have?" This is a question no Chinese official is willing to answer.

One of the old Russian habits the inhabitants of the northeast have kept up is drinking. While in the rest of the country the average consumption of beer is half a liter per person per year, in former Manchuria the average is 11.5 liters. One night, four drunken Daqing workers driving in a jeep from Harbin back to their oil fields went off the high bridge that crosses the Sungari River and fell to their deaths on the ice down below. A frightening hole in the guard rail of this major communication artery remained for many months.

For the large majority of the Chinese people living in the northeast at the end of World War II, the arrival of the communist armies was a real liberation. Life under the rule of Manchukuo had been terribly hard and humiliating.

"We were confined to certain areas. If a Chinese was caught crossing the main street, the Japanese would send their dogs after him. To eat rice was a crime, for it was all reserved for the Japanese," recalls Hung Wenli, a 62-year-old waiter who has lived in Changchun from his birth. Today people eat rice, have enough clothes to defend themselves against the cold weather, and their children go to school, but Changchun has not changed much since the old Japanese days. The majority of its 2 million inhabitants still live in conditions that only patient Chinese people could endure for so long.

In the crowded neighborhoods around the railway station, the standard accommodation is a brick hut with no water, no toilet and so tiny that families have to keep their reserves of cabbage for the winter in something like tiny dog kennels. Piles of garbage which nobody takes away obstruct the sidewalks, but they do not spread disease because the sub-zero temperature freezes them into sterility.

In Harbin, just outside what used to be the Russian railroad concession near the river, thousands of Chinese coolies used to live in a ghetto of stinking hovels and misery. Today that area is still a kind of ghetto with its expanse of brick and wooden huts patched with cardboard boxes, the windows broken and covered with plastic sheets.

The only clean, orderly place in the whole neighborhood is the newly reopened mosque. Built in 1935, this temple was heavily damaged, like all the others of different faiths, during the Cultural Revolution. The Imam and his closest followers were sent to a labor camp to be re-educated. In 1979, after 13 years of detention, they were released and were given 200,000 renminbi to repair their mosque. Now, on Fridays, some 400 people come here to pray while 14 young people have started to study Arabic in order to read the Koran. Religion seems the only field where "readjustment" has not cut funds.

In Changchun, the Chinchen Mosque has been almost completely reconstructed after the Red Guards had turned it into rubble. At the Santa Theresa Catholic Church, once the home of French missionaries, 71-year-old Father Roch Lu, who survived 14 years of manual labor, has been given 300,000 renminbi to rebuild the church. In Harbin, repair work is proceeding at the old Chinese temple and at an Orthodox church. The old Protestant church, where a German pastor lived until 1950, has also reopened after 300,000 renminbi worth of repairs had been completed. A few old Catholics now gather regularly in the church around an old Austrian piano and greet the visitor with a surprising "hallelujah, hallelujah."

"My head does not follow anymore," says a young guide who used to be a Red Guard. "I now agree that it was wrong to destroy these places, but I don't understand why we rebuild them now when there is no money to open new factories and give us jobs." With the freeze on employment in the old plants and with no new factories being built, the cities of former Manchuria are clogged with a growing number of unemployed youngsters hanging around the public parks, doing such odd jobs as transporting goods, taking pictures of people in front of monuments, selling old clothes and homemade cakes, or "forming counter-revolutionary gangs of ruffians who hate the socialist system, hate the Communist Party and feel that living in our society has no significance," as the *Shenyang Daily* wrote about a group of young robbers.

Recently, when an American teaching in Harbin let it be known that he was looking for a personal servant, he received more than 200 applications, most of them from educated boys who had not been able to find any other job.

In the past, students who graduated from middle schools were sent to the countryside, and these recurrent "learn from the peasants" campaigns turned out to be a clever device to avoid urban unemployment. With the fall of the Gang of Four, this unpopular "down to the countryside" policy was abolished. The result has been that people stick to the cities and the underpopulated countryside of the northeast remains short of laborers.

Until recently, one of the secrets wrapped in the remoteness of the Manchurian steppe was the existence of dozens of concentration camps, or "lao gai" (reform through labor camps) as the Chinese call them.

Since the founding of the People's Republic, but particularly since 1958 with the launching of the Anti-Rightist Campaign aimed at dissident intellectuals, millions of people have gone through this Chinese gulag, many spending more than 20 years in one camp or another. These people have in their way contributed to the economy of the northeast by opening virgin land for cultivation, by helping the exploitation of remote mines and forests.

After the fall of the Gang of Four, the majority of these prisoners were rehabilitated and much of the work done in the past in the countryside by the inmates of the lao gai camps and by the "learn from the peasants" youth now remains undone.

The province of Heilongjiang has 130 million mu (7,670,000 hectares) of cultivated land. According to the local authorities, 70 million more mu (4,670,000 hectares) are ready to be reclaimed, but there are no volunteers to do the work. The forests of Jilin have plenty of timber that Japan would be ready to buy, but the local authorities have difficulty finding people who want to go for long periods of time, for small salaries, into the wilderness.

"Today's youth ask too many questions, talk about their freedom and don't understand the principles," says a Party official in Shenyang.

Since the fall of the Gang of Four and the complete reversal of the radical policies of the Cultural Revolution, political lectures and indoctrination meetings that used to hammer slogans and produce at least an apparent conformity among the masses have been greatly reduced, and people now indeed ask questions unthinkable in the past. One person asked the *Workers' Daily*, "if socialism is so good, why is it that we cannot catch up with the capitalist world?" Another wrote, "Workers are exploited under capitalism, but they live better than we who are not exploited. They have cars, refrigerators and color TV." The newspaper, now posted on the boards of factories, answered them with an editorial titled, "Only Socialism Can Save China." The paper concluded that, "If it was not for the destruction brought about by the Gang of Four during the 10 years of chaos, the difference between us and western countries would be very small."

Not everybody is convinced by this argument. One does meet people who whisper about the Communist Party having lost the "mandate of heaven," a traditional way of saying that the emperor no longer has the moral right, the legitimacy, to rule, and there are reports of worker strikes and of student demonstrations.

At the end of January, 1982, a dozen young people were arrested at Shenyang University for having organized a protest against the living conditions there. The Party may not tolerate for long these manifestations of dissent, particularly in a region like the northeast which is so sensitive and vulnerable due to the long common border with the Soviet Union (some youngsters have recently defected to the other side). "Here we are basically conservative. We are slow to change," says Huang Rongqi of the Harbin branch of China Travel, trying to explain the different mentality of the Chinese in former Manchuria.

The northeast was one of the areas of major influence of the Gang of Four. Mao's nephew and closest relative, Mao Yuanxin, was the region's overlord until he was arrested in 1976, together with Jiang Qing. He is now awaiting trial in Shenyang as a major accomplice of the Gang of Four.

The northeast has been the slowest region to purge radical elements, and many cadres who grew up politically during the Cultural Revolution are still in power. In addition, many who were purged then have not, as in the rest of the country, been rehabilitated or reinstated to their former positions.

In dealing with foreigners, Harbin has kept many of the habits that used to be common during Cultural Revolution days, such as guided tours to visit "model" families, discreet security controls by the guides and attempts to cut all ties between the visitor and the local population. Small signs of the different pace at which the political situation has developed here can be picked up everywhere.

When the foreign visitor is taken to the Harbin railway station, as in the old days he has to go through a special door and wait in a special room while the loudspeakers are turned full volume with some martial, revolutionary music. Departing for the north to the rhythm of the Candlelight Waltz is probably still considered decadent in Harbin.

While in Peking most of Mao's portraits have been removed from public buildings and offices, in the northeast one sees the quotations of the Chairman painted on the walls, and all the cities still have dozens of big statues of him. The biggest, the biggest in all of China, is in the main square of Shenyang. The massive monument put up at the height of the Cultural Revolution has Mao surrounded by the heroes of that time, most of them holding the "little red book." There are peasants of Dazhai, oilmen of Daqing, soldiers of the People's Liberation Army, young Red Guards with Mao badges over their breasts. The "little red books" have been chipped away from the stone hands of the various figures, but most of those "heroes" of the past, now vilified or downgraded in the rest of China, still stand in their revolutionary ardor around the Great Helmsman in the heart of Manchuria.

"What do they know in Peking about our problems, about

our factories?'' asked one guide when I was refused permission to visit a factory. The visit had been approved by the Foreign Ministry in Peking.

"Our resources would be enough for us, but we have to share them with the rest of the country,'' said another official complaining about the fact that the northeast had to work according to a national and not a regional plan. Regionalism has been a traditional problem in Manchuria, which from 1911 to 1949 was not under the control of the central Chinese authorities.

Manchuria, due to its geographical position, has traditionally had very close relations with the Soviet Union. This is a sphere where the region today once more differs slightly from the political line prevailing in the rest of the country. There are streets, squares, parks and shops named after Stalin in every city of the northeast. Among the monuments and vestiges of the past that have been destroyed or converted (like the tall obelisk the Japanese had built in Harbin for their dead soldiers, and which the Chinese have since turned into a parachuting training tower), all the statues and monuments put up by the Soviets, when the Red Army was stationed here after World War II, have survived even the worst moments of anti-Moscow resentment and hysteria.

In Changchun, a tall column topped by a model of a Russian plane still has intact an inscription in Chinese that says, "The friendship of the Russian and Chinese peoples will last for ever." Young couples stand under it to have souvenir pictures taken.

In Harbin, the only cemetery is the one where some 150 Soviet soldiers are buried. Once it had thousands of tombs, for it used to be the cemetery of the Russian community at the time of the concessions. During the Cultural Revolution, the Red Guards destroyed them all and turned the whole area into a cultural park. But the gray stones with the red star of the "Soviet heroes and martyrs" went untouched, and are now honored with fresh flowers and wreaths at each anniversary of the founding of the Red Army.

Party officials in the northeast give briefings to visitors without ever mentioning the otherwise routine question of the

"Soviet threat." In no way does the presence of 1 million Soviet soldiers along the common border seem to affect the life of the people in the region.

Since 1976, the population has no longer been asked to take part in civil defence exercises. The elaborate, terribly expensive, and ultimately ineffective tunnels dug under the cities after 1969 to shelter people against possible Soviet air attacks are now being converted into storage depots, dormitories or shopping areas.

In Harbin, the first department store in the city center recently took over part of a three-level underground tunnel, and among the items on sale are Russian TV sets, New Dawn brand. "The border is open. People go back and forth. Here we have fewer tensions than in Xinjiang," says political cadre Lo of the Heilongjiang administration.

The Manchurian border with the Soviet Union, formed mainly by the Ussuri and Amur rivers, does not look like a front line. Once a week the Peking–Moscow train crosses it, and every day tradesmen from both sides meet to exchange Chinese pork, mutton and vegetables for Russian radios, television sets and vodka.

The bloody battles on the Ussuri in 1969, when Chinese and Russians killed each other for control of an insignificant island in the middle of the river, seem absolutely forgotten.

The present flourishing Sino-Soviet barter trade along the border is in miniature the kind of functional exchange which took place in the fifties and could resume on a large scale at any time.

Soviet Siberia and former Chinese Manchuria have economies that can be easily integrated with mutual profit. Soviet factories across the border produce machines and consumer goods China wants, while the Chinese agriculture of the northeast produces fresh meat and vegetables which Soviet Siberia desperately needs. Furthermore, the 120 major plants and dozens of smaller factories the Soviets helped build in the fifties are all equipped with old Soviet machines whose replacement is long overdue.

Basically, the whole industrial infrastructure of the northeast today is Soviet, and its modernization would naturally be less expensive and more functional if done with Soviet machinery, rather than with equipment imported from the west.

Seen from former Manchuria, a return to good neighbor relations and even close cooperation between China and the Soviet Union is on the cards and cannot be ruled out. "Everything is possible," says a young Harbin student, "what was good yesterday is bad today but can be good again tomorrow. One day we are told to hail a man, another day we are told to damn him. In the hands of our leaders we are like a screw: sometimes we are turned on, sometimes we are turned off."

5

Heavenly Voices

Chinese games with crickets and pigeons

The old general had just climbed to the rostrum and was about to deliver his speech at a People's Liberation Army conference when the whole audience burst into laughter. From a pocket inside the general's padded jacket a cricket, kept there inside a small gourd, had started to chirp away happily and its song, amplified by the microphones, had echoed throughout the hall.

"I am sorry to have indulged in the small game," apologized the old general.

The "small game," as it is known, is the old-fashioned Chinese habit of keeping all kinds of animals, including some unusual ones, as pets.

The habit, severely condemned as "bourgeois and wasteful" during the Cultural Revolution, is now officially tolerated again, and for a year has been at the center of a great popular revival.

Every Sunday on the bank of Long Tang Hu (Lake of the Dragon) in the southern district of Peking, thousands of people, many of them teenagers, gather at the crack of dawn to discuss and admire, to buy and sell animals, cages, fodder and all sorts of paraphernalia connected with the "small game" and its many pleasures.

Since man's best friend, the dog, is still illegal in the urban areas of China, and thousands more dogs in Peking alone have recently been rounded up and electrocuted or clubbed to death by the police, people now confine themselves to the raising of fish, cats, monkeys and rabbits, but above all of birds and crickets.

The fondness of the Chinese for crickets is old and a whole literature exists on the subject, dating back at least 1,000 years, with each successive dynasty reprinting a famous manual that

98

taught people how to breed crickets and how to make them sing beautifully or fight bravely.

Cricket stories belong to Chinese folklore. One tells of a small boy who committed suicide in order to become a cricket himself, thus saving his father from disgrace for losing a valuable insect belonging to a magistrate. This has been told to generation after generation of Chinese children as a classic example of filial piety.

It is said that the women of the imperial household started the custom of keeping crickets in golden cages under their pillows in order to find solace and company in the lonely nights at the palace. It is also said that was the reason why, in the old days, peasants were required to supply the court and the provincial mandarin with crickets, as a form of taxation.

With the passing of time, this old custom of the imperial seraglio was imitated by the common people. Until the Cultural Revolution almost every Chinese family had a special bamboo basket, padded with cotton and warmed with a hot water bottle, in which the crickets were kept in winter. Various little bamboo cages in the form of palaces, towers and boats housed the insect musicians in summer.

The custom has been resumed. After many years of silence, in Peking one hears again the street call "Guo-guorrr... Guo-guorrr," as peasants come to town with clusters of little round bamboo cages, each one holding a green, chirping cricket for sale.

In August and September, one costs only 1 mao (5 cents), but in January or February it is worth at least 50 times as much, for in their natural state all crickets die with the first cold.

To breed crickets out of season is thus a good business for skilled and patient peasants, some of whom have again started small cricket farms around Peking. For those who buy them it provides the old refined pleasure of listening, in the midst of winter, to that surprising, warm trill of spring, while all around is ice and snow.

"Sadness and joy I feel as its chirp now pauses, then continues, vibrating yet prolonged, a heavenly voice, a sound

99

appropriate for the man of leisure," wrote Tun Lichen, a Manchu gentleman in 1900.

Different in color (they can be yellow, green, black, white, purple or oily brown), different in shape (they can look like a watermelon seed or a grain of rice), there are many kinds of crickets. For each of them the Chinese have a name, for each of their sounds a poetic description.

There is the "jin zhong," the golden bell, whose pure monotone stridulation has been compared to "the sound of drums and trumpets," or to "the sound of water rapids" by two Chinese authors. There is the almost invisible, not-even-3-millimeter-long "jin lin zi," which produces a sound similar to "that of sacred bells in Buddhist temples." There is the popular "hu lu," with its moving voice full of ups and downs, like that of a sobbing human.

For the Chinese, keeping a cricket is like keeping a dog for Europeans. One has to feed it (some eat carrots, lettuce or chestnuts, others only worms); one has to bathe it (this is done with lukewarm water); and also take it along when going out so it doesn't feel left alone.

People have special pockets sewn inside their coats and jackets so that their pets, comfortable in their hiding places, can be taken everywhere (even to political conferences) and feel cozy near the warmth of the human body.

The winter abode of a cricket has always been a gourd. Not a natural gourd — the Chinese would not be satisfied with it — but an artificially shaped one.

The Chinese have been masters for centuries at shaping these gourds. Gourds are raised in molds. When the gourd flower blossoms, the flower is forced into the hollow of a clay mold and there it grows, taking the shape of the mold and getting embossed with all the designs that have been previously carved into the mold. Thus there have been gourds with bas-reliefs of poems or landscapes, gods or human figures on them.

The covers of these gourds were made of ivory, wood, jade or turtle shell and were carved in the form of dragons, lions and symbols supposed to bring luck to the owner. People of the old days, especially the Manchus, used to spend fortunes in order to have the best artisans of the time manufacture the most exquisite habitations for their singing companions.

But not only could crickets sing, they could fight as well, and even bigger fortunes were invested in the breeding of these tiny warriors, and were won or lost in the betting over their deadly struggles.

The Chinese knew long ago about the fighting abilities of crickets and through the experience of centuries they managed to achieve a natural selection of the best kind. Good fighters were said to be reincarnations of heroes of the past and were treated with great respect.

"Rearing crickets is like rearing soldiers," wrote a famous author of the twelfth century. Indeed. Special attendants were required for fighting crickets, as grooms are required for horses. The crickets, each one in his own expensive earthenware pot furnished with a bed and a tiny porcelain cup for water, were fed daily on a special, varied diet consisting of fish, honey, rice and chestnuts. Special trainers were used to bring the crickets up to their best form and psychological tricks, such as having them fight against weak adversaries, were used to boost their egos and to strengthen their self-confidence during battle.

On the day of the real fight, two warriors of the same kind, size and weight would face each other in an open jar on which the eyes of dozens of spectators and gamblers were glued. The referee was called the "director of battle;" the small brush with the ivory handle, with which the crickets were irritated and stimulated to fight, was made of the whiskers of a country rat.

Often the battle lasted only a few minutes: amid the chirping battle cries the crickets would get at each other's legs, wings and heads. At the end one was dead or maimed and sometimes even eaten up. The victor was then nominated a "general." A cricket which had survived various fights would get the title "everlasting marshal." Small carved silver coffins were used to bury the remains of the defeated cricket.

All this is the story of the past. In today's China, man himself may not be buried and gambling is strictly prohibited.

Yet, at Long Tang Hu market on Sunday mornings, peasants are again offering good "generals" for sale, and children again search the fields looking for their own fighters. "A good cricket is found guarded by two centipedes or by a snake," advises a legend. In one of Peking's new free markets, the Guan Yuan, just across from where Mao's widow Jiang Qing used to live, an array of old jars, ivory ticklers, cricket beds and cricket feeders have reappeared for sale, together with tiny packages of traditional medicines to cure cricket illnesses, such as dizziness, colds, overeating and asthma.

Besides crickets, birds remain the most popular pet of the Chinese, and a common way of wishing happiness to someone is that he may "get old and be able to take care of a bird and a grandson." Often one sees this dream realized as an old man pushes a shaky bamboo perambulator down the street with a small boy and a bird cage inside.

For the Chinese, to have a bird does not mean to keep it at home as part of the decor. It means to have a companion one wants to walk with, to play with. Long before the sun rises one sees in Peking dozens of old men with one cage in each hand walking rhythmically toward the public parks. There the cages are hung in the branches of the trees and while the birds sing to each other the old men under them talk about birds and their pleasures.

Bird cages, even the simplest ones, are miniature masterpieces, with sliding doors, porcelain pots for grain and water, and often even a tiny vase for little flowers which the bird is supposed to admire and then sing to for joy.

Chinese cages, unlike western ones, don't have swings. Therefore, during their walks, old men let the whole cage swing on their wrists. The effort the birds have to make to hold on to their perches is thought to be the best exercise against rheumatism.

The variety of birds available again in the free markets of China is immense. Their value varies with the quality of their voices. A "lao shizi" (old lion), a kind of sparrow which can only make a strident sound, is worth 7 mao (35 cents). A "hua mei" (painted eyebrows), with its prolonged soprano

102

trills, is worth ten times as much. A "bai ling" (100 elves), which according to the Chinese can imitate the voices of 100 animals, including those of the cat and the dog, costs up to US$70.

After the silent years of the Cultural Revolution, when the "small game" was prohibited and birds were no longer kept as pets, cities have come to life again with all kinds of known and strange sounds which people are free again to produce for their pleasure.

In a city like Peking, at any hour of the day one can be attracted by a mysterious, howling sound, a sort of outer space melody that approaches and disappears. Against the blue sky one then sees scores of pigeons flying past: somebody has released his pets from their cages and is playing a concert in the air.

The Chinese started to make pigeon whistles during the Southern Song dynasty (1127-1279). They make them today in exactly the same way, out of bamboo, gourds or reeds. The whistles can be made with only two or three tubes, like a small organ, or be big as a fist and have up to 30 pipes. Each whistle is fitted with a bone or ivory handle, which is fastened to the bird's tail feathers by a fine wire. When the pigeon flies, the air passes through the different-sized pipes and produces the sound. By fitting various pigeons with different whistles, one obtains something like an orchestra with different instruments.

The Chinese call that sound "heavenly music" because, as an old Peking gentleman who has a collection of over 300 different whistles and over 20 pigeons to play with says, "If God had a voice, it would not be very different from this sound."

6

When the Peasants Are Content the Empire Is Stable

Shandong and the end of the communes

A man hacks the ground with a primitive iron spade. Another has tied himself to a cart and pulls it with the help of his children. A woman trudges around a stone slab, pushing a heavy granite wheel to mill her corn.

Hacking, pulling, pushing, sweating with the same tools, the same gestures. Generation after generation, today as hundreds of years ago.

Shandong is one of the oldest provinces of China, the second most populous one. The mountains, eroded by man and time, show the barren rocks of their spines. The earth of the plains, turned upside down millions of times by laboring peasants trying to grow enough food, seems as exhausted as the people by centuries of work with inadequate compensation.

Shandong (East of the Mountain) is one of the cradles of China's civilization. Some of the early Hans settled along the Yellow River and here the mythical man who tamed its waters was made emperor. Yet, the mighty dragon that flows from the Tibetan plateau and generates life along the more than 5,000 kilometers of its course often brought sudden death, famine and pestilence as well, with its floods and its unpredictable changes of direction. The Yellow River thus came to be known as "China's Sorrow." To this day, it is one of Shandong's major worries.

North of the provincial capital, Jinan, under the huge span of the railway bridge first built by the Germans, the reddish, muddy waters whirl and crash. The level is frighteningly high, due to heavy rains upstream, yet there is no way to use that mass of water in this province, where the reservoirs are empty and the fields dry. For months not a drop of rain has fallen over the whole region. The peasants are experiencing the worst drought in 60 years, but now they have no gods to pray to as in the past. Shandong is China's Holy Land, but no temples are open.

Confucius and Mencius were born in Shandong. In Shandong is the most sacred of China's five sacred mountains, Tai Shan. Here Taoism had its center. It was from the shores of Shandong that the Eight Immortals set off for their legendary voyage across the sea. For centuries, religion has been an essential part of the peasant's daily life. Every village had a temple and pagodas were part of Shandong's landscape. Now they are all gone, destroyed, dismantled, transformed. A few shrines were recently reopened, but mainly for the benefit of foreign tourists.

A century ago Shandong, more than other regions, suffered humiliation by foreign powers. Here the Germans came. "Show the Chinese with full severity, and if necessary with the most brutal ruthlessness, that the German emperor cannot be made sport of and that it is bad to have him as an enemy," Kaiser Wilhelm II ordered Admiral Diederich on November 7, 1897. Two German Catholic priests had been murdered in Shandong and that became the long-sought excuse for Germany to acquire a foothold in China. The German navy occupied the bay of Kiaochow and forced the Chinese Empire to sign a 99-year lease for the area. Shandong became the German sphere of influence in China.

The Germans stayed only 16 years, but when they returned home, defeated by the Japanese, they left behind Qingdao (Tsingtao), an example of modern city planning unmatched in China. They left behind a harbor that is still the best, they left the embryos of industries still active (beer, silk, embroidery) and a railway system that is the most important in the region.

Traditionally, Shandong has been a land of rebels as well. The Taipings were active here. The xenophobic Boxers were born here. The first resistance against the Japanese invasion of 1937 was organized here. Here the communists had, from the beginning of their struggle, secure bases. And here they had the upper hand against the Kuomintang during the civil war.

"If the peasants are happy the empire is stable," was a

105

saying in the old days. The landlord system had pushed large masses of peasants into famine and despair. These peasants wanted to own their land and Mao Zedong promised it to them. As a result, many of them joined the Red Army. In vast areas of Shandong, communist land reform was carried out before 1949. Expropriated landlords fled to the zones under Kuomintang control, and peasants still tell the story of one who left saying to his tenants, "I shall be back and slaughter those who took my land. I myself will open a restaurant with human meat."

The Kuomintang ultimately was defeated and the landlords came back, but only to face kangaroo trials for their "crimes against the people." Several million of them were executed throughout China, and their fields were confiscated and distributed to those who worked on them. Agricultural cooperatives soon started to operate and the peasants were happy.

Then, in 1958, Mao Zedong launched the movement for the establishment of People's Communes in the whole of China. Shandong was in the vanguard. All vestiges of private property vanished, garden plots and livestock were confiscated, rural free markets closed. The commune owned everything. The commune controlled everything and the peasant, as a member of this large unit (usually a commune was made up of 30,000–50,000 people), was just a laborer detached from his land and required to work today on a dike, tomorrow at the construction of a road, or at an iron-melting plant. His income was a share of the income of the group to which he belonged. Half of this income was in the form of the Seven Guarantees which the collective granted him — food, clothing, medical care, education, housing, childbirth, and marriage and funerals.

Mao Zedong thought he had found the shortcut to the ideal communist, egalitarian society in which "each contributes according to his capacity and takes according to his needs." The result was disaster. "In 1961, the overall output of grain, sugar and pork dropped to the 1951 figures. Other crops were lower than in 1949," one reads in a confidential book, *Problems of Agricultural Economy in China*, printed recently in Peking.

In Shandong, just as in the rest of China, millions of people experienced famine, hundreds of thousands died unseen and unreported by western observers, while Peking's propaganda spoke of immense successes. A few corrections to the rigidly collective communal system were attempted in the early sixties (e.g. with the reintroduction of private plots which the peasants aptly called "life-saving plots"), but these reforms were short-lived and the Cultural Revolution swept them all away, creating millions of new victims and reimposing Mao's leftist ideology.

Much of the political struggle in communist China (Liu Shaoqi against Mao; Mao against Deng Xiaoping; Deng against Hua Guofeng; and now Deng against what is left of the Gang of Four) has been about what to do with the countryside, where 800 million Chinese live. The success or failure of the farmers determines today, as it did in the past, the stability of the ruling dynasty.

The struggle still goes on, because the problems are immense and there cannot be a consensus on how to solve them...if they can be solved at all:

— China has only 7% of the world's total arable land, but with it she has to feed 23% of the world's population;

— China's population steadily grows, while her arable land diminishes, due to the expansion of human dwellings and industrial sites (during the last 35 years China's population grew from 551 million to over 1,000 million, while cultivated land shrank from 107 million hectares to 99 million hectares, despite massive reclamation of wasteland and deserts);

— China's grain production (which per person is the same today as it was during the Han dynasty 2,000 years ago, around 300 kilograms per year) is not quite enough to meet the country's requirements;

— China's countryside conditions have not significantly improved since the communists took over the country, and even the official press now admits that only one-third of the peasants live above the subsistence level of 120 yuan per person per year. Another one-third barely make it and one-third of the peasants have an average income lower than 60 yuan, and therefore "...they depend on other occupations, as well as on government relief and frugality, to make ends meet," according to a recent issue of the Party's theoretical journal, *Red Flag*.

Shandong Province, with its 73 million inhabitants, mostly peasants, is a mirror of the situation in which the 800 million peasants of China live today. Shandong, with some of the poorest and some of the richest communes of the whole country, is a good example of:

— the generally unbalanced development of China's agriculture;
— the attempt by the present central authorities to dismantle the People's Communes system;
— the local authorities' resistance and opposition to it;
— the state of confusion over what system should replace the one inherited from Mao;
— the mood of the peasants, who profit from the present liberal policies and pursue in haste their own private interests, doubtful as they have become by experience whether the official line of today will last.

In a tiny village in Anqiu County in eastern Shandong, the market square had been eliminated and covered with buildings. During the past 20 years no market was allowed. Now, every five days a crowd of some 3,000 peasants gathers on an unpaved field for a typical country fair, where everything from piglets to chickens, from vegetables to medicines, from mousetraps to clothes and sunglasses and watches, is offered for sale. Agricultural products come from the private plots of the people. The consumer goods come from Weifang, a city 35 kilometers away, where enterprising peasants have gone to sell their goods and have bought things they now sell to their own people.

Each day, streams of peasants enter the big cities of Shandong and squat along the sidewalks, offering vegetables and eggs that are fresher than those in the state shops, and chickens that are tastier than those from the state chicken farms.

The profits are good enough for each of the 42 families of

a village in Zouping County in Shandong to have bought a TV set, although they cannot yet watch TV because there is no re-transmitter nearby.

Only a few years ago, all these people would not have been able to leave their communes, would not have been allowed to sell their products, would not even have been allowed to plant a few cabbages along the banks of a canal. Personal use of land was criticized as "capitalist." But all this has been encouraged since the publication in 1979 of Document 75, which established the responsibility system on the farms. This system, the brain-child of Vice-Chairman Deng Xiaoping, is now revolutionizing the Chinese countryside.

In theory, the system means that the individual peasant no longer shares the income of the large group to which he belongs, but that he and his family are responsible for a specific quota of production on a specific piece of land, and that what they produce above that quota will be theirs. In practice, the responsibility system means the breakup of the commune system and the de facto redistribution of land, household by household.

Liu Zonghe, 35 years old, is a member of a poor commune at the foot of Shandong's sacred mountain Tai Shan. In March last year, he and the other 127 members of his production team (a commune is divided into brigades, a brigade is divided into production teams, a production team is formed by several families) were told by their leaders that work could be done according to the new system. They decided to try it.

The land at the disposal of their production team of 24 families was uneven; some plots were better than others. So, each plot was given a number, the numbers were put in a hat, and each family drew its luck. Liu Zonghe and his family (his two parents, his wife and two small children) got a total of 8 mu of land (a little more than half a hectare) divided into four plots, each a kilometer away from the other. The tools of the production team were divided as well, and Liu got two brooms, a rake, a pitchfork and the wooden frame of a wheelbarrow. Unfortunately, the wheel went to another family. In return, Liu committed his family to produce and to sell to the state, at a fixed price, 1,600 kilograms of grain per year (200 kilograms per mu). Anything above this quota would be his. "At harvest time, my wife and I could hardly sleep, we worked so much and we worried so much," he recounts. "But all went very well."

The Liu family's total production was 2,600 kilograms of grain and, with what Liu got from the sale of the 1,000 kilograms in excess on the private market, he bought himself an ox (420 yuan), two pigs, and the first batch of bricks for a "five-room house" which the Liu family plans to build. "The responsibility system has kindled the enthusiasm of the peasants," writes the *People's Daily*, pushing the political line approved by the central government.

In some cases the enthusiasm has even gone too far. In a faraway commune of Heze County in Shandong, the peasants proceeded to reoccupy the fields which their forefathers had tilled. In another commune, the rumor spread that land would be returned to its original owners, and some people went to the Party headquarters and produced old documents proving their ownership. In other places the allocation of land caused terrible quarrels, some of which ended in fights with hammers and knives.

In some areas the peasants, led by their cadres, first divided the land and then went to the collectively owned buildings of the brigade headquarters to share out among themselves tables and chairs from the conference room. In the end, they even pulled down the building and shared the bricks. In Zhinfang Commune, in Jiaxiang County, five cadres organized the sale of land and of 50 collectively owned rooms, and divided the 29,525 yuan among the commune members. "Certainly, the introduction of the responsibility system has created some ideological confusion among local cadres," says Liu Zongchen, vice-governor of Shandong.

Over the last few months the Chinese press has embarked on an almost daily campaign to explain that "fixing of quotas per household does not mean transferring property or the land," and that "agricultural land cannot be rented out or sold away."

"We want to replace egalitarianism with productivity, but without changing the principle of collective property," says

Guo Xingjiang, director of the Shandong Province Planning Commission. Egalitarianism used to be the social ideal of the Maoist days. Now egalitarianism, expressed with the Chinese phrase "everybody eats out of the same big pot," has become a kind of unforgivable sin.

"Those who produce more must get more," says planner Guo. In the past, people who did work hard ate as much from the same big pot as those who did not or perhaps could not work at all, and this was frustrating for many. Yet the same big pot also fed the old lady whose son was in the Army and could not till the fields, fed old people without children to support them, and fed widows and orphans.

In the rural communes, where people get neither pensions nor sick pay as in city factories, the big pot functioned as a welfare fund for the old, the sick, the widows. These are now the people who are losing out under the new responsibility system because they are left to themselves.

The complaints are serious, especially from the military. "The rural economy is booming and we have to worry for our families back there. We ourselves, by serving in the Army, are losing a bicycle the first year, a house the second and a bride the third," wrote a group of young recruits of the People's Liberation Army to a local paper recently.

Peasant families whose sons are in the Army find themselves deprived of able-bodied contributors to the household budget. That is one reason why there are fewer and fewer volunteers presenting themselves for service and why many soldiers of peasant stock are now asking to be demobilized in order to return to their farms and take advantage of the change in rural life. High officers are unhappy, and resentment against Deng Xiaoping's policies runs deep among the ranks.

"There are people among us who do not correctly understand the reforms in the countryside and call them bourgeois liberalization and retrogression," the official *Liberation Army Daily* said recently, acknowledging strong leftist opposition within the military to the political course of the post-Mao era.

The responsibility system has brought to the surface another grave problem which the egalitarianism of the communes had

111

managed to contain and to keep under control: the massive surplus of labor in the countryside. Out of the 800 million people who live on farms in China, 300 million are the labor force. One-third of this group (that is 100 million people) is unemployed, according to official Chinese sources.

Under the old commune system, these people shared whatever there was to do and ate whatever there was in the same big pot. Now, on the contrary, with each unit trying to increase its own productivity and with each family pursuing the interest of its own members, the tendency is to cut down (on what?), and an increasing number of country people are kept away from the big bowl of rice.

A natural solution would be gradually to move these people toward the cities and employ them in factories; but the cities already have masses of unemployed people and the present program of economic readjustment leaves no hope for new jobs in the near future. Moreover, readjustment and the responsibility system have given factories greater autonomy, thus turning them into rather independent units, geared to the pursuit of profit for the exclusive interest of their own members and managed as if they were large family businesses.

The Jinan Number Two Tool Factory (1,500 workers and staff) has had a 30% cut in production this year; no new people have been hired due to readjustment. The last to be added to the payroll were 300 young workers in 1980, all of them relatives of old workers who retired to leave their jobs to other family members. "It is impossible to think of hiring outside people," says Yi Hungjiang, factory manager. "We still have to find jobs for another 300 unemployed young people of our own."

In every city in Shandong, as in the rest of China, unemployment is now a visible phenomenon. Along the streets of Yentai, the rich northern city, able-bodied men squat for hours in front of a plaster of Paris bust of a naked lady or a few handmade keyholders they hope to sell. Around the Jinan railway station, built by British architects in the 1930s, there are dozens of people who sell bowls of hot noodles to travelers out of baby prams transformed into small moving restaurants.

Groups of peasant girls have come from faraway with only

cardboard boxes of peanuts or sunflower seeds to sell. In the back streets one meets people going around on bicycles and announcing either with a trumpet or a bell their readiness to sharpen knives or fix broken umbrellas or mend shoes. Beggars in rags lurk again around market places and bus stops in search of food, and more and more troupes of acrobats try to attract the attention and the contributions of passers-by with children doing dangerous contortions, swallowing nails and pushing daggers down their throats. "This is a form of torture. Many children are hurt and crippled," writes the *People's Daily*, while the police have issued a nationwide order to stop these practices. But in vain, for the acrobats have no other way to make a living.

Though it creates these and other problems, the reintroduction of private incentives in the economic life of China is certainly contributing to raising the average income of peasants, especially those from the poor communes. The 1979 average yearly income of a Shandong peasant was 81 yuan per person. In 1980, it was 105 yuan. In Shandong's Heze County, one of the poorest in China, peasants made only 40 yuan per head in 1979, but thanks to the introduction of the responsibility system they reached 71 yuan in 1980. This is true for the rest of the country as well. Material incentives and private interest increase productivity. The experience of the last 35 years is there to prove it.

The story of China's pig population, as told in a confidential report published "for use of cadres only," speaks for itself. In 1954, there were 100 million pigs in the whole of the country. With the movement to establish the cooperatives, the number of pigs went down to 84 million by 1956. Pigs were up again to 146 million in 1958, but the communes came and in 1959 only half the pigs were left. The same happened during the Cultural Revolution.

"The three big decreases in the pig population have taken place every time pigs have been collectivized and private plots have been confiscated," concludes the report. The present Peking policy of liberalization of the economy is based on these and similar conclusions and the orders are "to push ahead quickly with the reforms." But the orders are not

113

necessarily followed once they reach the provinces, the prefectures and the counties, where the influence of the old Maoist leftist ideology is still strong and the Party apparatus holds things up.

Shandong, a province still run by a first Party secretary, Bai Rubing, who was appointed in 1975 at the height of Gang of Four power, shows signs, like other provinces, of this silent opposition to the reforms. The full implementation of the responsibility system is slow: only 40% of the villages have replaced the old distribution system of the communes with the new one. The expansion of the private plots which the central authorities want to give back to the peasants is also going slowly. Private plots are tiny pieces of land allocated to rural families for their own exclusive use without any conditions. Whatever the peasants grow there is their property.

People put a lot of effort into tilling these gardens and a visitor recognizes them as private plots immediately by the way they are intensively exploited and well cared for. "A mu of private land yields two or three times more than a mu of communal land," admits the director of the Planning Commission of Shandong. But although the central government has given instructions to distribute private plots for a total of up to 15% of the communal land, in Shandong, as in other areas of the country, private plots still represent only 7% of the land collectively owned. "We would like to increase it but we are affected by ideology," says Mr Guo Xinjiang of the provincial government. "For a long time we called these plots 'the tail of capitalism.' Regarding them as incompatible with socialism, we did our best to cut these tails off. So it is only logical that we now face some opposition."

"We eliminated the private plots in 1961 and we don't want them back," says Wu Zhongrong, leader of the Shijiazhuang Brigade in Shandong's Anqiu County. "We are already beyond that stage." This brigade is a model one, visited by thousands of foreign tourists during the past 10 years. Besides farming, the brigade collectively operates workshops producing pajamas for export, plastic bags for the internal market and a modern rabbit farm with the best breeds in the world. People live in pleasant, newly built public buildings. The guest house and cinema are large and clean. Here land has not been redistributed to families and there are no private plots. This year each brigade member has, out of the common pot, received an income of 400 yuan. People here have a point in being opposed to the reforms. "We are an advanced socialist unit. Why should we go back to a less socialist organization?" says one of the team leaders.

A different but more important form of opposition to Deng Xiaoping's liberal reforms comes from the local Party cadres whose positions are at stake with the changes. Peasants call them "fan tong" (rice baskets) because without doing any productive work they fill themselves with a lot of food. One easily recognizes them, as they walk around the communes with their hands behind their backs ("because carrying tools is not their custom," the people say), always present at the banquets for visitors.

These people used to run the communes. They decided what the peasants ought to plant, they fixed their quotas, their share of the income. Now, with the extension of the private plots and the new responsibility system that leaves peasants free to choose what to produce, and when and how to produce it, these local cadres have lost most of their functions and thus their jobs. In the poor areas of the country, where the peasants have opted for the new responsibility system, many of the fan tongs have been given a piece of land and requested to work it. Obviously, they don't like it. But there is more to it.

Mao's idea of a commune was of a self-sufficient unit, collectively responsible for production, administration, and welfare. The commune structure ought to encompass everything. A man was born in a commune to die there, for he had no reason to leave it. Now with the breaking up of the communes, with the introduction of the private element into the daily life of the people, the commune is losing control over the income and therefore over the movements and actions of its members. A Chinese village, like any other social body, if left to itself solves some of its problems by itself and this is exactly what worries many communist cadres accustomed as they are to controlling, if not solving, every single matter.

Shidao is a gray, gloomy little town on the most eastern

tip of the Shandong Peninsula. Beside a naval base, the life of the town is determined by a string of embroidery factories filled with young girls, and a fleet of fishing vessels loaded with young men. It would be enough to have a meeting place where the youngsters could gather for an occasional dance or something similar in order to solve some of the natural problems of people. No. In the evening, as soon as the sun is down, Shidao sinks into pitch darkness, everybody retires into his stone hut or dormitory and the problem of finding husbands for girls and vice versa is left to the communist trade unions. The reintroduction of a private element, the granting of free choices to people, is something profoundly contrary to the beliefs of local Party cadres, and they do their best to attach new strings to the newly granted freedoms.

Zhao Liquan is a 58-year-old barber in a village of Shandong's Linqiu County. His commune has established a form of responsibility system and he has made a contract with the collective to cut hair for at least 300 yuan per year (one hair cut is 0.20 yuan). He can keep 80% of what he makes above the 300 yuan for himself. "This is to encourage him to work more," says brigade leader Zhao Yindai.

Peasants, however, are not allowed simply to go to his shop, get a haircut, pay and go home. With the establishment of the responsibility system the commune has assigned one of its accountants to keep the barber's records. Thus a peasant who decides to have his hair cut has to go to the commune headquarters, get a special ticket, and bring it to the barber, who then sends it back to the commune. At the end of the year, the peasant is debited for his various haircuts and money is withdrawn from his sales of grain to the state while the barber is credited for the number of coupons he has delivered. All this is to prevent people from handling cash and to prevent the "suspected village barber" from taking "the capitalist road."

Mao Zedong was sitting in his book-filled study and US President Richard Nixon, next to him, was complimenting him on the great changes he had brought to China. Mao listened and slowly replied, "No...no...I have only been able to change a few places around Peking."

116

Shandong is a province 500 kilometers away from the capital and in many ways it proves how right the old Chairman was in his pessimistic assessment. After 35 years of collective life and socialist education, 35 years of struggle against Chinese traditions and human nature, 35 years of attempts to build a "new man" and around him a new society based on new values, peasants here, as in the rest of China, are still pretty much what they have been for centuries: parochial, selfish and family-oriented. As soon as a breach in the rigidly collective frame of the communes was opened and some freedom was granted under the new responsibility system, one could see all the old attitudes and problems surfacing again in the Chinese countryside.

Xiaozheng is a commune in Shandong's Qiyun County, where peasants have been assigned a specific plot of land to till. Whatever they produce above a certain quota is theirs. In order to expand his plot, a certain peasant went to the collectively owned irrigation ditch and took some earth away from it. Since his land was not too fertile, he went again to the irrigation canal and took away 10 cubic meters of good soil to spread over his own. His neighbors thought that was a good idea and did the same.

The result was a big gap in the ditch and damage to the irrigation system that brings water to everybody's land. The commune convened a meeting, the peasants involved were severely criticized and an education campaign "to love the collective" was launched. Similar incidents have happened in various places and new posters such as "Love the factory as your own family," and "Be good in productive work, be good in collective love," have appeared in cities and villages.

Since they took power in 1949, the communists have concentrated much attention on one of China's traditional problems: irrigation. Particularly after the full collectivization of land and the quasi-militarization of people within the framework of the communes, immense canal and water conservation projects were carried out, with masses of people transferred from one place to another to do collective work. A confidential Chinese publication now claims that one-third of these water projects of the past, including dikes, were badly done and might at times represent a danger. However, they served their purpose.

Now that peasants are concentrating exclusively on their own plots of land, it is not clear who is going to take care of the projects of common interest. Some villagers already complain about people who no longer do their collective job of cleaning leaves out of the canals and strengthening the ditches.

The 1958 campaign to kill all sparrows, because somebody in Peking (some say Mao himself) thought they ate too much of the crops, turned into a scourge. Peasants throughout China stood in the fields, on rooftops, on trees with drums and banners and made a great deal of noise for days and days. Frightened and unable to rest, the birds dropped dead by the millions. Soon afterwards insects and plant parasites increased out of all proportion and caused much more damage than the sparrows ever had.

The 1969 campaign to build tunnels under every city and village to protect the population in case of a Soviet attack also turned out to be immensely wasteful. Millions of people worked for months to construct shelters which in most cases could not withstand a carpet bombing. However, those tunnels cutting through the underground water networks caused a lowering of the level in rivers and lakes, and Jinan, Shandong's capital, has suffered serious water shortages ever since.

In the past, the possibility of mobilizing millions of people, particularly peasants, for one project or another was a great asset for the authorities. Now that people depend on what they themselves produce for income, such appeals for collective work have become less and less successful.

Another even more serious problem created by the new responsibility system in the countryside is that of population control. Shandong already has 472 inhabitants per square kilometer. One can travel for days through the countryside without ever finding a stretch of land without a village or a cluster of mud houses. In the twenties and thirties, in order to escape from famines, thousands of people left Shandong for Manchuria and other less inhabited areas of the country. Now they don't leave, and their number constantly rises.

"Late marriage late childbirth," says a huge poster in front

118

of Qingdao's railway station. Here, as in all other Chinese cities, the new policy of "one couple one child" seems to work because the penalties for doing otherwise are heavy and the living space in the cities so small (3 square meters per person). But in Shandong, as in the rest of China, the urban population is just a minority (roughly 25%) and the rural households do not follow official policy. "Now less than before," says the director of the Shandong Province Planning Commission. With the introduction of the economic reforms which gave families their own plot of land to till, peasants have gone back to the traditional idea of regarding children as additional manpower contributing to the household budget. "We now work on our own. We don't ask the state for grain, we don't ask for cloth. If we produce more children it is our own problem," says a peasant in Shandong's Shouguang County.

Some communes have tried to establish a fine of 100 yuan for those who have a second child, but with no success. "I prefer to play with an extra child than with an extra 100 yuan," says a woman who had paid the fine. Some counties made abortions compulsory and sent out militia patrols to catch women without the birth license issued by their units (the license is given according to the number of deaths in each unit). This practice had to be stopped for fear of violent reactions by the peasants.

At the origin of China's tremendous population problem ("basically production growth is eaten up by the population growth," says a foreign expert) is Mao himself. "More people mean greater ferment of ideas, more enthusiasm, more energy," he said in 1958. It was Mao who opposed birth control policies immediately after Liberation. At that time Ma Yingchu, professor at Peking University, warned the Party that unless China stopped its population growth it would never develop. He was accused of not having "sympathy for the Chinese people" and was later labelled a rightist.

The present tendency toward a baby boom in the countryside as a consequence of the introduction of the responsibility system ("since 1979 we have had a jump in birth rates," admits a commune official in Shandong) will end up aggravating the rural unemployment problem (already one-quarter of the labor force is technically jobless) and further postponing the plan to modernize agriculture.

"We will achieve basic mechanization of agriculture in two years," promised then Party Chairman Hua Guofeng when in office. Such a slogan is no longer heard, and a common sight in the Chinese countryside is that of people working with old-fashioned implements, pushing and pulling carts, at most helped by a sail to catch the wind, as they have done for generations. Families who have been given small plots of land to till have no use for tractors and other machines. Communes which have not yet fully adopted the new system have no great interest in mechanizing, for this would only increase the number of unproductive people. More tractors mean more unemployed and that is why the number of tractors produced is being reduced.

The tractor factory of Yentai now produces bicycle parts; a tractor repair shop makes electric fans; another produces the bodies of wrist watches. Instead of agricultural machines, the peasants are now being given consumer goods ("We respond to their demands," says a top Shandong provincial official). The peasants are happy. Whether in the long run this is a good policy for China is another question.

"Do you feel that cigarettes, detrimental to anybody's health, are more useful for building socialism than diesel engines?" a foreign visitor recently asked the director of the Yidu aluminum foil factory (970 workers) in eastern Shandong. Until 1979, the factory, built in 1970, produced 3,000 diesel engines a year. When its conversion was ordered, all heavy machines were given away and new machines producing aluminum foil for cigarette packets were brought in.

"The people want to smoke more and better quality cigarettes. We help them to do so. This is our contribution to socialism," says factory director Li, before entertaining the visitor with statistics on floor space, production plans and anticipated profits.

In the past, when touring around China to see factories, communes, universities or kindergartens, the visitor was taken to a special room and offered tea, while a local Party official, sitting under a portrait of Mao (later of Mao and Hua Guofeng), gave a long lecture on the political line of the moment. During the Cultural Revolution the visitor would be told about the crimes and damage caused by those who had taken the capitalist road. Soon after the return to power of Deng Xiaoping, he would be told about the crimes and damage caused by the Gang of Four and their followers.

Now, in the same rooms, often in front of the same officials sitting under a traditional painting of flowers or a landscape (Mao and Hua are gone, but one can still see a trace of their portraits on the unpainted walls), the visitor is given a few details about the unit, but no political speech. Traveling through Shandong Province these days, the only line one hears over and over again is, "since 1949, under the leadership of the Communist Party, we have made steady progress."

"And during the Great Leap Forward?" one asks, "when thousands in Shandong died of hunger because they were taken off the fields to build backyard furnaces?"

"Oh, not much damage. We only lost a few kitchen pots that people melted to make iron."

"And what happened during the Cultural Revolution?"

"We suffered no harm here," says Wu Zhongrong, leader of the Shijiazhuang Brigade of Weifang Prefecture. Only a few years ago, at the time of the great Peking show trial of Mao's widow Jiang Qing and her followers, Shandong, like all other provinces, denounced the damage and the suffering caused by the Gang of Four. Shandong, like other provinces, announced the arrest of some local followers of the radicals and promised a speedy trial for the most criminal among them.

In Shandong, as in the rest of China, not a single trial has taken place and today not a word is being said anymore about the "black hands" of Jiang Qing.

One theory among observers is that Deng Xiaoping and Hu Yaobang do not want to start digging too deep into the past because, after all, it is the past of the whole Party and not of the Gang of Four alone. Another theory is that in Shandong, as well as in many other provinces, the followers of Mao's radical ideology are still so strong that local cadres do not dare to move against them.

The fact is that one no longer hears criticism of the "10 years of chaos," as the period 1966–1976 was called until recently. It is as if the Gang of Four had never existed, as if the Cultural Revolution had never happened.

At the top of Camel Mountain, near the town of Lin Zi in Shandong's Yidu County, a splendid Taoist temple, built with heavy stones during the Tang dynasty (more than 1,000 years ago), used to dominate the breathtaking horizon of chains of blue hills and yellow plains. In its grottoes, devotees of ancient times carved some of the most beautiful examples of Buddhist statuary in China. Today the temple is a cemetery of broken and overturned stones. From the shade of caves, serene stone faces of statues of Buddha still look down benevolently over the valleys and their people. Some have lost their ears, their hands, their noses in hasty destruction. Others are left with only their elegant bodies. The heads seem to have been carefully sawn off, as used to be done at the beginning of this century when Chinese scavengers went around the country gathering material for foreign collectors.

"Most of the destruction was caused by religious wars between Buddhists and Taoists during the Ming dynasty," says Yang Zhizhong, curator of the Yidu County museum. "Some was caused by Kuomintang bombing during the civil war."

"And during the Cultural Revolution?" one asks, noticing much more recent damage among the rubble of beautiful carvings and inscriptions. "The Red Guards never came here...it was too far away for them," the curator replies. Yet, distance never lessened the destructive fury of red rebels unleashed by Mao.

Deep in the countryside, 12 kilometers away from the town of Qufu where Confucius was born, is the tomb of Shao Hao, one of the mythical emperors of China who ruled the country before recorded history (2,700 years before Christ). A guidebook recently published in Peking says, "this is the only pyramidal tomb in China." It would have been more correct to write "it was." Only the base of the pyramid is left. The rare wooden temple on its top was burned down by the Red Guards. The compound is abandoned. The huge marble turtle which once marked the approach to the temple now lies lonely in the middle of a cotton field. The stone message it carried on its back is lost.

The same fate befell many lesser-known temples, pagodas and churches throughout Shandong, once the Holy Land of China. And the destruction did not start with the Cultural Revolution. "We dismantled the temple immediately after we liberated this place in 1946," Bi Koyou, leader of the Dayudao fishing brigade on the coast of Shandong, says. "The people needed to be freed from superstition." Leader Bi, a fisherman himself before he joined the Red Army for 13 years, explains that in the old days, when a boat had caught an unusually big fish, the people would go to the temple, burn incense and yellow paper for the gods and free the fish in homage to the sea spirits. "Now we keep the big fish. We don't waste them," he says.

The massive destruction during the early stages of the Cultural Revolution, and later during the anti-Confucius campaign, was the logical conclusion of the communist policy intended to eliminate from the people's minds whatever had to do with the feudal past and to imbue them instead with the new values of a socialist society. "Fight against the old," and "Struggle against superstition and false beliefs," were the slogans of various campaigns. For 35 years now the peasants have been subjected to such campaigns yet the policy does not seem to have been a success.

In Shandong, old women still climb the holy mountain Tai Shan as an act of devotion; some peasant families have rebuilt at home small ancestor altars in front of which they place cooked rice, fruits and burning joss sticks. At market fairs one sees homemade images of Buddha and the Eight Immortals for sale. At the entrance of their homes, on the wall that was traditionally built in front of the courtyard door to prevent evil spirits from getting in, peasants write again the old characters "fu" (luck and happiness) and "cai" (wealth).

"The return to feudal superstition is not allowed," one reads on the blackboard of a commune near Shandong's provincial capital Jinan. Yet, on the Thousand Buddha Mountain near-by, peasants throw coins and tiny prayer sheets to the few Buddhas which survived the onslaught of the Red Guards and have been put behind glass for the benefit of the tourists.

"Don't spit. Don't make noise. Don't destroy the cultural relics," says a sign outside the Palace of Great Purity, one of China's oldest Taoist temples at the foot of the rugged Laoshan Mountains in Shandong. The cultural relics, as the labels on them say, were all "made in 1980." Wooden statues, scroll tables, bronze incense burners and candleholders were produced by a Jinan factory, after the provincial authorities decided to reopen the temple complex and assigned to it five monks and a woman who, in their newly government-issued robes, look more like actors from a film studio than people who have chosen a life of contemplation. "I work here eight hours a day, six days a week," says one of them.

The temple complex is on a marvelous, wide terrace between huge rocks and deep blue sea, 60 kilometers away from Qingdao. Chinese peasants have come here on pilgrimage for over 2,000 years. The Germans, who occupied Qingdao at the beginning of this century, built Mecklenburg houses for the members of the Alpenverein (Alpine Club) who came here for hikes and climbing. According to the legends, it was here that the Eight Immortals gathered to decide how to cross the sea. The place has lost its original mysterious, mystical spell because an Army barracks was built just behind the temple and because part of the mountain is used as a firing range.

Only foreign and Chinese tourists in special buses can come here. For the common devotee there is no public transport from Qingdao. The revival of "feudal superstitions," i.e. religion, among the peasantry worries the communist authorities and the Chinese temples that are being reopened in Shandong and in other provinces are not places of worship, but museums for tourists, with entrance fees and watchmen and policemen all around.

Christian churches have a different story. They reopened for worship in order to satisfy some small minority groups in the urban population, as well as to prove to foreigners that China guarantees freedom of religion after all. The Protestant church of Qingdao, built by Germans in 1908, is functioning again. The Catholic church, built by Americans in 1936, is now filled with workers busy restoring it at the cost of half a million yuan.

"I want to be Catholic," says a young man in Qingdao. "Catholicism is a foreign thing, therefore it must be a good thing." Traveling through China nowadays one is surprised to hear this and similar expressions quite alien to the traditional Chinese sense of superiority over what is foreign.

The visitor strolling around Qufu's free market, where thousands of peasants come to sell the produce of their private plots and the surplus of their state quotas, will be asked by old and young men from which country he comes, and he is surprised to hear, whatever his answer might be, the very common comment: "Your country is better, much better than China."

The Chinese press has recently tried to tackle this attitude among people, pointing out the recent sports victories of the Chinese teams against the USA, the Soviet Union, and Japan as good reasons for a renewed Chinese pride. The point is that the opening of China to the outside world and its exposure to western values have come at a moment of deepest ideological and cultural confusion which has left people completely disoriented. The great Chinese past, of which they could be proud, was labeled bad and destroyed. What was put in its place by Mao and his followers has now been equally classified as bad and to be forgotten. The people are left with almost nothing.

For at least 2,000 years Chinese peasants have lived in an unchanging world, ruled by the same unchanging laws, the same customs, the same values. In the old days, an admirable mandarin, the official sent by the emperor to rule a province or a city, would leave things in exactly the same conditions he had found them years earlier.

Since the middle of the nineteenth century, when the old order was upset, China has been thrown into turmoil by interference and invasions. In 1949, the communists took over the country and promised to build a new order, a new society.

To achieve this they began to criticize the old society and to dismantle it. Old moral laws, habits, customs, and old values were criticized, struggled against, their representatives physically eliminated. Yet, instead of a new order, the last 35 years

125

have brought people one disorder after another in the form of various political campaigns.

"Down with the Four Olds."

"In agriculture learn from Dazhai."

"Chairman Mao is the sun in our hearts."

"Down with the Gang of Four."

The walls of houses in the countryside tell many stories through these various slogans which the peasants, not bothering to erase, have left to fade in the rain. Only one slogan is freshly painted and prominent all over the Shandong countryside. "Beware of fires. Beware of robbers." Traditionally, Chinese villages were self-policed units where everybody was checking on everybody else and where each family was collectively responsible for the behavior of its members. The communes somehow reflected this organization. Now, with the breakdown of the commune structure, with the resurrection of private interests and the stimulus toward consumerism, crime is on the increase in the countryside and in the cities.

Peasants lock their houses when they go to the fields. Factories put spikes of broken glass on top of their surrounding walls. City parents do not leave girls alone at home for fear they might be raped by gangs of hooligans said to be roaming through certain neighborhoods.

The authorities have taken a tough stand to control this wave of crime. Outside the Qingdao Supreme People's Court, in front of the former colonial government house built by the Germans, people gather to read the posters of the death sentences passed by the local judge: eight in one week alone.

For centuries the basis of all Chinese correct behavior and policies had been the *Analects* of Confucius. The writings of the master contained the solutions to all problems, the answers to all questions. There was no situation in life that could not be settled with a quote from the great sage. The communists attacked this traditional wisdom as feudal and Mao proceeded to replace the *Analects* with the "little red book" of his quotations. An old system was replaced by a new one but the basic idea was the same: a man ought to be able to find in Mao's words the solutions to all his problems.

Hundreds of millions of people were put through obsessive

study sessions, peasants were forced to learn by heart sentence after sentence. They had hardly started to know and to apply some of them when the book was taken out of their hands and declared bad, for it had been compiled by that "traitor" Lin Biao. And photos of Mao himself, which many peasants had placed in their homes on the same altar where they used to keep Confucius, had to be taken down as well. What is now left for them? Some debris of the holy words.

One of Mao's most famous quotes, still written at the entrance to Army barracks since the military are the last stronghold of Maoism in China, was "Serve the people." This was the formula used to encourage people to sacrifice themselves, to do collective work, to replace selfishness with social consciousness.

Now, at the entrance of a small chicken farm in Shandong's Shilianzhuang village, which is run according to the new responsibility system, somebody has written in black ink on pink paper, "Serve the chickens." "The better we take care of them, the more we earn," say the peasants.

In the past, hard workers and model peasants were rewarded with a simple red flower or a red flag, were praised as fighters on the front of production, and were issued certificates still to be seen on the walls of Chinese homes. Now the same people are given more money. But today's heroes are not as admired by their colleagues as were those of the past.

"We have to keep our best workers in separate rooms, or they might be attacked by the others," says Qi Keqian, manager of the Shidao embroidery factory. With the new system, which has eliminated egalitarianism and pays more to those who work more, model workers are used, as in western capitalist factories, to set times of production and quality standards for the others. Obviously they are not loved by their fellow workers. The dismantling of the communes, the adoption of the responsibility system in factories and farms and therefore the reintroduction of the private interest element in Chinese life, have started a completely new game in which some people will win, others will lose.

Yet even peasants of the poor areas, who are profiting from the changes, are worried, for they do not know how long this new system will last. "For a long, long time," assures the *People's Daily*, trying to encourage peasants to invest in the plots newly assigned to them, the only requirement being to produce a fixed quota. It is, after all, the same *People's Daily* that in 1959 wrote, "the fixing of farm output quotas based on individual households is an extremely backward, retrogressive and reactionary way of doing things." Not long ago Xue Muqiao, a top Chinese economist, wrote that the policies of collectivization of the past were wrong because they were too premature, and that "therefore it is correct now to take a step backward."

Thus, the logical conclusion would be that what is given today may be taken back tomorrow. The ups and downs of Chinese politics seem not to have reached their end. Mindful of the bitter past experiences of liberalization and collectivization, of small freedoms and great repression, everyone tries to improve his own position as best he can and forget about the rest.

Shandong's peasants have a simple way of describing it:

In the fifties we helped each other,
In the sixties we killed each other,
In the seventies we feared each other,
In the eighties each one thinks for himself.

7

We Are Building for a Hundred Years

The former German colony of Qingdao

The hangar where young German Lieutenant Gunther Plueschow used to hide his plane, The Pigeon, after flying his daily daring missions of reconnaissance over the Japanese lines during the dramatic siege of autumn, 1914, is no longer there. But most of the other buildings of the time are and, seen from the sea, Qingdao still looks pretty much as it must have looked in those days. In the center is the copper-green spire of the Protestant church, built in 1908. Behind it is the sturdy stone castle of the German governor. Along the bay to the east are the German Asiatic Bank, the Grand Hotel and the massive building of the colonial administration; and, toward the west, the imposing structure of the German police headquarters, the railway station and, finally, the roofs of the German-Chinese University.

"In Kiautschou we see a port which should hold the key to the economic and commercial domination of this country," wrote the famous geographer Baron Ferdinand von Richthofen after two trips into the area, the first in 1860 as the geologist of the Prussian expedition to East Asia.

As latecomers in the race among the big powers to divide the crumbling Chinese Empire, the Germans saw in Shandong their chance to make up for lost time, particularly against the British, who were already well established in their colony of Hong Kong.

Conditions seemed favorable. "Shandong is a province with a good climate, where agriculture, mining and industry could be developed far beyond their present levels, and where an enormous amount of cheap and intelligent manpower is at hand," wrote von Richthofen.

The Germans needed an excuse to grab what they had already chosen as their prey and the excuse came on November

1, 1897, with the "timely" murder of two German Catholic priests (Fathers Franz Nies and Richard Henle) by a Chinese gang in southwestern Shandong.

Two weeks later, in a bloodless battle, the German fleet took over the Chinese fortifications along Kiaochow Bay and seized the whole area. In March 1898, a treaty was signed under which China granted Germany a 99-year lease for Kiaochow Bay, the right to build two railway lines through Shandong, and a concession for the exploitation of all mineral resources within 15 kilometers along both sides of that railway.

China thus recognized the whole of Shandong Province as Germany's sphere of influence, and the Germans did not waste a day in beginning to turn their new colony into a model of the western presence in the east. They did wonders.

The Germans never numbered more than 5,000 at any one time, but, with the help of local laborers, German architects and engineers quickly established a harbor and built the railways to transport precious coal from the interior. At the mouth of Kiaochow Bay, on the tip of the eastern peninsula, on the site of a tiny little fishing village, they built Qingdao (Green Island), a city of imposing public buildings, churches, hospitals (eight of them), schools and dozens of elegant villas.

Facing due south, Qingdao was built according to a modern, well-conceived city plan. A special commission had to approve all construction, after checking their engineering and architectural standards. Sewerage and public utilities were provided and, at the end of its first year of life, Qingdao already had a telephone system with 26 private subscribers.

Soon it acquired the fame of being the cleanest and most orderly city in the far east. The Germans had established eight different police units (including one, the "servants" police, exclusively in charge of cooks and maids) to maintain order in the city. Strict rules kept the 100,000 inhabitants of the Chinese districts under control. One said: "No Chinese is allowed to enter the city between 9 p.m. and sunrise without a lantern."

Foreigners residing in the far east came from Hong Kong and as far as Saigon and Japan to spend their holidays in the healthy climate of Qingdao, "The pearl of the east."

A completely German pearl. Prinz Heinrichstrasse, the central thoroughfare, looked like the typical main street of an elegant German town. It still does. Few of the original buildings have been pulled down and most of them, here as in the rest of the city, are used today for the same purposes for which they were originally constructed. The old government house, where the German colonial administration used to work, is now the seat of the Qingdao People's Government, guarded by soldiers of the People's Liberation Army; the main German hospital, recently expanded, is still used as a hospital; and the old German police station is the seat of the city's Public Security Bureau.

The romantic hunting castle of the German governor, built outside the city on a rock overlooking the Yellow Sea, at the end of what used to be a large forest infested by wolves, has now been turned into a Party guest house. The huge and somehow sinister governor's residence, on a hill in the middle of town, is used to house high visiting leaders and foreign guests. Mao Zedong, Lin Biao, Jiang Qing and Ho Chi Minh all spent some time here.

Chinese guides of Qingdao like to tell the story of the first German governor, Diederich, who was fired by the jealous German emperor because his residence in Qingdao was an exact copy of the emperor's house in Berlin. "The governor may have been a bad man, but we take good care of his villas," says Liu Baiyuan of the foreign affairs office of the Qingdao administration.

The German character of the city was so imposing that, even after the Germans had left, German-style buildings continued to be built by the Japanese, who ruled Qingdao until 1922, and then by the Chinese themselves. The communists, who took over Qingdao in 1949, have since continued to repair and restore the main structures, while most private dwellings have decayed under the pressure of dozens of families living in space originally built for one.

The German inscription on the hilltop overlooking the harbor is gone and so is the German cemetery. The last tombstones were smashed during the Cultural Revolution. Yet, Qingdao is still quite a foreign city. "Red roofs in a green

131

forest," is how the Chinese describe it today. For many of them a trip to Qingdao is something like a journey abroad.

The Chinese have expanded the economic activities which the Germans so efficiently started during their short presence here. Shandong silk is still a major industry of the region, and embroidery is still practised in the same manner and according to the same patterns introduced by the Germans. The brewery, which started producing Germania beer in 1913, later called Rising Sun brand under the Japanese, now produces the famous Tsingtao Export quality beer.

The old Protestant church, built by the Germans near the governor's residence so that he and his family could walk to church, has been reopened and has regained its northern European look. Even the clock on the bell tower works again. "The Christians repaired it themselves, after the state shop asked a fortune to fix it," says Pastor Andrew Kuang. That church, like other buildings in Qingdao, is a solid structure of stones and iron for, as the Germans used to say, "we build for 100 years."

Qingdao, as the Germans planned it, certainly had all the prerequisites for becoming a German Hong Kong on the China coast. But history wanted it differently and instead of 100 years the Germans were there for only 16.

The end came unexpectedly. The growth and wealth of the German colony had raised the envy of both the Japanese and the British, and the outbreak of hostilities in Europe gave London and Tokyo an opportunity to put an end to German competition in the area.

On August 23, 1914, Japan declared war against Germany and Japanese and British forces moved against her Chinese colony. Qingdao's defence apparatus was minimal. A large part of the fleet had left the harbor for the South Seas and the 5,000 garrison soldiers, with their 600 Krupp guns, were no match for the 60,000 Japanese who came to lay siege, or for the British fleet moving in from the sea.

However, the Germans decided to fight. It soon appeared that their best weapon was the funny-looking single-engine plane of Lieutenant Plueschow. The plane had aroused laughter when it was unloaded in the harbor and even more so when, during a test flight, a gust of wind made it crash on the racecourse. But with the help of a Chinese kitebuilder, who used glue and silk to reconstruct its white wings, Lieutenant Plueschow put it together again.

The Pigeon now became Qingdao's pride, Plueschow its hero. In the half-light of dawn, Plueschow would take off, fly over the Japanese artillery emplacements and signal their positions to the German gunners. During the night, the Japanese would move their cannons, but Plueschow would spot them again and have them knocked out with the Krupp fire. The Japanese tried to bomb the hangar where Plueschow kept his plane, but at night he had his Chinese helpers build another hangar and a dummy wooden Pigeon. The Japanese were fooled. Day after day the "pilot of Qingdao" rose into the air and came down with a plane that needed to be glued together again after the trip. But the information he brought back each time was vital.

At the beginning of November 1914, the Japanese and the British closed in on Qingdao. The German forts Iltis, Moltke and Bismarck fell one after another. Plueschow kept going up into the air. Then came his last mission. At the request of the German governor, he flew to neutral territory with the colony's documents and a last message for the German emperor: "Qingdao has fallen."

At 7:30 in the morning of November 14, 1914, the Germans surrendered and the German imperial flag was lowered from the roof of the stony government building of Qingdao, never to fly over the Asian continent again. Chronicles of the time say that the German soldiers marched toward their prison camp singing the old soldier's song, "Ich hatt' einen Kameraden."

"They came with bad intentions," says a Chinese official of the Qingdao administration today. "Nevertheless, those imperialists left behind quite a nice city that we still enjoy."

8

We Teach Them Not to Rebel

Qufu: the birthplace of Confucius

The latest joke is that, if Confucius were to return now to
this little city in the heart of Shandong Province where he
was born 551 years before Christ, the people would welcome
him like a hero and the local secretary of the Communist
Party would invite him to be seated in the shade of the famous
apricot tree under which he used to teach, and ask him to
impart a few lessons of ethics to the young of today.

After the violent ideological attacks against him during
the Cultural Revolution, and the systematic destruction of
everything that recalled him, Confucius is returning to the
center of a cautiously growing attention. His revival is being
encouraged by the Communist Party itself as it looks for values
and ideals to inspire a new generation of ever more apathetic
and confused Chinese youth.

The mansion in which Confucius was born, the enormous
temple built in his honor, the gigantic cemetery-forest where
the Great Sage and his descendants were buried until very
recently, are now being summarily restored to what they looked
like before the Red Guards descended upon them with their
vandalism, looting and burning. Confucius himself is being
rehabilitated as a "great educator" and much of his "wisdom"
is being propagated once more in schools, even though its
source is not explicitly mentioned. Should all this continue,
the great teacher would be rising from his ashes for the
second time.

Two thousand two hundred years ago, the great Qin
emperor who unified China and built the Great Wall along
its northern frontiers, thought that in order to keep the whole
country under his firm control and to prevent "doubts and
disorder among the people" he had to eliminate old ideas and
old ideologies. Therefore he ordered all books, except those

on medicine, astronomy and agriculture, to be destroyed. This was dutifully done and, together with burning thousands of books, 460 scholars were buried alive, to prevent their minds from remembering and passing on what had to be totally erased. Thus, Confucianism was wiped out in China. Or so he thought.

Only 70 years after the great purge, one of Confucius' descendants, wanting to enlarge the house where the Great Sage was born and where he himself lived, knocked down a wall. Behind it he found a copy of Confucius' writings that his grandfather had bravely hidden there, at the risk of his own life.

From the reproductions of that copy, millions of Chinese studied their Confucian ethics for over 2,000 years. For 2,000 years people passed the imperial examination by knowing the content of that book by heart, and were appointed as mandarin-administrators throughout the country. Confucianism became the cornerstone of Chinese society. Qufu, the little town in the center of Shandong Province where Confucius was born, became, just as Mecca or Jerusalem, the goal of millions and millions of pilgrims. Confucius' descendants, entrusted with the care of his temple, his mansion and his tomb, were revered by the highest authorities of the country. Until our times.

Then another great unifier of China, Mao Zedong, also thought that in order to build a new society and eliminate doubts among the people he had to eliminate Confucianism. The destruction started again. The first wave came in August 1966, with the launching of the Cultural Revolution; the second in 1974 with the campaign to ''Criticize Lin Biao, criticize Confucius.'' Books were burned, scholars beaten and killed, and Qufu was attacked by gangs of Red Guards who in the name of revolution burned some of the temples, smashed the invaluable collections in the museum, and knocked down with ropes and hammers statues and steles, some of them dating back 2,000 years. ''The worst ones were the students of Peking Teachers College. For days and days they went on the rampage,'' says a Qufu resident who to this day is scared to talk about what exactly happened.

Although the central government has already spent almost

2 million yuan on the restoration of Qufu and the Temple of Confucius, the scars are visible everywhere. The big statue of Confucius which used to stand in the main temple, copies of which had stood in every administrative building of China throughout the centuries, has vanished and been replaced by a modern scroll painting of the great master. Of the more than 1,000 heavy stone tablets, many 3 to 4 meters high, which once stood in the temple courtyard, only a few dozen remain. Most of these have been badly put together again by cementing pieces found in heaps of rubble.

From the northern city gate, a one and a half kilometer long country road flanked by ancient tuya trees leads to the cemetery where Confucius and 74 generations of his descendants are buried. In 1900, German engineers building the Shandong railway wanted to cut this avenue, but they had to change their plans for fear of a popular uprising against the desecration of this holy area.

Red and black slogans painted on the marble arch on the way to the tombs have been superficially wiped off, and Confucius' tomb itself has been carelessly repaired. An ugly, low brick wall has been built in front of it and the old Chinese characters, calling the master "highly accomplished and saint," have been gaudily repainted. Dozens of children and old men hang around the place.

"What is your name?"

"Kong."

"...and yours?"

"Kong is my name."

People are no longer ashamed to say so. Of the 50,000 inhabitants of today's Qufu, at least 75% carry the name Kong, like the Master himself, and all of them consider themselves to be his descendants in one way or another. His direct descendant in the 77th generation, Kong Decheng, left Qufu in 1948 and fled to Taiwan, where the Chinese Nationalists gave him the title and honor of Rite Official of the Great Sage and Master.

Although Qufu is now being restored and the Temple of Confucius has been opened again for the first time since 1966, the place is in no way a religious center. No joss sticks are burning here (in today's China the smell of incense can only be associated with the toilets of hotels for foreigners). "We want to turn Qufu into a tourist attraction rivaling the Great Wall," says a local guide.

However, the partial rehabilitation of Confucius (last year, during a symposium held in his birthplace, he was called "one of the glorious figures of China") is more than a simple matter of tourism. For centuries, the Confucian idea of a perfect society, resembling a pyramid in which everybody, at his own level, has moral duties toward his elders and superiors, permeated Chinese life. To this day, millions of Chinese are still aware of Confucian values, such as filial piety, benevolence and obedience, even if unconsciously today. Precisely these values seem to be being stressed again to reintroduce some elements of morality into a society which has lost its orientation and its traditional ethics through the Cultural Revolution and its aftermath.

"We don't teach them to rebel. On the contrary, we want our students to love the Party, to love the socialist system and to respect their elders and teachers," says Qu Siguang, Party secretary of Qingdao's 17th middle school. "The aim of our education is to have physically and morally good students."

When asked to give examples of "morally good students," the Party secretary mentioned those who this year had been publicly praised for handing over to the school a watch they had found on the street, helped old people to return home, and made cushions for the chairs of their teachers.

9

Like Dogs with Broken Limbs

Tibet after decades of Chinese occupation

Awesome. Majestic. Bewitched. The Potala, fortress of stone, straw and gold spread over a mountain of rocks, rises like a sorcerer's dream from the middle of the Lhasa valley, symbol of man's desire to reach the sky, a defiant construction built by slaves for their god-kings.

For centuries, millions of Asian pilgrims, obsessed with the hope of this sight, traveled on foot for months to see it before dying, and many died in the process. A few brave western adventurers and missionaries, who had heard about this mythical forbidden place beyond the icy curtain of mountains, came, charmed by its remoteness, to unveil the last mystery of the east.

He who reaches it is taken by its magic spell. One cannot avoid it. Like hundreds of eyes, at times benevolent and consoling, at times threatening and terrifying, from the top of the white and dark-red, alive, man-made mountain among the barren, dead mountains of nature, the windows of the Potala follow the wanderer wherever he is in the valley. Under the first rays of the sun, its roofs of pure gold glitter in the mist. In the shadow of the night, its ghostly presence hovers over the city, heavy with memories of murder and sorcery, but also of salvation.

The Potala. For the Chinese, who now occupy Tibet, it is a museum of the horrors and superstitions from which more than 30 years ago they "liberated" the Tibetans. For the Tibetans, it is still the holy temple, the seat of their divine sovereign.

On Sundays, when the Potala's huge door of wood and brass is opened at the top of breathtaking staircases of stone (entrance fee 0.30 yuan), tens of thousands of Tibetans stream inside, wander through a maze of dark corridors, prostrate themselves in front of the 10,000 shrines, knock their heads against holy stones, climb steep wooden stairs toward hidden altars, and pour yak butter into hundreds of trembling lamps in front of the 200,000 images of gods, demons and ogresses, many of solid gold. They bring all kinds of offerings — from money to safety pins — to the embalmed bodies of the former lamas; crawl under huge shelves heavy with piles of holy scriptures so as to be imbued with their wisdom; and make their children wash their faces with — and drink — the purifying water allegedly springing from a vast underground lake with golden islands, hidden in the bottom of this fortress-cathedral. They kneel silently under the empty apartments of the Dalai Lama, their king, now in exile. They walk past wall after wall of magnificent and terrifying frescoes and, stunned and possessed, mumble invocations and vows. In a trance they turn their prayer wheels while endlessly repeating the holy refrain, "aum mani padne hum" (hail the jewel of the lotus flower).

Among them, a few uniformed Chinese soldiers on an outing look on incredulous and lost.

Since 1959, when the last popular anti-Chinese rebellion was crushed by Peking's troops and the Dalai Lama fled to India with 85,000 of his followers, the Potala was barred to Tibetans.

Then in January 1980 it was opened again, only once a week, and the violent explosion of repressed religious feelings took everybody by surprise, most of all the Chinese. They had granted this limited freedom of worship as a safety valve for hidden unrest among Tibetans. It turned into an alarm bell. Peking got worried. It quickly ordered a complete review of past policies, sent to Lhasa some of its top leaders (including Communist Party Secretary Hu Yaobang and Vice-Premier Wan Li in May 1980) and, in the hope of regaining the allegiance of the disaffected province, recently embarked on a policy of concessions and sweeping reforms far more liberal than in the rest of China.

Tibet represents one-eighth of the whole of China's territory. With its long common border with still-unfriendly India, and not so far away from Soviet-occupied Afghanistan, Tibet is one of the most sensitive areas along China's frontiers. It is the only province of China where a minority people constitute the majority of the population (the Tibetans number 1.69 million out of 1.83 million).

An explosion of popular dissent, or eventually another open revolt against Chinese rule in Tibet, could have disastrous effects upon China's image abroad and destabilizing consequences within China itself, where most border provinces are peopled with grumbling minorities. China can simply not afford trouble in Tibet.

For 30 years, but particularly over the last 20, Peking has ruled Tibet with a strong hand and has tried to impose there the same policies, through the same harsh methods, as in the rest of the country. The system has not worked, and Peking is changing its course.

"One cannot comb different kinds of hair with the same brush," I was told by Chinese Party boss of Tibet, Yin Fatan. Yin is the successor of the recently sacked general Ren Rong, who for 20 years was the undisputed overlord of the region.

Tibet has indeed proved to be a different kind of "hair." Twenty-five years of Marxist–Leninist ideology and scientific socialism have not even scratched the surface of the scalp. Even if Tibetan houses or huts are now adorned with portraits of Marx, Engels, Lenin and Stalin, and if among the people prostrating themselves in the Potala some don Mao badges, which have disappeared in the rest of China, the new ideology and the new sages have sunk no deep roots here, nor have they changed the age-old image of this strangest of all lands, haunted by other gods and by other sages bigger than gods.

Tibet still appears to be a country under a supernatural spell which through the centuries attracted people of all kinds. Lao Tzu, at the end of his life, sat on an ox and started off for a mysterious land from which he never returned: Tibet.

Seventy million years ago, Tibet was a land on the shores of the sea. When the continents of India and China began to collide, the Himalayan chain took shape. In the middle of it the Tibetan plateau was thrust toward the sky.

Giant shells of vivid colors, stone sponges, and ridges of coral are still today to be found on the highest peaks, from whose foothills spring some of the mightiest rivers of the world:

the Brahmaputra, the Mekong. The lakes of Tibet are still salty. The collision is not yet over and "the Himalayas still grow at the rate of ten centimeters every year," says the head geophysicist of a French mission now in Lhasa to study this phenomenon, which is at the root of the disastrous earthquakes that continue to ravage China.

Isolated from the rest of the world, and forced by nature to survive in the most beautiful but most inhospitable surroundings, Tibetans developed from Buddhism, Tantric practices, and an old local faith, a form of religion called Lamaism. It made people endure all kinds of suffering, made them build immense monuments to their gods, originated a system of values that cannot but be called civilization, and educated selected men and women to master powers beyond our imagination. There are people here able to survive naked for long periods of time in below-zero temperatures. Others can communicate by telepathy over great distances, or travel at inhuman speed through this landscape where every spot has a legend and every rock has within itself a spirit stronger than the rock.

Tibet was known for centuries as a depot of all treasures. "There are ants as big as dogs, throwing up huge piles of gold as they burrow," wrote Herodotus. And, more recently, Heinrich Harrer, the Austrian sky master who during World War II escaped from a British prison camp in India to spend *Seven Years in Tibet* (the title of his book), wrote, "You can see gold dust glimmering in the sunlight when you swim."

Yet Tibetans, bound by taboos and terrified by their own superstitions, never dug for minerals, nor did they ever try to build roads, for they believed that this would make the soil infertile.

Their religion slowly caused the population to dwindle due to the growing number of monks vowed to celibacy (there were 12 million Tibetans 10 centuries ago, 4 million at the end of the eighteenth century, and barely 1 million in 1949). Tibet remained frozen in a form of material non-development which is comparable to Europe's Middle Ages.

When Mao Zedong ordered the Liberation Army into Tibet in 1950, and into Lhasa in 1951 (a move that some

Tibetans resisted by force, but which now is called by Chinese propaganda "peaceful liberation"), Tibet, ruled by a theocracy of lamas and nobles at whose head stood the Dalai Lama (Ocean of Wisdom), was a country that had long ago ceased to keep pace with time.

There were no roads, no schools, no hospitals, no factories. In the 1930s, the thirteenth Dalai Lama had three cars imported in pieces on the back of men and yaks through the Himalayas from India (they were soon idle for lack of gasoline). Otherwise, in the whole of Tibet the only wheels that turned were the prayer wheels. An old prophecy had warned that "when wheels come into the country, peace will go."

The Chinese came in trucks. They brought with them tractors, water pumps and machines, and Peking committed itself to integrating Tibet with the rest of the "motherland." So far it has not succeeded and today's Lhasa is a symbol of this failure.

At dawn a Chinese soldier sounds reveille on a trumpet from the same fort which British troops occupied in 1904. Loudspeakers all over the valley blast out the notes of *The East is Red* before broadcasting Peking's propaganda in Chinese (a language most Tibetans do not understand), and two cities awake. One is a modern, clean, well-lit, new Lhasa, with paved roads and square brick houses which the Chinese have built for themselves, and the second is the old, dirty, dilapidated Lhasa of the Tibetans, with its mud houses and flat roofs, its crooked streets paved with a mixture of mud and excrement, a city wrapped in the stench of rancid yak butter and yak dung, which, in this country without forests, is still the most commonly used fuel.

In the old city, the Chinese have given names to the streets, numbers to the houses ("so as to better control us," say the Tibetans), but people still defecate in open trenches, for the first sewers are only now being built and water has not yet been brought in.

After two full decades of socialist construction, Lhasa, with its dark, malodorous courtyards where children play among pigs and goats in the thick smoke of cauldrons in which women boil wool, looks very much like the city seen by the Austrian

Jesuit Johannes Gruber, the first westerner to reach it; the city Abbe Huc described in 1847.

New Lhasa, now expanding toward the western valley, and old Lhasa, clustered at the foot of the Potala, meet along one main boulevard. In the morning, the Chinese do their calisthenics and jogging on one side of it; on the other side, the Tibetans, fingers on their rosaries, start the daily routine of prayers.

The two communities are separate, distinct, often without communication. Sometimes they seem to live in two different ages. Along the road to the airport, a People's Liberation Army unit puts up the telephone wire by which Lhasa is now connected with the rest of the world. Groups of Tibetans follow them and tie their prayer sheets to it.

In the whole of Tibet there are only 120,000 Chinese (6% of the population), excluding soldiers. Seventy thousand of them live in Lhasa and are the leading cadres, the technicians, the administrators of this province. Although official statistics say that 46% of the high cadres are already Tibetan, wherever one goes all managers, as well as the employees of the local branch of the Bank of China, those at the central post office, or at the tourist bureau are almost exclusively Han (as the Chinese are called).

The overwhelming majority of them do not speak Tibetan ("I would rather study English. It gives me more opportunities," says a young girl, originally from Sichuan, now in a government office), and dream only of going back "inland," as the rest of China is called here.

Life at 4,000 meters (13,000 feet) is not easy for people from the plains. In the Lhasa Valley, the Chinese have planted thousands of trees, thus increasing the level of oxygen by 1%. But the rarified air of the "roof of the world" causes respiratory problems, not only to the passing tourist, but to the resident Han as well. Here water boils at 89 degrees. Many germs therefore do not die and people complain about stomach trouble. To compensate for all these hardships, Peking pays its Han cadres a 30% premium on their wages.

To garrison Tibet, Peking has stationed some 300,000 soldiers of the People's Liberation Army in the province. There is no active resistance to the Chinese rule and the stories of Tibetan guerrillas ambushing Han patrols are at least 15 years old.

Yet, there are indications that an underground passive resistance movement survives among Tibetans. In 1979, when in Peking Democracy Wall had its spring, a wall poster appeared one night in Lhasa asking for the independence of Tibet. Since 1980, when Tibet was opened to foreign tourists for the first time in 30 years, visitors have been approached regularly by Tibetans who discreetly slip handwritten messages into their palms and disappear. Usually these notes, written in Tibetan (I received two of them), complain about the "Han occupation" and appeal to the United Nations to help Tibet regain its independence. The wording of these messages is similar; the places where they are passed on differ.

Though still quite impotent, a clandestine organization must exist, and the Chinese are sensitive and don't want too much publicity about it. Journalists are rarely allowed into Tibet, and the number of tourists, which was scheduled to rapidly increase, will remain limited.

The most spectacular expression of defiance against Chinese rule over Tibet was seen at the end of 1980, during the visit of a delegation sent by the Dalai Lama to investigate conditions in Tibet. When the small group of exiled Tibetans arrived at the site of a temple which had been destroyed during the Cultural Revolution, they found themselves surrounded by a large crowd weeping and shouting "Long live the Dalai Lama!" Seventy-three Tibetan drivers had commandeered the trucks of their working units to transport some 3,000 people there. The Chinese cut the visit of the delegation short immediately, and made them leave Tibet. The drivers had their licenses withdrawn.

Since 1959, Peking has made an enormous effort to change Tibet. It has poured US$3 billion into the land; started 252 factories; opened 6,624 schools; and built 22,000 kilometers of roads, such as the one from Chengdu in Sichuan Province which crosses 12 rivers and 14 mountain ranges, all at an average height of 4,000 meters.

Like other colonialists, the Chinese are proud to show these remarkable achievements, but fail to understand why, nevertheless, they are not loved.

"Because they made us pay with our souls," says Lobsan K., a 32-year-old teacher who one evening waved me into his house to drink barley beer with a group of other Tibetans, all of whom seemed to share his views. "The Hans built roads, but destroyed our temples; saved people with their hospitals, but killed lamas with their guns. We Tibetans are like dogs with broken limbs."

In 1959, after the anti-Chinese rebellion was crushed and Peking started what it calls the period of "democratic reforms," there were still 106,000 lamas and nuns in Tibet. Now, there are fewer than 1,000. Of the 2,464 monasteries, 10 are left.

In a huge cave in a valley 20 kilometers away from Lhasa, Tsong Kapa, the great reformer of Buddhism, the Martin Luther of Tibet, had built in 1409 the great monastery of Gadan. He built it secluded and hidden because an oracle had told him that one day Buddhism would be overthrown and therefore he wanted to provide his followers with a hiding place in which to preserve the tradition. That was the first monastery the Red Guards attacked during the Cultural Revolution. Not one single brick of the old, enormous structure still stands.

The destruction of religion was planned, systematic, relentless, and fundamentally changed the Tibetan landscape.

Every district had a "dzong," a kind of religious fortress on top of a hill. All of them were leveled. The fields had stupas: the Red Guards turned them into scarecrows. Every household had clay figures of gods on their altars. They were all smashed. Religious instruments were destroyed, prayer flags that waved over roofs were taken down and replaced with the red flag of the Party. Carved and painted Buddhist figures on thousands of rocks on the mountains were erased.

In front of the Potala, on top of the Iron Hill, was the famous Medicine College which served for centuries as a medical school for the lamas. Here Tibetans used to go to scrape off the limestone and eat it as a medicine. Now there is hardly a trace of it. Chinese artillery smashed the temple in 1959, saying it was a nest of the reactionary forces. The Red

Guards did the rest, taking away the last stones and effacing the whole side of the hill and its hundreds of carved figures.

Even a sacred willow tree in the middle of Lhasa, reputed to have sprung out of Buddha's hair, was not spared. Now only a dry stump of it remains, covered with prayer sheets.

Burning of butter in the votive lamps was considered a waste and therefore prohibited. Dogs were called "parasites" and devout parents had to watch helplessly as their children were indoctrinated to stone and club them. Like all other beings, dogs are thought by Tibetans to be reincarnations of the souls of men.

The holy refrain, "aum mani padne hum," which brings merit not only if pronounced, but also if read or seen or turned inside a prayer wheel, was written on rocks and walls. The Red Guards diligently erased it everywhere and replaced it word by word with "Long live Chairman Mao."

"The Gang of Four caused very serious damage," says Lo Sanchichan, vice-governor of Tibet. To most Tibetans, this distinction between the Gang of Four and the Communist Party is a difficult one to make. To them they are all Hans.

Now that time and rain have begun to bring justice, one sees in many places the old script surfacing again under the red paint of the Maoists. Tibetans are trying to put together whatever they can find of the pieces left from the disaster. They are rebuilding small stupas along the roads. At Gadan, groups of young people regularly use their spare time to rebuild a shrine on the site of the old vanished monastery.

At Sera, half of the once magnificent complex of houses, cells and temples built at the foot of a rocky mountain north of Lhasa is still in shambles, a frightening testimony to the violence that must have been used by the Red Guards. A courtyard in the western part of the monastery is gutted by fire. Only a black skeleton remains of the cells and the balustrades. Everything in the adjoining chapel was smashed, slashed and clubbed. Not one image of the frescoes can be recognized. The wind blowing from Lhasa brings the cacophony of the loudspeakers with their Chinese propaganda. It also moves the dozens of small golden bells on an intact roof to jingle in the solitude.

An old lama, seeing me wander alone through the rubble, calls me into the cell to which he has recently returned. From the garden he has dug out a Tanka (scroll with religious figures) and he is still busy scraping the walls which he had covered with mud in order to save the frescoes from the Red Guards. On the table stands a new Shanghai-made thermos flask which the government has given him as compensation for the things he lost.

The government now pays a salary to the few surviving lamas, and is spending US$500,000 to restore monasteries such as Drepung, 5 kilometers west of Lhasa, to which foreign visitors are now shepherded.

Drepung was the biggest monastery in the world. In 1959, there were over 10,000 lamas living there. In 1962, only 700 were left. The Chinese, by implementing their "democratic reforms," forced the majority of the monks to go to work or get married. In 1966, the Red Guards finished the job, chasing everybody away and killing those who resisted. "How many?" Nobody seems to know or wants to remember. Under the vigilant eyes of the Chinese guides who accompany visitors, the voice of "comrade" Lama Gandun Icacuo, responsible for the spiritual work in Drepung, sounds quite strange as he explains the superiority of Marxism over religion and forecasts the doom of Buddhism in Tibet. "Marxism in the end shall prevail," he says.

At the moment, the biggest threat to the Buddhist tradition in Tibet is the fact that there are no new lamas in the monasteries. Chinese government propaganda says that anyone who wants to become a monk is free to do so. But a basic political decision on this issue has probably not yet been taken, for fear that thousands of fit men might present themselves to the monasteries. So far, a number of administrative measures (for instance, no person in China can abandon his working unit without a special permit) have discouraged Tibetans from doing so.

Nevertheless, the recent liberalization has already brought back some of the old Tibetan ways. At the Drepung monastery, old lamas are assisted by young boys, according to the traditional master–pupil relationship. Word of the new freedom of worship, fully granted again only in 1980, has gone quickly around the country, and Lhasa has become a city of pilgrims again.

Every day, from all parts of Tibet and from neighboring Sichuan, Gansu, Qinghai and Mongolia, where another 2 million Tibetans are scattered, hundreds and hundreds of herdsmen and nomads, many on foot after a trip of months, enter the holy valley and go to camp around the holiest of the temples, the Jokka Kang, built 1,300 years ago over a hidden lake in which, according to the legend, one can read the future. For some of these people, wrapped in their heavy wool clothes or in yak leather coats, this is their last trip, for they have come to die.

Old Asia hands described the Tibetan ritual of sky burials and I had heard it still happened. In old books I had read where it used to happen: behind the hills, east of the Sera monastery. The vultures were my guides over the last stretch of road. I saw them squatting on the top of a high rock. Then I saw them disappear, fly away behind the hill and come back with their spoil in their claws.

I climbed the hill and stood on that rock. Down in the next large valley, beside a silver stream of water, under the bluest of all skies, upon a huge flat stone, I saw the ritual the Tibetans have performed for centuries. In this country where the soil is too hard to dig, and where no wood is available for making cremation fires, sky burials have been the most pious way to dispose of the dead.

I saw the bodies being brought in by the families. The breakers unwrapped them and put them face down on the stone. First, with a blow, they split the head to help the soul wander toward a new incarnation. Then they opened the chest, giving the heart and liver to the biggest of the vultures. Then they began to cut slices of skin and flesh, and the ravens also arrived for their meal. A man at the side took the bones and pounded them with a stone hammer until they, too, were fodder for the birds. In the end, there were only three tired men, resting on a huge stone, and an old woman bringing them buttered tea.

The river was glittering in the valley, and from the distance the all-seeing Potala with its hundreds of windows was levitating in the haze. Over my head, the crowing of the ravens and the rustling of the wide-opened wings of the vultures.

"What is the difference? You let your dead be eaten by the worms, we by the birds," a Tibetan said to me that evening. "Once the soul is gone, the body is nothing but a thing, like this table."

For other pilgrims the trip to Lhasa is the fulfillment of a vow, or the long-expected opportunity to gain merit for their next incarnation. For the Tibetans, Lhasa is Mecca, Lourdes and Jerusalem at once, and walking clockwise around the Jokka Kang twice a day, always keeping the temple on the right, is a sacred duty.

The Jokka Kang houses the oldest image of Buddha in Tibet, the statue of the most famous Tibetan king, Songtsang Kampo, and has dozens of dark, malodorous niches with golden images. The road round it is filled with a continuous stream of marching, crawling, limping bodies — an immense court of miracles.

Along the sidewalks there are beggars holding out their palms, lepers offering their stumps to the pity of the passers-by, readers of sutras, old women selling yak butter, traders who buy from the pilgrims the coral, turquoise and amber with which they finance their pilgrimages, butchers who cut slices of raw meat on the pavement in front of sleepy dogs waiting for the leftovers, while on the road the procession of animals and people continues, some crippled, most in rags, all dirty, stinking, ailing, elated in the happiness of the sacrifice. Old men, young women with babies on their backs, young children, some with their eyes already destroyed by trachoma, all of them walk in the midst of clouds of dust, the permanent stench of rancid butter, and the smoke that billows out of huge brass cauldrons burning perfumed herbs.

Within a few hours one day I saw a woman giving birth, a man dying in the crowd, and an old woman drinking the urine of a little boy beside her.

Many do the tour of the Jokka Kang by throwing themselves on the ground, hands forward, then raising their backs again like earthworms, then thrusting themselves down again, their

149

faces a mask of dust and sweat.

Some protect their hands with wooden gloves; some simply leave a trace of blood in their path. At night the pilgrims light their campfires, and each group gathers around their elders. From a common bowl they pour buttered tea on balls of barley flour which they knead with their hands, while an old man keeps the fire alive with a pair of bellows made of a cat's skin.

In front of the closed red door of the Jokka Kang, under its roof of pure gold, dozens of people keep prostrating themselves over stones that have been rubbed and polished by millions of pilgrims over the centuries.

"Now there is freedom of religion. Religion is a theory. It cannot be prohibited by force," says Lo Sanchichan, the vice-governor of Tibet.

In 1978, when the Jokka Kang was discreetly reopened twice a month after the damage done by the Red Guards had been repaired, Tibetan government employees were prohibited from going there. Now the temple of temples is open every morning (entrance fee 1 yuan), and among the crowd of pilgrims arriving from remote parts of Tibet one can glimpse the odd Tibetan with a Mao jacket doing the same prostrations and mumbling the same prayers.

Two years ago, a man who sang a song in honor of the Dalai Lama in public was arrested. Now Yin Fatan, Communist Party secretary of the province says, "The Dalai Lama? He is an old friend. He is very welcome to return to Tibet. And he is free to leave if he does not like it here."

The night of March 17, 1959, the Dalai Lama, the fourteenth in succession, left his summer palace of Norbulingka disguised as a soldier with a gun slung over his shoulders, and never came back. Yet, the Dalai Lama is everywhere in today's Tibet. His image is on the laps of the gods in the Jokka Kang and the Potala. He is in the daily prayers of the lamas at Drepung and in the minds of most Tibetans. Almost every Tibetan household in old Lhasa has, in addition to an entrance room which is usually adorned with the paraphernalia of Marxism–Leninism and Maoism, another room where the religious images and portraits of the Dalai Lama are kept. In the countryside people don't even take this last precaution.

In the hut of the "model peasant" of a horse-breeding commune 30 kilometers outside Lhasa, where the visitor is brought
by Chinese guides, the portrait of the Dalai Lama has simply
been slipped into the frame that once held Mao's picture.

Old peasants brighten up, some weep at the simple mention of his name. People have around their necks threads of
cloth he once blessed. Most Tibetans still don't smoke, because
he once prohibited it. At the newly reopened market of Lhasa,
some enterprising merchants (including some young Chinese)
are now making small fortunes by selling reproductions of an
old picture of him at 0.50 yuan each.

The Dalai Lama is neither pope nor king. According to the
Tibetans, he is the reincarnation of Chenrezigs, the Protecting Buddha. Therefore, he is also the best ruler possible. When
a Dalai Lama dies, it is believed that within two or three years
his soul again takes human form in a boy born somewhere
in Tibet. Usually the search for the successor is a long and secret
process in which the highest lamas of the country take part.

"These are my prayer beads," said a 4-year-old boy, now
the Dalai Lama, when 43 years ago a party of monks disguised as servants and carrying some of the personal belongings of the deceased Dalai Lama, entered a small farmhouse
in eastern Tibet. The dying Dalai Lama had turned his face
toward the east, thus giving an indication of where to look
for his reincarnation. The boy recognized that the visitors were
not servants, but lamas from the Sera monastery. He spoke
to them in the official court language nobody in his family
knew and he identified, beside the prayer beads, a series of
other objects belonging to the late Dalai Lama.

This boy, now a 47-year-old man, is the fourteenth Dalai
Lama. He lives in India, heads a Tibetan government in exile,
is the undisputed leader of 100,000 Tibetans around the world
and continues to be regarded by the largest majority of
Tibetans throughout China as their spiritual leader.

Peking is now building golden bridges to bring him back
to Lhasa. In 1979, the government released the 376 surviving
followers of the Dalai Lama imprisoned in Tibet since 1959.
Every year it calls on all exiles to come back, and promises
the return of their properties (some of the old houses of the

151

former nobles in Lhasa are now being thoroughly repainted).

Five delegations of special emissaries from the Dalai Lama, including his sister, have been received by Peking and allowed to tour Tibet. Probably as a subtle sign of respect, the Chinese caretakers of the Dalai Lama's summer palace, Norbulingka, have made his bed, which until recently was shown to visitors in its ruffled state, as he had left it when he hurriedly escaped over 25 years ago.

"Tibet is a game of chess. It is only over when you have the king," the British used to say. They invaded Tibet from India in 1904, and lost the Dalai Lama when he fled to Mongolia.

The Chinese lost him too, in 1959. But they thought they could do without him. Now that their plans for changing Tibet have proved a failure and religion has proved to be as alive as ever, the Chinese see in the Dalai Lama their best card for helping them rule Tibet and pacify a people brought to the brink of unrest by Red Guard repression and wrong policies.

The disaster in the economy has been the straw that broke the camel's back. The pilgrims who gather today around the Jokka Kang temple provide a good example of the situation in the various parts of Tibet into which no foreigner has been allowed in the past 35 years: poverty, disease, destitution.

"Yes, 70% of the people's communes are worse off today than they were 20 years ago," admits Vice-Governor Lo Sanchichan.

Up to the arrival of the Chinese, Tibetans had "more taxes to pay than there are hairs on a yak." The Chinese eliminated all of them. But their so-called democratic reforms meant, as in the rest of China, forced collectivization and rigid People's Communes. This did not suit the Tibetans, who were accustomed to a semi-nomadic life and economy. They found themselves in a straight jacket and saw their crops being taken away by the state in pretty much the same way as they used to be taken away by the lamaseries, which in the past used to own almost all the land.

The worst mistake the Chinese made was to force the Tibetans to grow more winter wheat instead of their beloved chingko, a kind of barley that has been their main staple throughout the centuries.

Chingko does not need to be cooked. A handful of chingko flour, poured into a cup of tea together with a spoon of yak butter, is a readymade meal. Wheat, on the contrary, needs to be cooked. In a country without fuel (trees are extremely rare), this is an immense disadvantage.

Moreover, winter wheat impoverishes Tibet's particular kind of soil and renders it progressively less fertile. Yields dropped sharply, but the Chinese insisted on replacing chingko cultures with winter wheat, for this was the national policy. In 1979, 790,000 mu of land in Tibet were still cultivated this way.

Supplies of barley became scarce and "rising prices created urban unrest," says a high Chinese official in Lhasa. In 1980 alone, Peking had to ship to Tibet 40 million kilograms of grain to avoid starvation.

"We are far from self-sufficient," admits Vice-Governor Lo Sanchichan. In the late seventies, the New China News Agency announced triumphantly that Tibet was producing more than it ate, and the Chinese-made film, *Tibet: The Roof of the World*, still shown to visitors in Lhasa, portrays happy Tibetan peasants in the middle of winter wheat fields while a voice says that Tibet now provides grain for the rest of China.

After Communist Party Secretary Hu Yaobang's visit to Lhasa in 1980, and his unprecedented, open assessment of all these failures, Peking ordered a complete reversal of past policies.

Tibetans are now exempt from paying agricultural taxes, and they are no longer required to sell their crops to the state at a fixed price, but may bargain and sell them independently. Their private plots of land have been enlarged, and the number of private animals and private trees they can keep has been increased. The entire People's Commune system has been shaken, and Chinese officials have announced that in remote areas of Tibet private farming has started again. Private markets have reopened and Tibetan and Nepalese traders have been granted 400 licenses to reopen their shops in Lhasa.

The results have started to show: yak butter made privately is now on sale at half the previous price (from 15 yuan down to 7 yuan per kilo); meat, slaughtered by Tibetan Muslims, is now freely available on the sidewalks of Lhasa. Until recently it was a rarity.

If the economic system China has tried to force upon Tibet during the past 25 years has proved disastrous, the modernizations the Chinese introduced into the province have proved to be useful only to them.

The roads, the Tibetans say, were built by the Chinese for purely strategic reasons and are not of much use to the people since there is no system of public transport in Tibet. Schools have not changed much in the province, with 70% of Tibetans outside Lhasa still officially illiterate. The industrialization plan, launched by the Chinese in 1959, has not affected the Tibetans much as most of the 74,000 industrial workers in the province are Han anyway. In the electric power station of Lhasa, out of 330 workers only 90 are locals; out of 59 administrators, only eight are Tibetans.

Lack of planning and bad implementation have wasted big investments. A glass window factory built in Lhasa, where people still have to defend themselves against wind and snow with buttered paper in their windows, has only managed to produce small glasses for "maotai," the Han liquor.

Another factory, meant to produce sugar, which in Tibet is terribly expensive due to the huge transport costs, was discovered not to have enough raw material to maintain output.

The aquaduct, meant to use a former private well of the Dalai Lama and channel its waters to Lhasa, does not yet work properly, for the pipes are so exposed that in winter the water freezes.

Within the framework of the new policies, the glass factory is going to be closed down, as is a radio plant and a coal mine now described as unprofitable. The sugar factory is going to be converted. Moreover, the large majority of Han cadres and workers are going to be withdrawn from Tibet within the next three years.

"It will be impossible for all the Hans to go," says Lo Sanchichan. "We still need doctors, teachers and scientists. But very soon Tibet will be ruled by Tibetans."

Apart from sheer incompetence, "Han arrogance," as the Tibetans call it, has been one of the causes of Tibetan–Chinese animosity and of Chinese mistakes in Tibet.

The story of the Lhasa Municipality Carpet Factory is a case in point. Tibetans had woven splendid wool carpets for centuries. It was a home industry. They made them for themselves, to use over their beds, or for the monasteries. When the Chinese arrived, first they forced Tibetans to deliver all the wool to the state (and caused the disappearance of most Tibetan handicrafts as well). Second, they organized and modernized the carpet industries, calling in Han carpet experts from Tianjin and Peking to manage them. The classic Tibetan patterns were changed. The weaving method was modified and even the traditional Tibetan dragon, with its four claws, was woven with five claws, as is the Chinese dragon. Its contours were embossed by shears, as is done with Tianjin carpets.

The Lhasa Carpet Factory still runs at a loss, and, among the 140 workers, 20% are still Chinese who came to teach something the Tibetans knew better.

Now the official policy is to encourage everything Tibetan, to revive Tibetan culture, to respect Tibetan habits. (The Lhasa Exposition Hall, which was used in the past to prove the barbarism of Tibetans before Chinese rule, is now closed to the public, and opens by appointment to foreign visitors only). But all of this is easier said than done.

In 25 years the Chinese have pushed aside Tibetan culture and rewritten Tibetan history, to prove their point that Tibet is an inseparable part of China. The five million Tibetan books which the Chinese claim to have printed are mainly works on Marxism–Leninism and Mao Zedong-thought. The only book on the Tibetan past available in the Lhasa bookstores is one written by a Han offering the usual historical inaccuracies and lies, such as one which says the Jokka Kang was built by the Chinese to celebrate the marriage of the Chinese princess Wen Chen to the Tibetan king Songtsang Kampo. The truth is that he had three wives, and that the Jokka Kang, with its main door facing west, was built for the Nepalese one.

There are no more intellectuals in Tibet. When I asked to meet a Tibetan writer, the Chinese produced one whose only claim to literature was to have translated the famous Chinese novel _Water Margin_ into Tibetan.

In 25 years, the Chinese have brought to Peking and trained a small group of Tibetan cadres. Most of them are more Han than the Han. "They are like frogs in a well who have never seen the ocean," as a visiting Tibetan exile I met in Lhasa describes them.

As the old intelligentsia who fled into exile with the Dalai Lama is dying out, a new generation of Tibetan intellectuals, who have studied in western universities and live in India, Switzerland and Canada, could well contribute to the modernization of Tibet by Tibetans. The return of the Dalai Lama would bring many of these exiles back. For the time being, the main obstacle to this solution is that refugees still dream of an independent Tibet and that the Dalai Lama refuses to dissolve his government in exile.

Although Tibet has historically endeavored, and many times succeeded, in eluding Chinese control, today Tibet is irreversibly part of China, and the mere idea of an independent Tibet is politically absurd. China will never relinquish control of the region, for all her borders are inhabited by minorities with problems similar to those of the Tibetans.

On the other hand, China cannot afford a destabilizing unrest in that province. What Peking basically needs is to have her troops and missiles stationed in Tibet to counter the Soviet threat. It also needs to have access to the vast mineral resources of Tibet for her own modernization. The price Peking is now prepared to pay is a larger degree of autonomy for that region. The return of the Dalai Lama would help this plan considerably.

"Will he have political powers?" I asked the Communist Party secretary of Tibet, Yin Fantan.

"In China, religion and state power are irreversibly separated," he answered.

Realistic Tibetans hope that the Chinese plan will work and that Peking will understand the meaning of an old Lhasa prophecy that says, "Only if Tibet is happy can China prosper."

10

I Knifed Him Four Times and I Was Happy

Communism against Chinese traditional culture

> Above, a thousand meters of sharp rocks
> Underneath, a hundred frightening cliffs.
> Stretch your hand and you touch the moon
> While white clouds flow into your sleeve.

Standing above the mute emptiness of the abyss, a lonely wanderer of ages ago committed to poetry the emotions of climbing up to the Xuanggong Si, the Flying Temple.

Indeed a surprising experience, because for a temple this is a most unlikely location. In a barren landscape of gray rocks, from a river bed of huge boulders, a vast, massive wall of granite rises straight toward the sky. There, on this awesome stone precipice, Taoist hermits came to build their impossible nest and to meditate over the sense of life and the meaning of the Tao. That was 1,400 years ago.

The Flying Temple still hangs from the cliffs, a magnificent structure defying the laws of nature, an example of the daring architectural skills of men who never thought of conquering the moon, for they had it already in the reach of their hands.

With its rows of red lacquered columns, holding curved roofs once made of turquoise blue tiles, the Flying Temple was the gate to one of China's five sacred mountains, the Heng Shan, south of the Great Wall, east of the Yellow River, in the heart of Shanxi Province. For centuries the monks of the temple went to put water kettles on the fire to offer tea to the pilgrims when they spotted them, climbing up slowly, like dark dots in the shadows of the gorges.

Now an old, trembling Buddhist monk, whom the communist authorities have ordered to this Taoist sanctuary to entertain foreign tourists, goes to put on his yellow robe to offer himself to the indiscreet curiosity of their cameras.

The rest of the mountain is off limits. The other 28 shrines are destroyed ("some with dynamite during the Cultural Revolution," says a guide), but the Flying Temple, the only one left, has just been repaired in order to be a tourist attraction for foreigners chaperoned from the nearby city of Datong.

In the past, those who visited China were taken exclusively to see People's Communes, red flag factories, kindergartens, schools and revolutionary museums. The simple inquiry about temples and pagodas brought harsh reprimands from the official guides. "That is old, feudal China," one was usually told. "What we want you to see is new, socialist China."

Now, with the opening of the country to a mass influx of tourists, the communist authorities realize that foreigners have to be shown what they want to see if they are to keep coming and bring foreign currency with them. But the problem is that much of old China is gone: smashed, burned, ransacked, obliterated. The authorities are now hurriedly trying to put together what is left.

Shanxi Province, one of China's oldest cultural centers, is a good example of what is happening in the entire country. In 1982, the provincial government asked every county to prepare a list of the monuments which could still be salvaged and put on tourist itineraries. A restoration program was quickly approved and some previously forbidden localities have already been opened to foreigners.

Visiting these few isolated places which have been hastily repaired, one realizes the appalling magnitude of past destruction and the foolish policies of present restoration. Parts of different temples are pieced together, old ruins are moved from one place to another, remnants of statues, religious images, and inscriptions are taken from their original sites, badly restored and senselessly reassembled somewhere else.

China is in the process of putting together a cultural and historic monster, a kind of archeological Frankenstein, for the exclusive benefit of foreign consumers.

Twenty-five kilometers southeast of Taiyuan, the capital of Shanxi, dozens of workers are busy building a Ming dynasty temple next to a half-finished Yuan dynasty pagoda, while tiles of another structure brought here from a faraway village wait to be put on top of a wooden frame still in the making. A few more months and the old, elegant, quiet Jingci sanctuary, built 1,000 years ago around three legendary springs to honor the Mother of the Waters (the wells are already dry due to pollution from a huge chemical plant nearby) will be transformed into an amusement park, The Garden of Temples, with a selection of various traditional Chinese buildings.

"Tourists will no longer need to go to too many places," says the local guide. "They can come here and see them all. This will be very convenient for our foreign friends."

Old stone carvings, wooden and bronze statues, old furniture and even old house doors are being bought from peasants throughout the province to give life to the Garden of Temples. Here at least the surroundings are real.

In Guangdong Province in southern China, the local authorities have found so little left to put at the disposal of the tourist industry that they are now considering a US$70 million project proposed by a California company for the construction of a Chinese "ancient cultural and entertainment center," a Disneyland-like replica of an old city at the time of the Warring States.

Shanxi Province is in the heart of China. In past times, few western travelers ever ventured into this wind-beaten loess country, and Shanxi was known as the "hidden province." When in 1900 the International Expedition came to break the siege of the legation quarter in Peking and "punish" China for the crimes of the anti-foreign Boxer Rebellion, it stopped at the mountainous borders of Shanxi. They were too arduous to cross.

Far from the sea coast, where foreigners built foreign cities like Shanghai and Tianjin, far from Peking, the former capital of the empire, Shanxi was the home of the Han, the "black-haired race," the original stock of the Chinese long before history was written.

Near the city of Linfeng, the capital of mythical times, there is a mountain still called "the peak of the ancestors of man," for an old legend says that at the time of a great flood it was there that two human beings were brought on the back of a

159

lion, thus saving them from drowning. This was China's version of Noah's Ark. In Shanxi was born the man who is thought to have invented the Chinese ideograms; from Shanxi came the emperor's concubine who is reputed to have discovered the quality of the silk cocoon and learned how to breed it.

Tall, elegant, timid and stubborn, the Shanxi people resisted all intruders — they never surrendered to Genghis Khan — and became known to the rest of China as the "cow-skin lanterns," dark outside, bright inside. Old men and women, who roam around the village markets of the province today, Homeric figures wearing the padded black cloth peasants have worn for centuries, are the direct descendants of this unspoiled Shanxi race.

Everywhere in the province, myth and history have left traces of China's ancient greatness. In the north are the Yonggang Caves, where hundreds of Buddha figures were carved in limestone to the glory of the new religion that had arrived from India. In the center are the temples to honor China's emperors of the mythical age, when "there was corn in the fields, fish in the ponds, gold rained from the sky, and people were happy." In the south are the great shrines of Taoism which expanded to the rest of China.

In 1949, when the communists took over the country, 78% of all the temples of China were in Shanxi. Shanxi Province was a huge, open, natural museum. Now it is a saddening cemetery, dotted with ruins. Along the winding road that the visitor travels to reach the Flying Temple, across the mountains from Datong, one sees dozens of villages made up of caves cut into the hardened mud. Above the flat roofs of each of them there is the curved roof of a temple. All of these temples are no more. Their front entrances are walled and their colored tiles removed; some have been turned into granaries, some have simply been left empty to rot. They were victims not of the Cultural Revolution, but of the consistent policy of the Chinese Communist Party, methodically trying to eliminate all influence of past feudal culture from society.

The first blow came in the fifties with the Land Reform Campaign. Each temple had fields whose rents were used to finance its religious and educational activities. When all the land had been confiscated, the means of subsistence ceased and the monks were forced to return to civilian life and work. "We were starving and we had to come down to the plain," says Zhong Lian, the 77-year-old monk now in the Flying Temple, who in 1960 left the sanctuary of the Wu Tai Mountain where he had lived for 20 years.

Another blow came with the Anti Four Olds Campaign (old culture, old habits, old customs, old thoughts) and the Cultural Revolution, when thousands of Red Guards were unleashed to close the last temples, beat up the remaining monks and destroy what had survived.

One is now told that the campaign got out of hand because the ultra-leftists, the Gang of Four, took over. But the ideology behind it was the same as that during the War of Liberation when soldiers were sent to take the "idols" away from the temples, to throw them into the village square, to break their limbs, to smash their heads in front of the peasants, to show that "idols" had no power whatsoever. The Buddhas were an obstacle to modernization. Religion was holding China back in underdevelopment. Those statues — people were told — could provide no salvation. Shanxi people were told instead that "Mao Zedong is the saving star of the people."

For centuries, religion had dominated the hearts and minds of the Chinese. Their art, philosophy, ethics, were determined by it; and religion, having "produced China's finest thoughts," according to Ernest Fenellosa, was an intrinsic part of China's culture and history.

When the communists took power in China in 1949, they considered their revolution the cut-off point in history, and their declared policy was to eradicate all the influences of the past. In order to build new socialist China, old feudal China had to be eliminated. To build a new man, the old had to be pushed aside. By wanting to make China "a blank, white page," Mao started a trend that has developed into one of the greatest, still-unsolved, contradictions of communist policies.

"China has a history of 4,000 years," the visiting foreigner is told and retold by the tourist guides and the government officials he meets. Yet that history, being a history of gods, emperors, heroes, temples and palaces, is a feudal history and as such is withheld from the Chinese people. The contradiction is this: in the context of her relationship with the outside world, China boasts of her glories of the past to compensate for the failures of the present; in the context of her social development, that past is refuted and destroyed. The people are being asked to be proud of something they know nothing about.

"China is one of the countries of the world with the longest history," reads the new Chinese constitution. "The Chinese people have created a splendid culture...." Which culture is not clear at all, for the communists have consistently denied that Chinese traditional culture has any value.

For three decades, schools have taught young Chinese nothing about the classics, about the dynasties, about old China. Chinese history has been exclusively taught as a history of peasant rebellions, and not as the history of "empires that wax and wane," as it is described at the beginning of China's classic novel *The Three Kingdoms*. A whole generation has grown up without knowing the myths, the legends, or even the names of emperors, heroes and gods that together formed the immense pantheon which animated Chinese life for millennia. Not even the simple word "emperor" can be found in primary school books today.

Official guides of the China Travel Service, the state organization which monopolizes tourism and is believed to be part of Peking's security and intelligence apparatus, know very little about the places they bring visitors to see. An exceptionally well-informed tourist guide in Taiyuan admitted that he learned all he knew about the stories of the Jingci sanctuary from a Nagel guidebook a visitor once gave him.

In the New China Bookshop of the Shanxi capital, once a main cultural center of China, one can find books on Marxism–Leninism, all the works of Mao, even the latest volume by Kim Il Sung, the North Korean dictator, but not a single collection of old poems, not a book on the history of Taiyuan, not a description of its historical monuments, not even a map of the city.

The basic idea is that old culture and old stories, with their feudal heroes and feudal values, have nothing to teach to today's youth, and that now people have to learn from modern socialist heroes.

In the center of Linfeng, where a beautiful drum tower, once the city's landmark, is still in ruins, stands a famous old pagoda constructed during the Tang dynasty around a huge iron head of Buddha with bulging eyes and a mysterious smile.

The legend says that Buddha went to sleep in Xian and, while reclining, his head dropped into Linfeng, hundreds of kilometers away. After 1949, the temple adjoining the pagoda was transformed into a school, but later, probably to avoid the "bad" influence of the place, it was made into an exhibition hall. For the last year, the various rooms of this rather large compound have housed a collection of pictures depicting the life of Lei Feng, a man who never existed. According to present-day communist legend, he was a soldier of the People's Liberation Army who always obeyed the Party, who always did something good for the people, and who died when an electric pole fell on his head. The place is empty. No visitors. No faithful. An incredible waste of space in a country where every square meter of construction is so precious.

"What was the name of this temple?" a visitor asks a group of youngsters playing badminton among piles of coal in the dirty courtyard of another temple in the old center of Taiyuan. "There is no temple here, this is a factory," they answer. Indeed, under the yellow tiles of the broken roofs that indicate the imperial origin of the complex, there are machines and men at work.

The buildings are disfigured by wires, chimneys and posters. Old archways are filled in with bricks, new windows have been opened. The spirit wall, with its five dragons protecting the entrance to the temple, has been taken apart. Along the external walls, dozens of worker families have built with bricks and wooden boxes shabby cubicles which they call home. Here, as in thousands of other such places — it has been a consistent policy to build factories in the grounds of temples — people live among the ruins of great monuments to which they no longer have any relationship. Completely estranged from

163

their own past, they move among the rubble of another world, surprised at the attention of a visitor to ruins they know nothing about.

Now that some of these places have been ordered to be repaired by the same authorities who ordered them destroyed, people are confused, some even angered. Particularly the young. "Why spend so much money to restore temples when we need houses?" asks a worker in Taiyuan. And a student in Datong commented that "we have to go forward and modernize the country. So why go backward and revive the old?" In any case, these places are not repaired and reopened for the Chinese.

In the yellow, monotonous plain, 70 kilometers south of Datong, where the flatness of the landscape is interrupted only by clusters of mud houses surrounded by mud walls within village walls of mud, rises the elegant, dark silhouette of a pagoda. The Yin Xian pagoda, made entirely of wood, has thrown her long, protecting shadow over the flat roofs of the surrounding peasant houses for nine centuries. This gigantic structure of wood, standing on a pedestal of stone, is a stunning testimony to the work of ancient carpenters. As early as the fifties it was declared a national monument, and a book was prepared to illustrate the splendor of this structure in every detail. The book was finally published in 1980, but by then the pagoda had changed.

In August 1966, Red Guards came here and in a single night wreaked havoc. They had come to break the chests of the unique clay Buddhas for legend said that they had hearts of gold. Indeed they had, for they contained the sutras, the golden sacred scriptures. The Red Guards burned these in disappointment and anger. The animals of stone, carved around the pagoda's pedestal, were smashed with hammers. The temple buildings behind it were given to the flames.

The pagoda has now been partly repaired. But an iron gate has been built in front of it and hundreds of villagers gather against it to stare mutely at the lonely foreigner who buys an entrance ticket and is shown around. It is no longer their pagoda. They have nothing to do with it. Old people are not allowed in to offer joss sticks to the statues. The place is dead.

While policemen keep the crowds at bay, a former communist soldier, now in charge of the site, explains the restoration project that foresees flower gardens, little kiosks, and a parking lot for tourist buses. Formerly the greatness of the temple lay in its essential simplicity, mirrored by a nearby lake. "We drained the lake because it bred mosquitoes," says the cadre.

Wherever one goes, the repair work is rough, the colors flashy, the details offensive and neither the religious nor the artistic arrangement of buildings and statues is respected.

In the courtyard of the Shan Huali temple in Datong, an iron ox and an iron horse, retrieved from a destroyed village shrine, have been placed in front of a five dragon spirit wall which in turn had been salvaged from another Datong temple wiped out to make space for a new hotel.

In Taiyuan, 200 stone tablets with some of the finest examples of Ming dynasty calligraphy have been placed in a new pavilion next to the city's Twin Pagodas. The tablets used to stand in an old temple in the middle of town, taken over since Liberation by the Communist Party's local headquarters. "The Party does not want to leave the temple; at least we have saved its tablets," says a Taiyuan official.

The ground of the Twin Pagodas is a depot of old bits and pieces scavenged from around town which are being used to refurbish this abandoned place.

Repair work needing expertise and knowledge is everywhere under the direction of local, ignorant authorities. "Who planned the restoration project?" I asked at the temple of Emperor Yao, 5 kilometers outside Linfeng. "We did it, after consulting with the masses," said the local cadre, a Party man, whose main previous cultural experience was to have been in charge of the Datong cinemas.

Yao was one of the five mythical emperors of China who, according to the legend, was 3 meters tall and reigned for 102 years. His was the golden time Confucius dreamed about, when China was at peace and people were honest. "Higher than the clouds, higher than the moon," says an inscription about him at the main entrance to his temple.

This was one of the sacred places in China, for every

emperor came here to pay his respects to Yao. His huge statue still stands, surrounded by his advisers, in the main hall. Part of this hall collapsed last year, and many of the other structures are gone, but the plan now is to rebuild a whole complex of new buildings to house both cultural relics and the employees in charge of them.

On the holy ground, once covered by a forest of ancient cypress trees, workers are planting young Canadian pines and tracing the foundations for the new dormitories. Three new access roads are being cut through the compound, completely upsetting its solemn balance. There are no experts, no architects; Party cadres decide everything.

The cadres are in blue uniforms, fat, always with a black plastic bag in their hands, chain smoking in the sitting rooms of the guest houses or in their offices. They are the rulers of the country. Ex-revolutionary people, Party apparatchiki with no understanding of traditional culture, whose principal qualification is to have joined the communist ranks before 1949. These are the cadres in charge of restoration.

For every temple that reopens, for every pagoda that is refurbished, there are six to ten caretaker jobs that become available and they are usually distributed among the children of the cadres. Young girls, chatting among themselves about the latest fashion in trousers, take the visitor around the compound, opening and locking again the various doors to the shrines. Most of them know nothing about the places and only upon request repeat by heart the contents of some "for internal use only" brochure that gives only the measurements of the buildings and concludes with, "since 1949 the Communist Party has constantly invested money and energy to preserve and restore the cultural relics of China."

If the experts are gone, so are the experienced artisans. At the Yin Xian pagoda there is only one 72-year-old man who can repair the clay Buddhas. Some months ago the work stopped because he fell ill. In Pingyao, there is nobody capable of removing the white paint splashed over the 1,000-year-old frescoes in the Double Forest Temple when it was turned into a warehouse in 1966. In Linfeng there is no carpenter who can reproduce the intricate lattice work of the doors of the lower

Flying Rainbow Temple.

In 1979, there was a conference in Peking which for two weeks discussed the problems of restoration in China. Somebody suggested opening a national school for restorers but the proposal was turned down. "We are still a poor country. We cannot afford it." Thus the damage continues.

Two years ago in the suburbs of Taiyuan, a 1,400-year-old tomb of an imperial official was discovered during construction of a new road. The entrance corridor to the tomb was covered with frescoes. Nobody knew how to protect them and soon after the fresh air had come in the frescoes vanished. The tomb was closed again.

In the wake of the present construction boom throughout China, great damage is being done to the archeological heritage of the country due to the lack of expertise. "Foundations are laid by mechanically applying the method of exploding rocks and earth," writes the *People's Daily*. "In the ancient capital of Loyang, for instance, a thousand tombs have been destroyed."

In January 1983, the *Communist Party Daily* condemned a beer factory for having blasted away, during the construction of a new wing, a rare tomb containing a hundred statues. One of them, a black horse 50 centimeters high, was only the second of its kind to be found in China.

Handicrafts were once an aspect of China's greatness. Thousands of artisans from time immemorial were able to work any kind of material from wood, to iron, to stone, to silk, to bronze, to jade. The record of China's culture was laid down not only by philosophers, poets and painters, but by a countless army of nameless carpenters, carvers, weavers. Now one can wander around the markets of towns and villages and never come across any skilled product from man's hand, except for a rudimentary mousetrap.

The handicraft tradition was interrupted soon after the establishment of the People's Republic and particularly at the time of the Great Leap Forward, when this sort of workmanship was considered useless and the whole nation was required to produce pig iron. Anything that was decorative and that beautified everyday life was considered superfluous. People

167

had to show their patriotism by melting down every piece of metal, from the handles of their doors to the locks of their cupboards. The fires were lit with their own old carved chairs, tables, beds.

In those days, a famous film was shown throughout China in order to educate the masses to this idea. It was called *The Present from the Summer Vacation* and told the story of a group of children who, having heard from an old man that at the bottom of a river there were some ancient bronze bells, spent the summer holidays salvaging them and finally melting them in a rudimentary furnace. As a present the state gave them a tractor.

Throughout China, invaluable works of art and simple handicrafts were lost in this way. The Twin Pagodas in Taiyuan lost 20 big bronze statues of Buddhas to the furnaces. The niches where they stood for centuries are now empty.

One of the prides of Shanxi used to be that all the cities and villages of the province were surrounded by impressive walls. They have all been methodically destroyed by people who were encouraged by the authorities to take away the bricks to build their own houses.

For centuries Shanxi peasants used to teach their children to "never burn a piece of paper if a character is written on it." But the peasants of Shi Go, north of Linfeng, were singled out as a positive model to be imitated by all when they removed the stone steles, carved with the history of their village, and used them to make a bridge. The Party paper praised them repeatedly. The Party cadre of Linfeng now responsible for the cultural affairs of the county, explaining to the visitor the new policy of restoration, says, "we have to educate the people to respect their cultural heritage." The people, if left alone, would have respected it, for it was their heritage.

On the outskirts of Yun Cheng in southern Shanxi, once a little town full of history and now a charmless gray cluster of shabby new houses not far from a salt lake, there is a vast temple built during the Sui dynasty to honor Guang Gong, a hero of the Three Kingdoms period. To all Chinese he is the symbol of trustworthiness and fidelity, the red-faced protagonist in many classic Chinese operas. For centuries the people paid tribute to the temple and made it the most lively center of the cult of Guang Gong. Even in 1957, a local peasant painter described in two large frescoes the glorious deeds of the red-faced hero. In 1966, when the Maoist rebels came to attack it, the people protected it.

Zhang Jiexiang, the lady in charge of the temple, and her six assistants closed all the doors from the inside and barricaded themselves in. The siege lasted three months. "You have the key, but no power!" shouted the Red Guards. Madame Zhang had the local population on her side. At night they threw food into the temple and finally the Red Guards gave up.

In 1969, the leftist authorities of the county ordered the temple transformed into a school, but Madame Zhang assigned only one courtyard to it and with her people built a high wall around the main hall to prevent anybody from using the school as a way of entry into the temple.

Today, the Guang Gong shrine is the only place in the province still completely preserved and with a religious aura. The various halls are intact, the altars still have their bronze vessels, the legendary weapons of hero Guang are still in the arsenal. In a dark corner of the main temple, a life-size statue of Guang Gong, which once a year used to be carried in a palanquin through the streets of the town, is still there. Made of straw, dressed in cloth, now covered with dust, the face of Guang Gong, hidden behind a string of pearls falling from his head, still seems to be alive and waiting in the dark for better days.

Madame Zhang now has a team of 16 people. In a garden next to the temple she runs a prosperous greenhouse producing flowers and vegetables. With the money she makes she repairs the leaking roofs of the temple which she hopes to transform, with the full approval of the authorities, into...a guesthouse for foreign visitors.

Ding Cun, a Ming dynasty village 30 kilometers south of Linfeng, was saved by sheer accident. Ding Cun is a jewel of architecture. Every house is a museum: heavy wooden doors, ceramic spirit walls, carved verandas and lattice windows. Every detail of the village is an example of refinement. The courtyards even had marble platforms used as stages for private theater performances.

The village was one of the richest in the region. The households belonged to businessmen, dealers in medical herbs and bankers, who also owned the land all around. For generations the best artisans of Shanxi had been called to work in this village. Even the poles to which horses were tied were of marble carved with lion heads.

In 1949, when like everywhere else in China the landlords were accused of crimes against the people and put on public trial, Ding Cun was vacated by its original inhabitants. Some landlords fled, some were executed, and each house was given to the peasants of the area.

In 1954, a few hundred meters away from Ding Cun, workers opening a new railroad line discovered the fossils of a prehistoric man who had lived there 400,000 years ago. That saved Ding Cun, for a team of archeologists moved into the village. Impressed with the uniqueness of the place, they made an inventory of all the houses and their contents.

Dao Fuhai, who as a poor young peasant boy had taken part in killing the landlord in his own village ("four times I stabbed him, four times, and I was happy, for he had done so much harm to my family"), was one of the specialists who had come to Ding Cun. He was the one who stood up against the Red Guards in 1966 when they wanted to wipe out all vestiges of the feudal past of Ding Cun.

Now he has to protect Ding Cun against the very peasants who 35 years ago moved triumphantly into the landlords' houses. "They hang their corn from the carved beams, they drive nails into the wooden walls for their laundry, they keep their animals inside the houses!" says Dao.

His plan is now to relocate the villagers somewhere else and to turn this old landlord domain into a tourist attraction. "We have to keep some of the heritage of our past if we want to continue to be a civilization."

Many middle-aged intellectuals who actively took part in the revolution, and many former Red Guards one meets around the country, now do not hide their embarrassment and even shame at the senseless destruction they caused. "We wanted to destroy the old in order to bring forth the new," says a former Red Guard rebel who admits having gone to burn temples in Peking in 1966 and who now guides tourists around Shanxi Province, "...but no new culture has come forth."

Wherever one turns, the new is uninspiring. All the old cities have lost their charm. Their hearts have been cut through by large boulevards. One town is like another, with a main Liberation Road meeting a Red Flag Street in a People's Square, where a huge portrait of Mao overlooks the shabby emptiness. At sunset, all places are dark and dead, except for a few white lampposts identical everywhere from Manchuria to Guangzhou.

Taiyuan was a fabulous city. Now, apart from a few new buildings such as the railway station and a few blocks of workers' flats, the city is an evil-smelling cluster of dilapidated houses with open, common toilets exposed to the street. From the old doorways, once decorated with carved beams, step children, old men and women with buckets full of urine, walking toward the common garbage pit. People wash their dishes and their hair under the street's only water faucet. Children play with pigs on piles of garbage.

In 1949, Taiyuan had 270,000 inhabitants. For the 2 million who now live there, there are not many places of popular entertainment. All the teahouses have been closed, there are no more temple fairs, and the old Chun Yang Palace, a Taoist temple that used to be the heart of the city, is now the provincial museum, with a collection of ruins brought from all over Shanxi.

The communists have always accused the rulers of the past of having built huge temples and palaces for themselves while the peasants had nothing. Visitors to the Ming tombs in Peking are still told today how many sacks of rice could have fed how many people with the money the emperors spent building a single imperial tomb. Yet something very similar has been done by the present regime. Every provincial capital has a big imitation of Peking's gigantic Great Hall of the People, with vast rooms, usually unused and empty.

In Taiyuan, next to the Twin Pagodas, the communists built a huge monument immediately after Liberation and dedicated a vast area to the martyrs of the revolution. Surrounded by

171

high walls, this area is still there. Now, to turn it to some use, the Party cadres, who for three decades have forced the peasants to burn their dead so as not to waste arable land for graves, have decided to use this place as their own cemetery.

Recently, the local government spent a considerable amount of money restoring the Chong Shan temple, but it is very difficult for normal people to have access to this pleasant island of peace and harmony in the middle of Taiyuan.

"You take advantage of the foreigner to sneak in here," an old cadre-monk says scolding the young girl who came to my help when she saw me banging at the main entrance. "It's closed, it's closed, there is no key," says the caretaker of the Double Forest Temple, south of Pingyao, to a group of peasants. They had tried to follow the foreigner for whom the main door, guarded by four huge painted clay warriors, had just been opened.

Temples now being reopened as museums, and pagodas, now called towers, are there mainly to satisfy the curiosity of tourists. The problem is that sometimes they are too far away.

One of the most famous Taoist temples of China is the Yongle Gong in southern Shanxi. It was built in honor of Lu Dongbin, one of the Eight Immortals, and it contains the most magnificent frescoes of the Yuan dynasty. In 1959, since the temple was in a valley which was meant to become a huge water reservoir, the central government, under the personal instruction of Zhou Enlai, ordered the removal of the Yongle Gong to a site 25 kilometers away, on the outskirts of Ruicheng. Now the temple can only be reached by a hazardous trip from a railway station some 80 kilometers away. The unpaved road takes the visitor across wild mountains with frightening precipices. The trip takes hours. "We should remove the Yongle Gong again and this time take it to Taiyuan where we have better facilities for tourists," says a provincial official.

In many ways China is still a closet full of skeletons and the Chinese authorities don't want foreigners to roam around freely through the countryside. Thus, the strategy is to concentrate tourist attractions in a few selected places and from there take busloads of people on one-day outings to visit more distant shrines, but not the villages in which they stand.

From the city of Datong, for instance, one is first brought to visit the Flying Temple, then to eat in a special guest house inside the town of Hung Yuan, but one is not allowed to visit the town itself. "This place is still closed to foreigners," says the local Party cadre.

From Taiyuan one is allowed to visit the Double Forest Temple in Pingyao, but once the visitor is taken for lunch inside the old magistrate's residence, now Party headquarters and government guest house, he is not supposed to leave the walled, isolated, guarded compound. "It is inconvenient," says one of the local officials.

The reason is that if one refuses to eat, as I did, and sneaks out to spend a couple of hours walking around before being caught, this forbidden city turns out to be a collection of all that the local authorities do not want the visitor to see. All the streets are unpaved and covered with a mixture of mud and excrement; rich old mansions built of stone are crammed with derelict people; an old stone bridge with carved lion heads, under which flows a dead river of flaming red water produced by a nearby plastics factory, is in shambles. All the temples and historic monuments described by a guidebook of the fifties are in ruins. The Catholic church that existed here has vanished; the old market tower with the sign of double happiness drawn over the yellow tiles is dilapidated.

On various houses somebody has drawn crosses with white chalk, and on the remnants of the city wall the same hand has written poorly, "habemus dominum." In the streets one meets child beggars, two screaming madmen, an epileptic woman, an old intellectual who after 20 years of labor camp is back selling the rest of his library to make a living. A former seminarian, speaking Latin in order not to be understood by the crowd, attempts to tell the story of the repressed Christian community. Going through the city gate one bumps into a group of some 200 youngsters with shaven heads, guarded by four uniformed policemen, returning to prison after a day of re-education through labor.

In spite of all precautions, the reopening of the temples for the sake of foreign tourists is posing some problems for the communist authorities. First of all with their own people. Now that the peasants see some of their old places of devotion used again, now that they know that some of their gods are back on the old altars, they feel attracted to them once more.

"They must have come at night," says the monk of the Flying Temple pointing to a clay statue mysteriously covered with an embroidered red cape. With a baby on his lap, the statue was known to provide offspring to childless couples, and the red cape seems to have been the present of somebody whose prayers had been successful.

In the past, people had a god for everything, a special heavenly protection for every circumstance. If no rain was falling, they knew whom to address. If someone was sick they knew of a remedy in some mountain monastery. The monks not only gave a charm written on paper that had to be burned and the ashes drunk, they also dispensed herbs which only they knew where and when to pick.

Thirty-five years of Marxist education and ideological campaigns against religion and superstition have not wiped out the power of these beliefs which have survived for centuries.

In Jie Xiu County in central Shanxi, peasants have started to visit an isolated monastery again in search of medicines, and recently even some cadre limousines have been seen at the foot of the mountain.

The old spirits of the Chinese supernatural world have not completely lost their power of attraction, and the *People's Daily* has just come out with a long article criticizing peasants who flock by the thousands to Mount Tai to thank the lofty goddess for the good harvest of the year.

Memories of the past still linger in the minds of people left disoriented and insecure by the policies of the past 35 years. Old legends still fascinate.

In the marketplace of Hung Yuan, an old lady sitting on the pavement sells turtles, telling an attentive crowd the story of their origins. "The turtle was made by God together with man to help him in his life," she says. People listen enchanted. In Chinese tradition the turtle is the protagonist of countless deeds. It was the turtle that helped the first emperor control the waters of the Yellow River and thus was rewarded with a life of 10,000 years. It was from the marks on the turtle's back that the Chinese established their calendar and fixed the seasons in which to sow and harvest. It was on stone turtles that the steles stood with the records of the emperors. The turtle is the symbol of longevity, of strength, of Chinese endurance.

"The turtle holds the secrets of heaven and earth," says the old lady pointing to the mysterious signs on its shell. "Chairman Mao changed the course of rivers and removed mountains, but he was never able to change the shape of the turtle."

People laugh and the old lady keeps telling her legend.

11

Good for the Individual and Good for the Motherland

The rebirth of kungfu

" **M** asters...I am ready. No sacrifice will deter me. No hardship will stop me. Let me come and I shall be your dedicated disciple."

The letter had arrived from faraway Europe and the old abbot of Shaolin monastery, hidden in the stony, barren slopes of Songshan, the central, sacred mountain of China in Henan Province, could not read it. So he passed it on to the local police. There the letter was lost among dozens of similar letters written' by young men from all over the world. All begged the monks of the famous temple, where Zen Buddhism and the deadly art of kungfu were born over 1,400 years ago, to take them as disciples.

The aspirant never got a reply. So much the better for him, for had he been allowed to come to Shaolin, he would have had the shock of his life. Much of the ancient monastery is in ruins, the statues of Buddha are new, made of plaster of Paris and painted in gaudy colors, and the few surviving monks are old and trembling creatures, unable to lift themselves out of bed, let alone break bricks with their fists and jump over high walls. The young novices are pale and weak, some even crippled. Kungfu is no longer practiced in the monastery.

The famous hall, where thousands of exercising monks left, through the centuries, deep depressions on the pavement by stamping their calloused feet on the ground, is covered with dust. The 11 2-meter-high wooden poles, on top of which the old masters made the young apprentices run after each other to increase their agility and strengthen their sense of balance, are now buried in sand and unused.

The only fighting monks one sees are those depicted in the splendid but badly damaged wall frescoes, which the monks

176

of the past used as a kind of textbook for learning their deadly kicks and blows between their meditation sessions.

Shaolin Si (the Monastery of the Young Forest) today is a center neither of Buddhist meditation nor of martial arts. It is simply another state-sponsored tourist attraction where every day thousands of Chinese and a few foreign sightseers come to browse around the uninspiring halls and the various stalls manned by monks selling bric-a-brac souvenirs, including absurd, shiny crucifixes with the word "Christ" embossed on the back.

"The rebirth of Shaolin has brought us a lot of business, and it is helping the modernization of our region," says Wang Zhizhou, director of the Foreign Affairs Bureau of Deng Feng, the county capital located 17 kilometers from the monastery.

The rebirth started three years ago when the central authorities in Peking decided to reopen the temple and allowed a Hong Kong film company to co-produce, on site at the old monastery, the first ever kungfu movie made in China.

Based on an historic episode, *Shaolin Temple* tells how Emperor Tai Zong, founder of the Tang dynasty (618-907 A.D.), was rescued from his enemies by 13 chivalrous monks of Shaolin, led by a young disciple named Zhang, the Tiger Cub.

Free from the usual political overtones of other Chinese movies, *Shaolin Temple* is pure amusement filled with thrilling scenes and bloody fights. It has been an instant success, seen by packed audiences throughout China, and has aroused the new craze for martial arts which has gripped the country.

The actor who plays the hero role in the film has become a national idol and he is now one of the few lucky citizens of the People's Republic to own a private car. Martial arts associations have sprung up in every province, with many millions of members, and more and more people dream of studying kungfu where it was born.

Since the beginning of this year alone, 20,000 people have written to the monastery. Over 100 of them have been children, the youngest a 9 year old. After seeing the movie, many of them have run away from home and have traveled by train, boat and bus to come and knock at the door of Shaolin, hoping, as in the legend, to be admitted by the monks as their disciples.

"We have sent them all back home because now we are a socialist state and kungfu has to be taught according to the state plan," says Liang Yichuan, deputy director of the Shaolin Martial Arts Association. A Communist Party controlled organization, the association has taken over the teaching of the deadly art which was once a monopoly of secretive Buddhist monks.

Shaolin was founded in 477 A.D. as a center where Indian monks came to help Chinese scholars translate from Sanscrit the sacred texts of the Buddhist religion which had just been introduced into the Middle Kingdom. Among them was an Indian prince, Bodhidarma, better known in China as Da Mo and in Japan as Daruma, the founder of the Zen sect.

Da Mo reached Shaolin in 520 A.D., after having crossed the Yellow River — says the legend — on a reed. In order to gain merits, Da Mo went into a lonely cave high up in the mountain behind Shaolin, and there spent nine years sitting motionless in meditation in front of a stone.

The cave is now inaccessible, though an enterprising peasant is making a small fortune by letting sightseers use a pair of binoculars to look at a black hole faraway on the mountain for 5 cents a time. The stone, according to the legend, on which the shadow of Da Mo was impressed during his nine years of immobility, has been taken down from the cave and is shown to the tourists among the sacred relics in the main temple.

It was to balance the immobility of meditation that Da Mo, and later his disciples (among them his successor, who chopped off one of his arms to attract the master's attention), developed a set of exercises to relax the muscles.

At that time Shaolin was surrounded by a thick forest, and it was through the careful study of the movements of the various animals living in it that the monks compiled their special form of gymnastics. They observed how animals fought each other, how they attacked, how they defended themselves, and they learned the strong points of each. They mastered the creeping of the snake, the jumping of the monkey, the leap-

178

ing of the tiger, and the dancing of the mantis.

Since the monks lived in isolation, and were often victims of bandits and robbers, their exercises quickly developed into the art of self-defense. Shaolin became a unique monastery, where the long hours of silent, motionless meditation were interrupted by equally long hours of noisy, violent exercises in which young and old monks trained themselves by imitating the gestures of animals.

"Zen Buddhism and kungfu were born together, as two faces of the same coin, as two ways to reach the same goal: internal peace," says De Chan, the 77-year-old bedridden abbot of Shaolin. "We combine spiritual concentration with physical strength into a harmony of body and mind. One cannot go without the other."

Strict discipline was the rule of the monastery from the very beginning, and the monks of Shaolin became famous throughout China for their unmatched skills. Peasants sought their help to fight bandits and despots, emperors to remain on their thrones. The monastery received honors, wealth and privileges, and Shaolin grew in size, wealth and fame.

At the height of its history, Shaolin had up to 2,000 monks, 500 of them fighters. During the Ming dynasty the masters of all the various forms of martial arts in the country gathered at the temple, and from that time the monks added the use of 18 different weapons to their practices, from the sword and spear to the flying fork and the meteoric hammer.

Yet the most fearsome weapon of all remained the body, strengthened through years of painful practice which did not change over the centuries. "The hands are the doors to keep the enemy at bay. The feet are the sledgehammer to kill him," says a former monk, now a kungfu instructor.

To strengthen their hands, young disciples were given a sack of beans, and hour after hour they had to thrust their fingers into them. After two or three years, sand would be substituted for the beans and the exercise would be repeated day after day until the tips of the fingers were like "steel needles that could pull the enemy's heart out of his chest," according to one of the monks.

To strengthen the palm of the hands, the disciples had to

bash them against a surface covered with iron filings. To strengthen his fists, the young monk had to punch a thousand sheets of paper glued to a wall. Over the years the paper would be destroyed, and in the end the pupil would be punching with all his might against the naked stone.

To strengthen the legs, young monks ran around the compound of the temple with 10 kilogram bags of sand tied to their knees. To harden their heads they had to beat them daily, first with a wooden stick and then, after a few years, with a brick.

To improve their stamina monks had to practice Qigong, a system of deep and controlled breathing meant to exercise willpower and to send one's vital energies to forgotten parts of the body to build up resistance against external pressures. To sharpen their eyesight, young monks threw cold water against their open eyes and looked straight at the sun and the moon for 15 minutes when they appeared in the sky each day and night.

To sharpen their hearing, they listened to the wind at night, trying to figure out its direction. This imitated Da Mo who, after nine years in the cave, was said to be able to listen to the movements of ants and guess their whereabouts.

Novices entered the temple at the age of 12 or younger, and their first test was the "bed." Five stakes were driven horizontally into the wall at a height of about 2 meters. The disciple slept on the stakes, and if he fell he was beaten by the masters.

After 15 or 20 years of these painful exercises came the final test. The disciple was placed at the far end of the temple and was asked by the chief abbot to go through the front gate. Thirty-six kungfu masters stood in the disciple's way, and each one of them was allowed one maneuver to stop him. If the disciple overcame them all and was able to get out of the temple, he was considered a Shaolin monk.

A monk was forbidden to teach his deadly art to anybody else except novices, and was under oath not to touch meat, wine or women. He was also not supposed to kill, but this prohibition became rather elastic. An old Shaolin saying goes, "If a tyrant is alive, ten thousand innocent people don't sleep in peace." Thus, getting rid of a tyrant was at times considered a great merit.

The day of a novice at the temple started at 4 a.m. and lasted until 10 p.m. Five hours a day were dedicated to physical training, and the rest of the time was spent in meditation, and in studying and reciting Buddhist sutras.

"In the beginning it was very hard and I cried many times, but with concentration I soon learned to overcome pain," recalls De Chan, the abbot. "To be a Shaolin monk and not to practice kungfu would have been a terrible shame." He entered Shaolin at the age of 7, after his parents bade him farewell at the doorsteps of the temple, never to see him again.

The combination of physical and spiritual practice made the Shaolin monks capable of the unbelievable deeds the legends attribute to them: flying over city walls with the help of a whip; leaping from the ground to the roof of houses; kicking a thick wooden door into a thousand splinters.

The adventures of the Shaolin monks have been part of the folklore of China for centuries. Almost everyone knows about the monk who fought a thousand enemies with a simple stick while pretending to be drunk (the "drunken stick" is still one of the standard routines of martial arts); or about the cook-monk who, during a peasant rebellion, used a poker to keep an angry mob of people at bay while the other monks continued undisturbed with their meditation.

The monks of Shaolin failed to live up to their fighting reputation at the time of the Cultural Revolution. When in 1966 the Red Guards came, like everywhere else, "to eliminate the vestiges of the past and to destroy the old culture in order to create a new one," none of the 200 monks who had survived under the communist regime stood in their way. The statues of Buddha were overturned and smashed, slogans were painted all over the walls, most monks were chased away and sent to work in the fields while a few old ones were locked in a separate courtyard, and Shaolin Si was closed.

Novels about the Shaolin fighters were burned throughout China, and even the practice of kungfu was attacked by the radical communist ideologues as "feudal garbage."

Yet, the lore of Shaolin survived outside China, for, according to an old Chinese saying, "all martial arts under

181

heaven are born in Shaolin.'' The adepts of various forms of boxing, from judo and karate in Japan to kendo in Korea, continued to regard the old temple in Henan as their original holy shrine.

In the early sixties the film *A Touch of Zen*, shot in Taiwan by the Hong Kong Chinese director, King Wu, launched a new type of Chinese "western" based on the adventures of kungfu fighters. The Hong Kong film industry jumped at the idea and dozens of films starring Bruce Lee made kungfu a popular sport throughout southeast Asia and Europe.

After Mao's death and the fall of the so-called Gang of Four in 1976, the new pragmatic Chinese leadership under Deng Xiaoping decided that kungfu was such a gold mine that China should not let others, who didn't even have Shaolin, exploit its fame and possible revenue. So the Peking authorities reopened the temple, allocated money to restore it, rehabilitated the surviving monks, and made Abbot De Chan a member of the county Political Consultative Council. Wind-beaten, gray and poor, Deng Feng, the holy city at the foothills of Songshan mountain, now deprived of its famous forests, was put on the tourist map of the country.

Kungfu was given a new lease on life and the officially controlled press started to promote martial arts as a major sport using the slogan, "good for the individual and good for the motherland."

The magazine *China Sports* has urged girls to learn kungfu to protect themselves against molestation. "No assailant could possibly anticipate this kick," wrote the magazine, showing the way a woman could stop a man's advances. "Feeling a sharp pain in his private parts, he will let go of your hand to protect his crotch. At this moment, you may deal him a blow he will never forget."

China Daily discovered the country's oldest kungfu master, a 97-year-old man now living in Harbin. He had learned his first kicks with the Boxers, when that xenophobic secret society tried to kill all foreigners in Peking in 1900. Other papers publicized Taiji Quan and the other five slow-moving boxing exercises, all derived from kungfu, as a means of keeping healthy and prolonging life.

182

Even Zhou Enlai was discovered to have studied kungfu in his younger years. *China Martial Art Magazine* revealed that the popular general Xu Shiyou, the one who led the only cavalry division of the Red Army during the Long March, and who is now vice-chairman of the Advisory Commission of the Communist Party, spent eight years from the ages of 8 to 16 as an assistant cook in the Shaolin temple, learning its deadly art.

Anecdotes about the 78-year-old general's kungfu abilities were reported in a series of magazines for young readers. Thus one learned how, during the anti-Japanese war, he managed to jump a 6-meter-wide ditch; how, during the 1950s campaign to conquer the wild areas of China, he removed trees with his bare hands; how at one time he humiliated a huge, strong, Soviet adviser, by taking a massive stone lion in his arms for a walk outside a Shanghai restaurant when the Russian had been unable even to shake it.

The screening of *Shaolin Temple*, and the almost contemporaneous showing on television in China in 1982 of a Japanese series on judo, loosed the final avalanche. Sleepy Deng Feng County, south of the Yellow River, was hit by a kungfu rush. Thousands of people descended on the county, wanting to see for themselves the holy shrine and learn its martial secrets.

To accommodate tour groups, the local authorities built a motel, while dozens of private "gan dian" (dry hotels, i.e. lodgings without water facilities) sprang up for the less well-to-do travelers. A 10-meter-wide road was opened between Deng Feng and the temple; a Friendship Store selling Coca Cola started operations next to the monastery; and a martial arts association was established to train young fighters and give, for a fee, performances for tourists. The actor-fighters currently give their show in the parking lot of the new motel.

Encouraged by the new policies of Deng Xiaoping, who has given peasants some freedom to enrich themselves if they can, local people have opened small workshops producing Shaolin souvenirs, and stalls selling drinks and food. A few peasants rent their horses to tourists who want their picture taken in front of the 230 stupas of the stone cemetery, where the great kungfu masters of the past are buried.

183

A thriving trade has started in teach yourself kungfu books and collections of Shaolin legends. The latest volume, now being sold by the monks themselves, is called *Secret Recipes for Healing Injuries Caused by Falls and Beatings*. It gives instructions on how to look for certain herbs in the mountains, how to dry them, and how to boil them in the urine of children. "The best urine of all is the morning urine of the first male baby of the morning," one reads in it.

To cope with the thousands of applications from people wanting to learn kungfu, some written in blood, the local authorities have given permission to open special schools in the tiny city of Deng Feng. The state has set a tough "three approvals" rule to screen the applicants. Anyone who wants to study martial arts there needs the approval of his parents, the approval of the authorities of his place of origin and the approval of the Deng Feng county government.

How about foreigners? "We have received many letters from as far as South Africa, the United States and Europe," says Wang Zhizhou, director of the Foreign Affairs Bureau of Deng Feng. "Some people are really desperate to come here from abroad, but this is something we cannot decide. Permission must come from Peking." So far such permission has not been granted and there are no plans to do so in the near future.

In the various schools that have sprung up in the area around the temple there are 500 children studying martial arts: 300 are local, 200 come from various parts of China. "I saw the film *Shaolin Temple* and begged my parents to let me come here. I want to learn kungfu and maybe one day I also can be in a movie," says a skinny, shy, 13-year-old boy who one year ago arrived here from a village in Guizhou Province some 2,000 kilometers away. He plans to stay in the school for five years.

The school is an abandoned kiln compound on the outskirts of Deng Feng on the road to the Song Yue brick pagoda, the oldest building of its kind in China (built in 520 A.D.). Living conditions are spartan: 13 students, two of them girls, sleep in a common dormitory and eat in a rudimentary canteen. Each day they practice from three to five hours.

The children no longer go through the painful, at times

gruesome, endurance tests of the monks of the past, yet they have blisters and scratches from punching and kicking the sandbags in their attempt to develop "steel hands and iron feet."

The school is run by an agricultural commune which had discovered, among its peasants, a former monk of Shaolin who abandoned the temple when the communist armies arrived there in 1949.

The school fee is 30 yuan a month (10 yuan for kungfu instruction, 20 for food and lodging). For the commune, it is a good income from what the state now calls a "sideline occupation." For the children and their families it is a significant investment, as 30 yuan is half an average worker's monthly salary in China.

In a country where youth unemployment is a growing concern, to be a young kungfu master, now that the old ones are dying out, means the assurance of a job and possibly even fame.

There are 12 of these kungfu schools collectively run by communes in Deng Feng, and three more are run by the county middle schools. In addition, some peasants who have or claim to have been monks in the famous temple have started to take "private" students (monthly fee 25 yuan). Not all the pupils are satisfied.

"I thought I could learn how to walk through walls and how to jump on rooftops, but all I practice here is gymnastics," says a 15-year-old boy who has come from Manchuria.

Kungfu instructors in Deng Feng say that disappointment is a common problem among students during the first weeks, but that very few leave once they have been admitted. "Some people arrive here with wrong ideas. They think kungfu is what they have seen in the movies," says the headmaster of Middle School Number 15. "We cannot teach miracles."

Beside "miracles," the martial arts schools of Deng Feng, now under the supervision of the local communist authorities, do not even teach some classic kungfu moves like the "tiger-slaying blow" and the "ox-killing kick," basically meant to bring sudden death to the adversary in battle.

"These moves are too dangerous and the state does not

185

encourage these activities,'' says Liang Yichuan. Thanks to his kungfu skills, he escaped death as a young boy when robbers entered his house and he and his two teenage brothers managed to kick them out. "Kungfu today does not need to be as deadly as it used to be. Now we have to train good fighters, but also good citizens.''

Students of kungfu today do not take the oaths that once bound the Shaolin monks. They have their own brand of oaths. "Part of the training is to teach our students the five stresses and the three loves,'' says master Liang. The five stresses are: stress decorum, manners, hygiene, discipline, morals. The three loves are: love the motherland, love socialism, love the Communist Party.

The revival of kungfu has created all over the country a great demand for anything connected with Shaolin. Fake Shaolin medicines are sold at market fairs throughout China, and people pretending to be former monks offer themselves as teachers of martial arts. Recently, even the *People's Daily* warned people against these imposters and wrote about a man who, posing as a Shaolin master, had created a Shaolin temple acrobatic troupe and made a good business traveling with it in six Chinese provinces before being exposed.

The revival of kungfu has also raised new worries among Chinese cadres, some of whom still see martial arts as a thing of the past "that glorifies the feudal society and gives youth the feeling that it would have been far better to live 1,000 years ago than to be working to build the country today,'' according to one newspaper editor. Recently, the *Tiyu Bao* (*Sports News Daily*) had to remind its readers that "the aim of learning kungfu is to render better service to society.''

Certainly the teaching of kungfu will render good service to Deng Feng. According to the state plan approved by Peking, kungfu is going to be the focus of economic development as the major tourist attraction and main export commodity of this so far poor, backward and isolated county. Four kindergartens will start to hold experimental classes in kungfu in September. The number of primary and secondary schools specializing in martial arts will be doubled, and more and more students from various parts of China will be enrolled. Tourist facilities in the county will be enlarged with new investments from the state and cooperation from some Hong Kong companies.

In five years Deng Feng will start graduating kungfu masters from among the students now in schools (it takes from six to eight years to become a professional kungfu fighter), and the total kungfu student population will have reached 15,000. "Deng Feng will provide the whole country with real Shaolin instructors," says Wu Chengde of the county Sports Commission.

What has all this to do with the Shaolin monastery? What has it to do with the monks?

"Martial arts don't need Buddhism to prosper," says Wang of the Foreign Affairs Bureau. "The monks will take care of their religion; we shall take care of the sport." In effect, the 11 old, surviving monks are not even free to take care of their religion because the state which now encourages the revival of kungfu does not want to encourage the revival of Buddhism at the same time.

Shaolin monastery is now under the control of three different units (the Cultural Relics Bureau, the Parks and Amusement Bureau, and the Patriotic Buddhist Association), all under the leadership of the Communist Party, and the monks now housed again in the temple are not allowed to recruit new disciples and teach them religion.

"Many young people have come here asking to become monks but we have had to reject them," says Abbot De Chan. "Only the state can make the selection. The state likes those with good motivation and good faces." Over the last year 14 novices have been recruited for the monastery: three have been sent to study Buddhism in Nanking, and the others work as assistants to the old masters. The one assigned to Abbot De Chan is 29 years old, has a limp, and looks as if the state assigned him to Shaolin because he would have been useless anywhere else.

"The old monks are dying out and we need new ones to keep Shaolin," says a Party cadre in the county. The monastery is an indispensable framework for the rebirth of kungfu and its exploitation as a sport and as a tourist attraction. That is why the temple has been reopened, why it is being restored, and why the few monks who survived the persecutions of the Cultural Revolution have been brought back to play the role of extras for this refurbished stage.

The last to arrive was old master Hai De, who is now 82 years old. He is famous because in his younger days he was able to stand on two of his fingers, and because for 60 years he has slept sitting up as did Da Mo, who inaugurated the tradition of Zen Buddhism and kungfu in his solitary cave on the mountain.

Now, 1,400 years later, that tradition of unity between meditation and action is over. Now, where that unity was founded, Buddhism and kungfu are bound to have different futures.

Sitting uncertain in his bed and knitting his brows, Abbot De Chan says, "The future of Buddhism I cannot see with my own eyes, but the future of kungfu is all around me." Next to the red walls of the temple, workers are busy building the new kungfu demonstration hall, while others are taking measurements for the foundations of a new tourist hotel.

12

The Best Baby Is a Dead Baby

The birth control policy

A young widow throws her two children into the waters of a Guangzhou lake so that she can get married again and have the right to a "first and only child" with her new husband. A peasant woman, about to deliver a baby in a commune in Shandong, implores the midwife to suffocate it immediately if it turns out to be a girl, so she will not be beaten by her husband and can try again for a boy. Women, some of them already at the eighth month, are rounded up in a commune in Guangdong Province, put on a truck and, amidst screaming and wailing, are brought to the local clinic for forced abortions.

These things are happening in China. The draconian birth control policy adopted five years ago to curb population growth produces these and other aberrations. But it does not work. Though couples are begged, advised, ordered to have only one child, though they are threatened with all kinds of consequences and punishments if they do have a second or a third, China's population continues to grow.

Every two seconds a new baby is born. Every day 42,300 come to life. Every year 16 million new Chinese add themselves to the over 1 billion Chinese counted by the last census.

Each Chinese couple still has on average 2.6 children. Unless this figure is sharply and quickly reduced, China's grand plan to achieve the Four Modernizations by the year 2000 is doomed to failure because whatever advances the country manages to make will be eaten up by the extra people.

"Chinese people will not be much better off by the turn of the century unless the population is kept within 1.2 billion," wrote Wang Shengquan in *China Daily* on February 17, 1983. Lack of cultivated land has already become a serious problem in the rural areas where 80 percent of the population lives.

In 1949, the average amount of land per person was only 0.2 hectare. Now it is half of that.

Though the total grain production has increased immensely, a Chinese person today has at his disposal a yearly quota of grain (316 kilograms) which it is estimated is half what he would have had during the Tang dynasty over a thousand years ago.

Among Mao's mistakes, not paying attention to numbers was one of the biggest. And this mistake is proving to have the longest-lasting consequence of all.

"More people mean a greater ferment of ideas, more enthusiasm and more energy," was one of the most quoted sentences of the Great Helmsman. Professor Ma Yinchu, who dared to challenge Mao by saying that without a population control policy the country would be heading for disaster, was labelled a "reactionary" and silenced for 20 years.

"Only someone who does not love the people can ask the people not to have children," was the accusation made against him. Professor Ma was right, but the Communist Party had to wait until Mao's death to change the policy on this issue. First the goal was two children per couple. Since 1980 the order has been to limit it to one.

"We are a socialist country. Since we are able to plan agricultural and industrial production we ought to be able to plan the production of life," said Minister Chen Muhua, the highest ranking woman in the Chinese communist hierarchy and an alternate member of the politburo. The plan called for a strict implementation of the rule of one child per couple.

The details vary from region to region, from town to town, but generally speaking the system of penalties and rewards now applied is geared to delay marriage and thus reproduction, to make all kinds of contraceptives easily available, and to facilitate and even to impose abortion in the case of an "illegal" pregnancy.

The strict system of social control brought to China by the communist victory in 1949 contributes to the efficient application of these measures.

Each citizen in China belongs to a "danwei," a unit, which can be your factory, the school in which you teach, the agricultural production team you are assigned to or even an official artists' association. The danwei, or more exactly the local Communist Party secretary who is in charge of it, oversees the life of its members. The danwei pays the salaries, assigns apartments, distributes food coupons, gives out the coupons to buy a bicycle, and so on. The danwei now decides if and when its members may have children.

"When is your turn?"

"In a couple of years. I still have a few colleagues ahead of me." This kind of conversation is quite frequent now among women workers in urban factories.

When a couple wants to have a child, the woman registers her name with her danwei. Since each unit has a quota of children based on the number of its members, each one has to wait for her turn. Some danwei even keep a calendar charting the menstrual cycles of women members to make it easier to assign turns for getting pregnant, and at the same time to check those who, without authorization, get pregnant "illegally."

If this happens, the danwei is responsible for the abortion. Social pressure is strong. The whole group wants to stay within the assigned quota of children, because all members then receive bonuses and prizes of various kinds. If a woman does not stay within the rules, not only she and her family but her danwei as well will be penalized.

In certain parts of China, such as in the city of Guangzhou, the pregnancy permit issued by the danwei must be produced for a woman to be examined by a doctor during pregnancy or to be accepted in a state clinic for delivery.

In certain areas, where overzealous Party cadres have installed a system of spot checks against "illegal" pregnancies, women are required to carry the pregnancy permit with them in order to show it to the "pregnancy patrols" that go around stopping any woman suspected of being pregnant. It was indeed one of these patrols that caused the incident of Dongguan in the southern province of Guangdong where a Chinese journalist from Hong Kong witnessed the rounding up of a number of pregnant women.

"Some were handcuffed, while others were tied up by ropes. They were all put on trucks. When the vehicles moved out one

191

could hear wailing noises." At the county hospital, the women were given an injection and soon afterward all had abortions.

In the past, abortions were a matter of routine within the third month. With the imposition of the one-child policy, it is now considered normal to have an abortion up to the ninth month. In some regions of China, doctors in hospitals in the countryside are under instructions from the Party authorities not to let a couple's third or fourth baby survive, and to tell the parents that the baby was stillborn.

Recently, at the main entrance of a country hospital in eastern Hebei Province, the Party secretary put up a big banner which said: "The best baby is a dead baby." The local doctors refused to work until the sign was taken down.

Forced abortions in late pregnancy are at the heart of big conflicts, especially in the countryside. In a commune in Shandong Province, a peasant whose wife had had two daughters and was eight months pregnant was forced by the local Party cadre to bring the woman to the hospital for an abortion. After the operation was completed, the peasant saw that the aborted baby was a boy and went crazy. He went to the house of the Party cadre, grabbed his 3-year-old son, and slaughtered him with a kitchen knife. He left screaming, "now we are even...we are even!"

Since the Party organization has been asked to implement as strictly as possible the new one-child policy, many clinics in the countryside have adopted as a standard practice putting an IUD into women who have just delivered their first child, and to make sterile (through tubal ligation) those who have delivered their second or third. No previous consent is required.

Removing these IUDs from peasant women who notwithstanding the prohibition want to have more children has become one of the underground activities in the countryside which some unscrupulous people or part-time nurses are using to get rich. The price varies from 5 yuan to 20 yuan to have an IUD removed.

The official press warns people against these quack doctors who often perform operations with rusty hooks, but the practice goes on because regular doctors are prevented from removing IUDs. Some who have done it have been indicted for "obstructing the birth control policy."

Since the enforcement of the one-child rule is entrusted to the local authorities, it is common for some areas to be more flexible than others. People quickly learn about this and there is already a sort of maternity map of China based on the good and the bad areas for delivering children. Migration of pregnant women is a well-known phenomenon. From the communes of Shandong, where controls are tough, women at the seventh or eighth month "go to visit some relatives" in the province of Shanxi, where the implementation of the same policy is less rigid. They have their babies there and then and after a few months both mother and child go back home, in most cases only to face the simple penalty of a fine.

A fine can be a lump sum of money paid to the state (in some areas fines are as much as 400 yuan for the second and 800 yuan for the third child), or payment by installments (in some counties in Hebei Province the penalty for a second child is a yearly fine of 50 yuan for 14 years, and, for the third child, 100 yuan each year for 14 years).

These monetary penalties do not seem to discourage the peasants very much. In southern China, where many families have relatives in Hong Kong and abroad, people ask and receive remittances from outside to pay these fines. In other places, peasants make all kinds of sacrifices to buy themselves the right to have more children. An old Chinese way of describing a disaster, "the family is bankrupt and the children are dead," is now being turned around to "the family is bankrupt but the children are alive."

The policy of one child has revived, in China generally though in the countryside in particular, the traditional attitude of preference for male children. Boys guarantee the continuity of the family line. Boys stay within the family and are responsible for the care of their elderly parents. Boys are an asset in the family. Girls are a liability. So if a couple is only allowed one child, it must be a boy.

The consequences are obvious. In some villages of Guangdong Province, the peasants keep a bucket of water by the mother's bed as she is giving birth. If the screaming infant turns out to be a girl, she is immediately drowned. In

Jiangsu Province, bodies of baby girls have been found dumped in rivers, in fields and even in public lavatories. Female infanticide has become such a widespread phenomenon that *China Youth Daily* wrote an article with the moving appeal, "Save the Baby Girls."

For their inability to produce male children, many women are beaten by their husbands, cursed by their mothers-in-law and despised by their neighbors. Some in despair have been forced to commit suicide. The Chinese newspapers, particularly the provincial ones, have been full of horror stories of this kind. A Shenyang worker, for instance, connected a door knob to electric wires so that his wife, guilty of having given birth to a girl instead of a boy, would get a shock.

"We Want a Second Liberation" was the title of a long letter written by the Women's Federation of Liaoning Province to the *Workers' Daily*. It listed maltreatment suffered by their members at the hands of disgruntled husbands. The problem is taken seriously within the Party, and both Premier Zhao Ziyang and Party Secretary Hu Yaobang have had to remind people of the importance of women in society and condemn the survival of certain "feudal ideas" about them.

The local and national press has also taken up the subject. The *Peking Review* published a note by the social editor reminding its readers that "infanticide is a crime," and quoted the special article of the Chinese marriage law which says, "infanticide by drowning and any other act causing serious harm to infants is prohibited."

The *People's Daily* sent two of its reporters around China to research the subject. Their conclusions were unequivocal. After a survey of several provinces and towns they found that: aside from sick and crippled infant boys, the great majority of abandoned, maimed and killed children are infant girls; in some district orphanages infant girls make up 99 percent of the total; in one unnamed county alone, 65 babies have been found abandoned in two months, all of them girls.

Not long ago *China Youth News* gave a chilling account of a peasant of Licheng County, Shandong Province, who drowned his already 4-year-old daughter after a fortune teller told him his pregnant wife would have a boy this time.

"On December 1st, the peasant Liu Chunshan told his daughter that they would go and visit her auntie. He took the girl on his back. Soon the child was asleep. When no one was in sight he bound his daughter's head with a towel, carried her to a well and threw her in. A chilly wind was blowing across the wasteland. From the bottom of the well the girl was screaming 'Ai baba, ai baba....' Liu Chunshan lit a cigarette and smoked while occasionally looking into the well, until the sounds of someone struggling down in the waters ceased."

The man was later arrested and condemned to 15 years in jail. The wife gave birth to the new baby, another girl.

This desperate search of countless families for a male baby under the new one-child rule has provided some enterprising people with a rare opportunity to make money.

Cui Yongxian in Huaxian County in Henan Province had manufactured a "miraculous sex-switching drug" that could change the sex of the foetus if taken within the first three months of pregnancy. "One hundred percent effective" was the slogan on 10,000 leaflets he had had printed and distributed in four provinces. The cost of the drug: 35 yuan. The consequences: a slight form of poisoning suffered by many women until the man was arrested and his drugs confiscated as fake.

Some hospitals in major cities have advertised their willingness to test the child's sex before birth (thus allowing parents to have an abortion in case of an undesired girl), but this practice has also come under attack by scientists who say this will only worsen the already apparent male–female imbalance of the Chinese population. A banning of all these tests has been proposed.

The 1982 census established that in China today there are 106.3 males for every 100 females. "This imbalance is dangerous. If it continues we will suffer the merciless punishment of natural law in 20 years, when our sons will not have a chance to form families," writes the *Gansu Social Science Journal*.

For the time being an even bigger worry of the authorities is the consequences the one-child policy, if successful, will have on the Chinese race as such. The average adult Chinese of today, having grown up during the civil war and the revolu-

195

tion, is a rather strong man used to surviving in a big family. Since his childhood he has known that food is scarce and has to be shared with others. The birth control policy now produces a completely different generation of children: lonely, pampered, overprotected, overfed. A generation of spoiled people.

A recent study conducted in Shanghai kindergartens has shown that the children have lost most of the old Chinese social characteristics. "They do not respect their parents, they do not respect the environment, they are fussy about what they eat and what they wear, they are selfish, they do not care about others and do not know how to take care of themselves."

A similar study, conducted in the kindergartens of the western districts of Peking, reached the same conclusions. "Single children are weaker than others." Chinese pedagogists are worried about this trend. More than 30 books have been written about the subject, most of them trying to advise parents how to educate this kind of child.

While the experts worry about the long-term consequences, the Party and the government do their utmost to apply the policy. Since the beginning of 1983 there has been a campaign to teach people how to avoid having children and to convince them of the advantages of having only one. "A single child is happiness," reads a poster plastered all over Peking. A printing press in Shanghai has produced a poster with Karl Marx playing with a little girl under the slogan "Happiness is a family with a single child." The poster does not say that the girl was the daughter of one of Marx's seven children, and it is now sold as a new year poster in every bookstore.

The *Peking Evening News*, more faithful to historical detail, has used the fact that he had so many children to show how this "affected in a negative way Marx's struggle and his living conditions."

Great publicity is given to the advantages offered to couples who commit themselves to having only one child. They are guaranteed food coupons, a place in a kindergarten, free education and even precedence in the allocation of new flats.

By presenting their "one child certificate," these couples can get a 30 percent discount on food, clothes and toys for their children in special shops. In some schools, single children get vaccinated before others; in some hospitals, single children affected by polio are treated before others.

So far 12.5 million couples throughout China have committed themselves to having only one child. Most of them are urban residents. In the towns, where living space is limited and where people have jobs that guarantee them pensions at retirement age, the traditional urge for more children as a form of social security is fading away and birth control measures have started to be successful. Not so in the countryside where 80 percent of the population still lives. It is in the countryside where the new responsibility system introduced by Deng Xiaoping is based on the principle "more production more money," and therefore "more children more production."

Another obstacle to the efforts to curb China's population is the fact that the children born during the great baby boom of the fifties and sixties (a boom inspired by Mao) are now reaching adulthood. They are getting married and will be the cause of another baby boom. Over the next decade at least 10 million couples will get married every year and will produce their own children. The implementation of the one-child policy will have to be tougher and tougher if the government wants to keep the population numbers under control. So far the very publicity given to cases of people being punished for their "illegal" children seems to prove that the policy does not work, not even among Party members.

In one Hebei commune, a lady was expelled from the Party because, after having had three daughters, she got pregnant a fourth time. Disregarding Party orders, she refused to have an abortion. A high Party cadre in Guangzhou lost his Party membership and even his job. His crime was really without excuse: after having had six girls he tried a seventh time.

13

Discipline in the Field of Perfumed Grass

*My children write about their experiences
in a Chinese school*

We lived in Peking for three years and spent most of the time in a Chinese school. That was quite enough.

Problems arose from the very beginning. The first major obstacle was overcoming the language barrier separating us from the Chinese children. Once we got over it, somehow we encountered many more obstacles. Since entering the school in September 1980, we had a lot of surprises and came across a great many habits and rules of which we would have known nothing had we not gone to the Chinese school.

In the long run, we discovered that the main barrier which kept us away from the Chinese children was not the language but the fact that we were foreigners. Even when we did begin to speak some Chinese, we still were not allowed to mix with them.

At the end of our three years at the Field of Perfumed Grass School, we did not have a single Chinese friend. Teachers kept our "foreign influence" as far away from the Chinese students as they could. Not once in our stay in the Chinese school were we invited to the house of a Chinese person. No Chinese student was allowed to come to our house. Not a single conversation could go much beyond greetings. We could not ask a classmate what job his father was doing or where he lived, without his turning his back on us.

We foreigners were all treated the same. We had to play among ourselves, talk among ourselves, and stay among ourselves. To help us stay away from the Chinese as much as possible, the school gave us a ping-pong room which the Chinese children could not enter.

Every Monday, school started with the hoisting of the red flag. All Chinese children, most of them wearing the red scarf showing that they were Young Pioneers, stood in straight lines and saluted the flag as it was slowly hoisted up the pole, while the national anthem was blasted out over the loudspeaker. We foreigners were not allowed to salute the flag, nor were we ever given a red scarf.

Each school day started with 30 minutes of compulsory morning exercises in the schoolyard. Morning exercises consisted of bending and stretching and quite a bit of marching. Then, led by our class leader, we would walk off to our respective classrooms.

Class leaders were usually hardworking students with correct political ideas. They must be willing to sacrifice part of their time to help the other students and must do extra jobs for the benefit of the people. Their responsibilities included leading the students in an orderly manner to their classrooms, and watching over their behavior all the time, even after school. They supervised the morning exercises, they corrected wrong movements when they spotted them, and they reported to the teachers any slackness on the part of the students.

Class leaders can be recognized because apart from the red scarf they wear three red stripes pinned to their sleeve. These class leaders kept discipline when the teachers were not there.

Discipline is very important in the Chinese school. During classes, every student must sit straight in his chair with his hands behind his back so he cannot fidget. All his books must be ready before class begins and should be in a neat pile on a far corner of the desk. Whispering is not allowed, nor is borrowing things or even sharpening pencils. Each student should have at least five sharp pencils handy, to avoid having to sharpen any during class.

Also required in our school were a drinking cup and a clean towel. Fingernails must be well trimmed and clean. Each student had a desk and sat on a mini chair. The teacher, on the other hand, towered high over the room, standing on a step in front of the blackboard. When he entered the room, the class stood up and chorused, "Good morning, teacher!" or "Good afternoon, teacher!" Definite, quick words. No slurring.

Until you heard them speak, the teachers did not look too

imposing in their blue Mao jackets and blue cotton trousers. But when they were cross, rightly or not, there was nothing a Chinese student could do but wait for what was coming. This could mean being publicly embarrassed, being grabbed by the ear or worse. The teacher's power over his students was total.

We foreigners had certain privileges and were usually treated with leniency. But nobody was allowed to speak unless requested, and if he had the answer to a teacher's question, the student had to raise his hand, elbow on the desk, with no waving in the air.

Another thing we were not used to was cleaning the classroom. Every day after school some of us had to sweep and mop the floor, clean the blackboard and put the desks in order. Once a month, the whole school — windows, corridors, ping-pong room and toilets — had to be cleaned. Many times we managed to avoid it, for other foreigners, the North Koreans, volunteered for the job.

Two different students were chosen weekly to supervise the class. This duo were given a red armband with yellow characters saying "on duty," which they had to wear for the whole week. Their duties were to check whether every student had what was required, to look out for bad behavior, to report on failure to turn in homework, observe social attitudes during recess, and check the cleanliness of the classroom. They wrote a report about all this in a special book which they then gave to the teacher.

Most of our lessons consisted of mathematics and Chinese. "We love Chairman Mao, we love the Communist Party," was the first phrase we learned to read and recite by heart. We read stories about Mao when he was young and fighting the Japanese; stories about the Chinese revolutionary leaders and the People's Liberation Army; there were stories about Mao being an intelligent, hardworking boy who had many friends and took good care of his sheep. There were also stories of Marx starting with "Marx and Engels were very good friends..." and going on with Marx being poor and having to sell his clothes to buy his bread. There were patriotic stories about how the communists fought the Japanese and the atrocities the Japanese did, such as lining people up in a row and firing through them to see how many people a bullet could tear through.

Many lessons told of important people when they were young, and of how hardworking they were. We even read a story about how bright Einstein was when he was a young boy! The more reasonable texts were often sentimental or served some obvious propaganda purpose. The only ones really worth reading were the old stories, but these were very few.

History seems to be left out in Chinese primary schools. At least in our school there was none whatsoever. Discussions about the present were also left out, so as not to get into the way of politics. Little was said about foreign countries. When it was, it always portrayed extremes such as poor people and slaves and so on. This leaves a Chinese student little to compare his country with. The only thing he can do is compare China under the Communist Party with what the Communist Party has told him of old China (which, by the way, is far from positive).

Politics, in actual fact, is all-important in the Chinese school, and the highest authority is not the principal but the Communist Party secretary of the school. He loomed around our school, controlling and directing every teacher. He gave orders on what films to see and he made the speeches launching the campaigns at school which were going on all around China: the campaign to learn from Lei Feng, the campaign to plant trees, and so on. We were the ones to tell our father that something must have happened to Hua Guofeng, because one day we saw the Party secretary taking down his portrait from the teachers' meeting room.

Later, all textbooks carrying the famous picture of Mao sitting with Hua Guofeng and telling him, "with you in charge I feel at ease," were collected from the pupils and replaced with new ones. What a waste! China is a poor country and millions of books must have been destroyed.

Learning to read and write Chinese was boring and monotonous. Every stroke in each character had to be learned by heart and repeated over and over again. For homework we had to write line after line of the new characters we were learning. When we asked about the origins of the characters, and why they were written in such ways, we were simply told to copy and learn them by heart.

In fact most of our work at school was copying. We copied characters for Chinese language, we copied drawings and paintings from a book for art. We used rulers to draw lines and every line had its fixed length: no longer, no shorter. The drawings in our book showed Tiananmen Square, Mao's mausoleum, Young Pioneers marching, red flags flying over roof tops, and a still life with a volleyball, pencils and a brush container. In the book there were also some traditional Chinese paintings: mountains, water, boats, and a little temple perched on top of a mountain.

When we had copied the drawing line by line, the teacher would give us some paints and tell us where each color must go. If the painting in the book was of something red, we couldn't paint it pink. If a flower was yellow, we couldn't paint it orange. When all the paintings were finished, they looked like one painting that had been reprinted countless times. You wouldn't recognize your own unless you had signed it with your name.

All this copying severely restricted the minds of the Chinese students. Creative writing was practically nonexistent. We were never asked to write our impressions or feelings about anything. The paths for thinking had already been laid down by the teachers. The student's job was to follow them without questioning and without diverting from them.

Boredom during school hours was the hardest thing to fight. At times we really had difficulty staying awake. After staring at the strokes of the characters on the blackboard and looking out of the window into the glaring sunshine, the eye exercises after class were a great relief. Over the loudspeaker came the squeaky, singing voice counting up to eight, and then starting to count again. The points to rub were under the eyes, the temples and behind the neck.

The most shocking aspect of the Chinese school, and the one we never got used to, was the sessions of criticism and self-criticism that sooner or later turned everybody in the school into a spy or an informer.

Once a week, each class would meet and the teacher would

point out the good ones and the bad ones and would ask the class to provide proof to support his judgement. Once a month, the same process was repeated with all grades gathering in a large room to listen to praise and criticism by a professional actress: the principal. When each class had settled down in neat rows of chairs, she flashed her teeth at us in a cold smile and greeted us. Promptly we got up from our chairs and greeted her back. Unfortunately, we were now ready to begin. "First of all," she would say, "first of all let us hand out red flowers to the really good students of this month. From grade one..."

All the people named went up to the front and she distributed a red paper flower to each. Then she would ramble on about what good deeds they did or how hardworking they were, and then she would collect all the flowers, one by one, and glue them onto a board with all their names on it. She would clap, flash her teeth into another fake smile, make us clap and then send the "good" students back to their seats.

Now for the "bad" things. They could vary from a bad word to the discovery of a peanut shell in the ping-pong room. In our school we were totally banned from eating anything during, after or before classes. Punishments consisted of attacking the conscience of the culprit and making him ashamed of himself or extremely embarrassed. They did this by bringing the offender out in front of everybody and criticizing his actions. Then from time to time, the criticizer would ask the audience if they agreed wholly on the wrongness of the action. They usually did (or had to), because they must never contradict or disagree with what the teacher had said.

It was the duty of a student who had witnessed the bad behavior of another student to denounce it. If he did not, he himself would be criticized.

I, Folco, discovered a teacher spying on his students. He was on the second floor, concealed behind a window, looking out for any "bad" things the students might be doing during recess. His purpose was to see if these "bad" things would be admitted or reported by other students during the criticism session. Those who reported the incidents would really be the "good" students.

Another day I watched the following episode. Four little

boys had turned on a water hose and were flicking a bit of water on each other for fun. They were playing like good friends and were not disturbing anyone else. Then a teacher came. Furious, he demanded whose idea it had been. They had all turned it on together, but one of the four boys shouted: "It was his idea, his idea!" The others saw their chance of getting out of trouble, and joined in with, "it's all his fault!" pointing to the same little boy. Friends turned against each other as soon as the teacher came, and the game was over.

Part of the punishment, if you have done something wrong, is self-criticism. For me, Saskia, one of the saddest episodes came right after our 10-minute recess one day. During recess a boy of my class had gone to the toilet. When he came out a boy from a different class pointed out to him that he had urinated on his coat. The boy looked down at his coat and noticed the wet part. He grabbed the corner of his coat and, out of embarrassment and anger, flung it towards the other boy and managed to wet his jacket. The boy ran straight to the teachers' office and reported what had happened. Promptly, he was praised for doing this and a staff member marched off to inform the offender's teacher. When the class was quiet, our teacher called the boy to come to the front of the class. Knowing already why and what would happen next, he stood straight, with feet together and his head lowered. The teacher told the story to the whole class and asked for an adjective that would describe the attitude of the boy. In a matter of seconds many hands went up. The first pupil stood up and said he was "rude." The second pupil stood up and said he was not "hygienic." A third pupil stood up and said he was "bad tempered." After 10 pupils had answered, there was a last pupil who said the boy was "ungrateful."

This was exactly the word the teacher wanted to hear, even though she agreed with all the others, too. The girl who had used the word had to explain why. "Shi Li (the boy's name) is very ungrateful because the other boy informed him for his own good, so that he could wash the coat. But instead he threw the wet coat at him, and that was very ungrateful of him."

Asked whether they agreed, all pupils stood up and said yes, except for two, who were Shi Li's best friends. The teacher ordered them to stand up as well, repeated the story and asked again if they agreed that Shi Li was ungrateful. But they still didn't answer. At this point the teacher became furious. "You two are bad children!" she cried and sent them out of the class. Then she turned to Shi Li again. "What do you feel now, Shi Li? Do you regret having done this? Are you sorry?" Shi Li's eyes turned red and tears ran down his cheeks. This infuriated the teacher even more. At last Shi Li started talking. His head was lowered and his words were unclear. "Speak louder!" screamed the teacher. "Speak properly, with your head facing the class!"

Shi Li lifted his head and said, "I have been very bad and I am not going to do anything like this again. I am very sorry for what I did to the boy and in future I shall learn to be grateful to other people. I have been too bad. Everyone may call me ungrateful...."

The boy went on apologizing and criticizing himself. The teacher then called in his two friends who, for fear of the teacher, were no longer supporting their best friend. They also called him ungrateful. That day for homework Shi Li had to write a composition on what he had done and what he had felt. The next day he had to read it out loud to our class and to the class of the other boy as well.

"Politeness month" was announced through one of the school reunions. It was the main topic and the headmistress made a great show of it. "Politeness month" was not an invention of our school, but of the leaders "up there." It was to take effect in the whole of China. While it lasted everyone was supposed to be especially good and helpful and well-behaved toward everyone else: parents, teachers, and people on the streets alike. All the students were to work especially hard and do still more extra work.

The model we had to follow was a communist soldier, long since dead, called Lei Feng. He used to help mothers carry their children during thunderstorms and to help peasants push heavy carts, and always wore a smile. Like him, we were supposed to help old people cross the road, carry things for elderly ladies and pick up apple peel from the road. This campaign went well and so, since the month was nearly ended, minds raced to find another topic.

Before we could have a break, the "beautification campaign" was announced. This meant still harder work, still less free time. First of all, the school was to be thoroughly cleaned — windows, doors, tiles, corridors, everywhere. Then we were encouraged to bring plants to school to make it more beautiful. The small trees which were scattered here and there in the courtyard were pulled down and slightly bigger ones were planted in their place. And last, but not least, we were sent during the weekends to clean the streets.

Everyone went with a broom in hand, led by red flags, in a perfect procession. All the dust was to be swept off the pavement. Hundreds of children swept, loudspeakers boomed and red flags fluttered. It could have been a great success had it not been for the wind. That day it blew especially strongly and at every stroke of the broom, clouds of dust rose into the air and obstinately settled down again on the pavement a few hundred meters further down the road, only to be swept up again by the sweepers down there.

It was obviously a total failure. But to admit that would have been a loss of face to those in charge. Anyway, they were not the ones who had to sweep, so the sweeping went on for the rest of the day. You really had to work hard for "the people."

Once a week each class had a "morals lesson." The Party vice-secretary of the school did all the talking, and the talking was about the Communist Party. She told us that it was the Communist Party that was making China modern and, if it had not been for communism, China would still be a poor country. During one of these lessons, I, Saskia, was listening to the teacher saying over and over again "socialism this... socialism that...."

Everyone was attentive and when the Party vice-secretary asked if we had understood, we all said "Yes!" Except for one, and that was the class leader. He raised his hand and asked, "What is socialism?"

The Party vice-secretary stood still for a few seconds and then started walking all over the classroom. She was nervous. She had no answer herself. She only had learned by heart how nice China is now that there is socialism, but she did not know the meaning of socialism. Yet, since she had been talking about socialism throughout the lesson, she had to give an answer. So she told him what socialism had done to China, which was exactly what she had been saying all through the lesson anyway.

The class leader already knew his question was dangerous, so he did not want to push it any further. This class leader was so much braver than any other student. He dared to ask many questions. I admired him very much, but I never had a chance to talk to him.

Once a week there was another lesson, probably about Party policies, but we never found out what exactly it was about. We foreigners were asked to leave the room and read some books when this lesson was held. One possibility is that our Chinese classmates were being told how to behave toward us foreigners.

The toilets in the Chinese school are worth mentioning. First of all because their smell invades every classroom, and secondly because of their design. I, Folco, was usually very hesitant to enter one for fear of meeting my teacher there, as I once did. Each toilet room is divided into three or four sections, with a little wall about 1 meter high between them. They have no doors! When I entered, I only saw an open newspaper in one of the sections. Hiding behind it was my teacher. He said "Hello!" The *People's Daily* had become the improvised door. I thought he would be embarrassed, so I became embarrassed and ran out. Later we got perfectly used to it.

We also had science lessons. I, Saskia, remember one in particular. The teacher came in holding a bowl with two goldfish in it. He told us, with a happy smile on his face, that he was going to cut one of the fish's fins off so we could see for ourselves what would happen. The class cheered with enjoyment. The teacher calmed the class by raising his hand, then dipped his hand into the bowl. Once the poor little fish was in his hand, wriggling about, the teacher took a pair of scissors four times the length of the fish and slowly cut the fish's right fin off. The class couldn't wait to see what the fish would do once it was back in the water. When the little fish was dropped back into the water, it couldn't keep its balance. Its body tilted to the left. Its only fin waved about and the poor fish kept on turning to the right. The class was laughing at the miserable fish and then shouted, "cut the other fin off too!"

The teacher, enjoying himself and feeling quite satisfied because he had attracted the class's attention, grabbed the little fish, which couldn't escape from his hands, and with no pity cut the left fin off too.

Men walk, birds fly and fish swim. It sank right to the bottom of the bowl and managed to move a few millimeters by thrusting its tail, but that was not for long. The class was crowding around the bowl now and was shouting, "cut the tail off too! Cut it right off!" Again the teacher, with great enthusiasm, caught the fish and snapped its tail off. The fish was not a fish anymore. It just lay at the bottom of the bowl breathing itself to death. The only ones who did not find it funny were the boy who had raised the fish and I.

Sports play an important role in the Chinese school: marching, saluting, spinning around on one's heel, learning some kungfu kicks, and hand grenade throwing. Of course the grenades are fake, but their shape is like a real one. The ones we used were made of wood with a metal top.

In the Chinese school, hand grenade throwing is one of many competitive events, like softball throwing in the west. Each year there was a school sports day, which was very well organized and took place in the schoolyard. Behind a large table covered with a white cloth, cups of tea and bunches of flowers, sat the Party secretary and some important guests, among them an old general who arrived in his big black Red Flag limousine.

Before the events and competitions came the parading. The best marchers, wearing white shirts, blue trousers and their usual red scarves, formed columns two abreast and advanced to the tune of a marching anthem. At the head of the columns, flag bearers held the bamboo poles of the red flags exactly vertical. The students in the very front of the procession supported a huge, rectangular piece of framed canvas with a saying of Chairman Mao written on it. Each group was organized so that the smallest marched at the front. They would separate, turn back and then flow into columns again; they would march in place, and they would snap to a stand-still at the last note of the anthem. It was all very even, precise and disciplined.

When each class, from youngest to oldest, was lined up in front of the Party secretary, he gave his speech. He would announce the beginning of sports day and what events would take place and where. Then he would remind the Chinese in particular that they should try their best to win. If they won they would bring honor and glory to their motherland.

Even in a race, a child has to think of giving all the glory to the motherland, and can keep none for himself.

I, Folco, ran the 800 meters. I ran as hard as I could, because I knew that if I won I would compete in the Peking inter-school competition. And I won. I had beaten all the Chinese. The second to arrive was also a foreigner, and the Chinese were far, far behind. Now, as the sports teacher had told me, I had qualified. I tramped up to him, first thing, and asked, "I can go to the inter-school competition, right?" The answer came as a shock. "No!" he said. "No, you ran fast, but not fast enough." And that was that. Fastest in the school, what more did he want? But no. The foreigners, although a minority, had won too many events. It wouldn't do to show that all the best athletes of our school were foreigners when we went to the inter-school event. He needed more, many more Chinese. And so I was replaced by a Chinese who had not even arrived second. It was another decision made, not by my teacher, but by the school Party secretary.

The presence of foreign students in the school created problems for the Chinese. The kite-flying competition was another such occasion. Each year, the school held a contest to see who could keep his kite in the air longest. The date had not been fixed, but people were talking about it and making their kites. Together with a foreign friend, I, Folco, made my own. We kept asking when the contest would take place, but the answers from the teachers were always vague and mysterious. It looked as if they really wanted to keep something secret from us. So we decided to stay on after school

209

for a few days to see if the contest was being held behind our backs. Nothing happened. Only later did we discover that the school had done something very simple and unbeatable: they had held the contest during schooltime, but during the hours when we foreigners had separate lessons. I wondered why. Maybe it was because, the year before, the two winning kite flyers had been foreigners.

We had music lessons, but they could not do without communist songs. Each person was given a sheet of paper with the words and the notes of the song. In the first lesson the class would sing the notes only; in the next lesson they would sing the words.

During the annual singing contest one year, there was one song that was sung by at least half of all the classes. It was called, "If There Wasn't the Communist Party, There Wouldn't Be New China." The second in importance was the "Politeness Song." Other songs explained how good Chairman Mao had been and others told you to work hard and be a good Young Pioneer. Some children were asked to sing by themselves in front of the audience.

Once again, foreigners and Chinese were separated in the singing contest. I, Folco, had a teacher who made his foreign pupils sing a song different from the standard ones. We sang "Old McDonald Had a Farm," and each of us stepped forward to make different animal noises, much to the enjoyment of the Chinese children for whom this was completely new. Among the foreigners, we won. Among the Chinese, one class singing the "Politeness Song" got first prize.

The teachers did not have much freedom in choosing their teaching methods or teaching materials. They had to follow the rules and methods laid down for them by the Party secretary. Yet I, Saskia, had the impression that all the teachers of the school had to work very hard, though they did not seem to get many rewards for this. The teachers' salary was very low and their living conditions were not very good either. The unmarried ones lived in poor dormitories within the school compound. Every day, at a quarter to 12, each teacher walked to the dirty kitchen and with his numbered key opened a drawer and picked up a metal container into which a few spoonfuls of soup had been dumped. You could hardly even call it soup. It was only boiled water with a few strings of noodles and tiny pieces of chopped-up meat and vegetables that had no taste. On special occasions or special days they were also given a bowl of rice in addition to this, but otherwise, that was their lunch. They did not get any drinks. The soup was both drink and food. I think this may be why all my teachers were so thin.

These teachers were all very kind to us and they did their best to teach us as much as they could. When we first entered the school, we did not know a word of Chinese and for four or five months the teachers tried their best to teach us as much as they could to help us catch up. They were all very nice to us.

When I, Folco, was once in hospital, two teachers took the trouble to visit me there and brought me some fruit. As people they were good people, but they had to follow the rules which the Party secretary laid down for them.

So, my final thoughts about the Chinese school are far from positive. I hated the spying, the criticizing, the apologizing to save one's own skin. I hated the teaching system that left no space for imagination. I hated all the copying, the learning of rules, learning the correct way to think. All the deceiving, the lying, the feeling that you cannot say what you really think, that you are not allowed to think certain things. Never again.

I learned a lesson which I will not forget. I learned about the system and I have no intention to go through all that again.

Folco was 11 years old when he arrived in China. Saskia was 9½. What they have written, above, are their own uncensored, unabridged recollections of three years in the Chinese elementary school, Fan Cao Di, the Field of Perfumed Grass.

14

We Welcome Them with Long Hair

Shenzhen and Guangzhou: experimenting with capitalism

Capitalism has won. Here, at least, it has won. After 35 years as the door to the puritanical and egalitarian kingdom of Mao Zedong and the forward bastion of Chinese communism, Shenzhen, a small town just within the border between the People's Republic and Hong Kong, has surrendered to the temptations of bourgeois prosperity. The order for surrender has come directly from Peking. "Stop opposing capitalism. Imitate it. We must learn its mechanisms, its systems," people have been told.

Shenzhen is the first strip of Chinese land the visitor sees when coming from Hong Kong. The border is just a little river. A bridge links two worlds. The British flag is flying on one bank and the red flag of China on the other. In the past, taking those few steps across that bridge was like going on a long trip between two faraway galaxies, each armed against the other. It is no longer so.

Shenzhen has been declared by Peking a "special economic zone." This means that, within the borders of this area, regulations are different from those in the rest of China; capitalism is allowed, and private initiative has the right to exist and flourish.

The concept of the special economic zone goes back to 1979 and is one of the daring initiatives taken by Deng Xiaoping since his return to power.

For a communist, the idea of experimenting with capitalism is certainly most sacrilegious. But a lot of people in China, including some leaders, were asking themselves questions that needed to be answered.

"How is it possible that the Chinese of Hong Kong have a standard of living so much higher than that of the Chinese of China? How is it possible for people who escaped from the

People's Republic with nothing to return after a few years with all the symbols of affluence people in China yearn for? Perhaps communism does not work?''

The system which has ruled China since the communists took over the country has certainly not been entirely successful. Thus came the idea of experimenting with something new on a small scale, at least for the time being.

Compared to the vast size of China, Shenzhen is just a tiny territory with a population of only 200,000 people, but the introduction of the special zone regime has completely changed its appearance. The new constitution has sanctioned this change and dedicated an entire article to it.

During the years when China had closed itself to the outside world while seeking the solution to its problems through self-sufficiency, tourist companies in Hong Kong organized trips to a spot in the British colony from which one could observe China through binoculars. All one could see was a quiet rural town surrounded by fields, where farmers dressed in blue were working to the sound of revolutionary music broadcast from loudspeakers.

Now Shenzhen is an enormous construction site: skyscrapers, factories, roads, residential buildings are all being built. Cement has taken over the fields, thousands of laborers have replaced the farmers. Eighty thousand construction workers, electricians, plumbers, all with their political secretaries, have arrived to make Shenzhen into a copy of Hong Kong.

With whose money? Much of it comes from the Chinese capitalists of Hong Kong. The law for the special zone offers huge inducements to foreign investors; and, for large Hong Kong companies, the opportunity to have land and labor at prices far more favorable than in the British colony is not to be forgone.

A construction company has just finished three large apartment buildings to be sold to Overseas Chinese who want a residence in China. Pepsi Cola is already operating a bottling plant. A company with European capital is manufacturing ship containers. A large toy company from Hong Kong has transferred the bulk of its production to Shenzhen, as has a

213

printing company. Some textile industries have been set up, and electronic goods are being produced.

The Peking government is handling the infrastructure: it is building roads and sewers, dredging a new harbor, planning a new airport and basically allows the capitalists, a term used in Shenzhen almost with a tone of respect, a free hand.

Although still unthinkable in the rest of China, companies in Shenzhen choose their own workers, fire the inefficient ones and handsomely reward those who are more productive. "Here we manage with economic criteria, not political ones," declares a manufacturing plant manager who came from Hong Kong, and the Chinese official standing next to him nods.

From the outside, the symbols of power are those of the rest of China: the Party cadres dress in blue and carry a black plastic handbag, the policemen have the same uniform as elsewhere. Only in Shenzhen they seem to be spectators. "They come here to learn how capitalism functions and they do not interfere," said an industrialist from Hong Kong. And somehow it is true.

In the evening, at a coffee shop called Garden of the Arts, a jukebox grinds out songs by a singer from Taiwan, forbidden in the rest of China because they are considered to be tinged with "pornography." In another dark, large room, scores of teenagers with long hair and leather jackets operate noisy electronic games that no one has even seen in the rest of China.

What in the rest of the country is condemned as decadent, in Shenzhen is allowed. It is almost taken for granted that, in order to have the production rates of Hong Kong and of the west, it is necessary to yield also to this kind of westernization.

"If having long hair contributes to the Four Modernizations, then long hair is welcome," said a political officer of the city. At the beginning of the experiment in Shenzhen, the Party opened an Office for the Propagation of Spiritual Civilization, a sort of center for teaching socialist morality. After a few months of useless effort it was closed. In Shenzhen, the danwei do not interfere in the private lives of the people. "We can do what we want," I was told by two young girls who stopped me during a stroll to chat one evening, "as long as one works and works well."

Now Shenzhen is like a place outside China: the workers earn four to five times more than in the rest of the country, they have access to consumer goods at the same prices as in Hong Kong, and enjoy a freedom inconceivable in the rest of the country.

In the past, Shenzhen was a set goal for those who wanted to escape to Hong Kong from China. Nowadays no one comes here to escape any more. On the contrary, now that the fairy tale of Shenzhen has reached every corner of China, there are many who want to come here not to escape but to work. The Party makes a careful selection of the workers who are to be sent to Shenzhen. For others it is simply impossible to reach because special permission is required, almost like a visa.

The idea for Shenzhen is still that of an experiment intended to attract foreign capital, import western technology, and train Chinese managers in capitalist ways, to enable them eventually to transfer what they have learned to the rest of the economy and the country. But in the meantime, how can the government protect the rest of China from the influence of this place which allows everything that is forbidden elsewhere?

Seven kilometers north of the actual border between Hong Kong and the People's Republic, an iron fence 7 meters high and 70 kilometers long has just been finished. It isolates Shenzhen from the rest of the country. It is called a "customs barrier." Only customs?

The more Shenzhen is developed and becomes a copy of Hong Kong, the less it functions as a border between two worlds. No one who passes over the bridge thinks any longer of two opposite worlds. In making Shenzhen a special zone, Deng Xiaoping has also thought of a way to take over Hong Kong without too many tragedies: absorbing it bit by bit even before 1997.

And what if it is Hong Kong, or rather capitalism, that absorbs China? The question faces me in Guangzhou, known to the west as Canton. Three street urchins pull at my sleeve begging for money. A shoeshine man squatting on the sidewalk pulls my trousers, trying to make me place my foot on his small wooden bench. A woman wants to sell me a papaya; an old man, an ugly plaster statue. A group of youngsters crowd around a man who hides his merchandise as soon as I approach. When it becomes obvious that I am not a policeman, Chinese clothes notwithstanding, everybody bursts out laughing, and smuggled watches shine once again in the darkness. A simple stroll at sundown along the Pearl River brings about endless surprises. Is this China?

Guangzhou is the capital of Guangdong Province. Hong Kong and Macau, islands of capitalism in this socialist ocean, are only a step away. For a century, thousands of Chinese migrants have left these shores to search for fortune elsewhere, and it is to Guangzhou that they return to show off their wealth and to tell how the rest of the world works for the successful.

During the Cultural Revolution, Guangzhou and the surrounding provinces suffered badly because of their suspected contacts from abroad. Now that Deng Xiaoping has given back a little bit of freedom, instead of a finger they have taken the whole hand, perhaps even an arm, and it seems that the situation is almost getting out of control.

If you compare it with the situation only two or three years ago, the changes are enormous. In the past, Guangzhou was the first sight the foreign traveler had of China: clean and crowded roads deserted at sundown; people all dressed alike; girls with braids; trills of bicycle bells. Now, as soon as one leaves the station, the first thing one sees is a neon sign for Seiko spread out on the entire roof of a building. It is longer and brighter than the one on the next building wishing "Long life to the Chinese Communist Party."

At one time the traveler had to drag his own luggage, and this self-sufficiency was considered a necessary aspect of socialism. This principle, as well as others, has been cast aside. Young farmers with bamboo poles crowd around the visitor, fighting for his suitcases, while other young men try to direct him to their own taxis — brand new red Toyotas. The money comes from the capitalists of Hong Kong, the manpower from China. In three years, when the financiers from Hong Kong will have recovered their investment plus interest, the autos will belong to Guangzhou.

On top of the fixed salary, the taxi drivers have the right to a bonus according to their proceeds. They happily accept a tip while at one time it was refused as an offense, and if the traveler pays them with the special certificates that are equivalent to foreign currency, the drivers have a tendency to give the change in local money (on the black market a certificate of 1 yuan is equal to far more than one normal yuan).

At one time, asking if there were prostitutes around would mean finding oneself at the police station or, at the least, putting up with a nasty political lecture. Now the occasional interlocutor will discuss at length the fact that prices have risen sharply, to 50 yuan, because of the many Chinese from Hong Kong who do not mind the expense. It has ruined the market for local men.

Hong Kong. Hong Kong. "Have you been there?" I ask a young man dressed exactly like anyone in the British Colony.

"In my dreams many times," he answers laughing. Almost every family here has a brother, an uncle, a cousin, or a distant relative who in some way, maybe even by swimming, has escaped or emigrated to the colony. A great many of the hopes of the people left behind are set on these relatives: a pair of blue jeans, a radio, a color TV, enough capital to open a shop. Now it is possible, and "the uncles of Hong Kong" come to visit their families loaded with all sorts of goods.

One can see the results everywhere: scores of hairdressers with modern equipment have opened shops downtown; a dozen coffee shops with rock music and tables on the sidewalk stay open until 1 a.m. Almost all the young women strolling with their fiancés along roads now well lit with neon signs have an imitation leather shoulder bag. Among the young workers, the Mao uniform has disappeared and a sort of cowboy outfit has taken its place.

"This was a room of my residence. Now we work here. We pay to the state a tax of 80 yuan per month, and the rest is all ours," says a young man who has opened a hairdressing salon with money from one of his uncles in Hong Kong.

With money from Hong Kong, two downtown restaurants have been completely renovated. With money and expertise from Hong Kong, a state-owned company has built the White Swan Hotel on Shamian Island, while a joint-venture company has put up the China Hotel, an extremely elegant and luxurious

217

complex where Chinese families bring their children on Sundays to show them what modernization means.

This capital coming in from outside has already changed the daily life of Guangzhou. The city has acquired the rhythm of every other city in southeast Asia where the Chinese work, trade, bustle and become rich.

In the evening, along the canal which at the time of the concessions separated the foreign quarter from the rest of the city, under the branches of centennial trees, tables and stools of improvised restaurants appear as if by magic. They offer seafood, fish soups, and, during winter, the specialty of the season — dog and snake meat. Under the arcades of old and decrepit buildings along the river, hundreds of peddlers appear. They offer at bargain prices a bit of everything, from medicinal herbs gathered and dried in faraway mountains, to porcelain vases and statues bought wholesale from the kilns of Foshan and sold retail by enterprising unemployed people.

The price of all these changes is obvious: the newspapers expose cases of corruption, and the police must make regular rounds to take down the TV antennas with which people watch Hong Kong programs because they disdain the local ones. "The dangerous influence of bourgeois liberalism" is frequently attacked in the official press.

Guangzhou has certainly changed, but Guangzhou is not China: an order from Peking would be quite enough to shut the lid on this boiling pot again. Besides, even here it is not true that everything has changed. Some old socialist habits still survive. In the People's Grand Hotel, completely renovated by a Hong Kong company, the young floor boy calls me with great urgency to demand that I pay immediately for a telephone call I had made four hours earlier to Peking. When he knocks relentlessly on the door to wake me up, it is 2 a.m.

15

Allah Has Given Man One Heart Only

The old city of Kashgar in central Asia

The houses are of mud. The streets are of mud. The mosques and the tombs are of mud. Only Mao is made of granite.

One of the few surviving gigantic statues of the Great Helmsman is where it belongs the least — in the middle of the Kashgar oasis, at the edge of the Takla Makan, the most fearsome desert of the world, at the foot of some of the highest mountains, the Pamirs, in the furthest western corner of China's western province, Xinjiang. Towering over the medieval maze of this ocher city swarming with ancient-looking people, sheep, donkeys and camels, the 18-meter-high Mao looks odd, out of proportion, out of place.

The inhabitants of Kashgar are devoted Muslims and as such they shun any image of deities. They are Uighurs, and they are resentful of anything that reminds them openly of the fact that they are dominated and ruled by the majority race: the Han Chinese.

The statue was put up in 1966, at the beginning of the Cultural Revolution, when Peking, 4,200 kilometers away, tried to impose in Kashgar the same radical policies as in the rest of the country. Mao's Red Guards, in an attempt to turn this remote, dusty corner of central Asia into yet another "red ocean," banned all religious activities, shut down the mosques, burned all copies of the Koran, prohibited private trade on which life had been based for centuries, closed the bazaar, and imprisoned its merchants as "speculators."

Now those policies have been repudiated as mistakes and Deng Xiaoping's reforms are being applied in this outpost even more liberally than in the rest of the country. Religion and private business thrive, the Koran is freely available at the New China Bookstore, the bazaar is again the bustling center of social life. All the signs and slogans of the past have been removed and washed away, but the huge granite Mao is still there, towering over Kashgar's skyline of mud, symbol of China's continuous determination to rule this part of the world.

In the recent past it was by violence, ideological pressure and terror (7,000 people were killed in the province during the Cultural Revolution); now it is by tolerance, more freedom and autonomy. The means have changed. The goal is the same.

The fight for the hearts and minds of Kashgar is part of the renewed, general effort on the part of the Chinese communists to gain the allegiance of the minority people and thus to overcome China's traditional weakness: the extreme vulnerability of her borders.

The land frontiers of the People's Republic run for over 20,000 kilometers from Vietnam in the south, to India and the Soviet Union in the west, and to Mongolia, the Soviet Union and Korea in the north. None of these border areas are inhabited by Han Chinese, but by Mongols, Tibetans, Zhuangs, Uighurs, Kazaks, people who for centuries have resented Chinese rule, have intermittently rebelled against it and can at any time rebel again.

The hinterland of China will never be safe and secure unless these minorities are pacified and assimilated or the border areas are firmly taken over by large masses of immigrant Han Chinese brought from the interior.

The loyalty of the minorities is questionable, for they are an easy prey to the propaganda of China's enemies on the other side of the dividing line, where similar minorities live, often under better conditions. Peking is well aware of the dangers. "Half of my family is in the Soviet Union, but I cannot even write to them," says a Uighur man in a Kashgar tea shop. "If I do, the police will immediately put me under surveillance."

Kashgar is 120 kilometers away from the Soviet Union, 310 kilometers from Soviet-occupied Afghanistan and 400 kilometers from Pakistan.

In the old days, Kashgar was the first stop along the Silk Road and it was here that Marco Polo's caravan rested before venturing into the desert on the way to the Mongol court. It was a flourishing trading post, a meeting place of different people and religions. During the last century, Kashgar became the center of intrigues and conspiracies, the nexus where "the three empires met" and where British, Russian and Chinese agents played "the great game," as the struggle for the control of central Asia and its riches was then called.

The Russian Empire kept moving the borders of its part of Turkestan forward by luring the local minorities into the tzarist fold. The British tried to halt the Russian advance by extending their influence from their base in India, and the Chinese Empire tried to re-establish its rule over the whole area by suppressing a series of rebellions waged by the minorities against Peking in the name of Islam.

Diplomats and spies, military officers and archeologists, explorers and adventurers of various countries and reputations mixed in Kashgar, often in interchanging roles. After the Silk Road had been abandoned in favor of the more convenient sea lanes, the oasis that had once flourished in the desert was evacuated and was slowly reconquered by the moving sands of the Takla Makan. Tales of lost treasures buried somewhere in the wilderness had been told for centuries, but those who went looking for them had never come back.

Toward the end of the last century, Kashgar provided the base for renewed attempts to find treasure. In 1890, Sven Hedin, then still a young student of Baron von Richthofen, arrived on his first journey to central Asia as a guest of the famous Russian consul, Petrovskj.

Albert von Le Coq, author of _Hellas Spuren in Ostturkistan_, stayed in Kashgar as a guest of the British consul MacCartney, after having taken the unique frescoes from the Buddhist caves of Bezeklik. The frescoes were later destroyed in the Ethnological Museum of Berlin under American carpet bombings during World War II. It was in Kashgar that Sir Aurel Stein stopped with his loads of invaluable manuscripts from Dunhuang before taking them to India and finally to the British Museum.

"All those foreigners came here to rob us," says Mrs Guan Yuru, a Chinese official of the Xinjiang administration. The Chinese have a point, for indeed they were the first among "the foreigners" to arrive in this part of the world, long before the others, in 126 B.C.

The Chinese Emperor Wudi had heard that people there had special horses that sweated blood and originated from heaven, and he wanted them for his cavalry. It took the emperor's emissary 13 years to return to the Chinese capital, but that mission opened the road from the hinterland of the Celestial Empire to the western areas beyond the desert. Ever since, the control of the oasis and its population has been considered vital to China's security. Yet that control was never complete; over the last 2,000 years, the Chinese succeeded in ruling over the oasis of Kashgar only intermittently, for less than 500 years.

Distance was one of the problems. At the beginning of this century it took five months for a caravan to cover the route between Peking and Kashgar. Still today Kashgar is not connected by train to the rest of China, and the road that skirts the southern rim of the desert is still partly unpaved. The little Soviet-made Antonov plane that hops to the oases of Aksu and Khotan before reaching Kashgar, does not take off from the provincial capital of Urumqi for its once-every-four-day flight unless the weather is clear along the whole flightpath and no winds are forecast. Kashgar remains the most isolated and remote city in China; a journey there is more a trip in time than in space.

To arrive in Kashgar is like landing in the Bible: people and animals clog the lanes of the old mud city; old men with curly white beards, all dressed in long black overcoats, ride tiny, skinny donkeys; women, their heads and faces hidden under brown shawls of heavy wool, gather in blind conversations; children go around collecting the droppings of animals to be used as fuel; open-air food stalls wrapped in clouds of smoke and fumes serve shish kebab and goat soup. There are hardly any cars. Bicycles are few and the transport of people and goods is done by an endless fleet of rudimentary wooden carts drawn by donkeys. "Posh...posh...posh" (give way...give way) is the constant refrain of the drivers and the first word of Uighur one learns. Sounds, smells, colors, the people's faces: one has great difficulty in remembering that this is still China.

Yet it is China, and Peking is absolutely determined to keep it that way. In 1949, the communists took over this region, then used the oasis of Khotan as a stepping stone to take Tibet. Since then, their grip has been firm and the "great game" for the control of central Asia is practically over. The Chinese are the winners.

The British long ago left India, and their former elegant consulate in Kashgar, now a dilapidated and decaying building, is used as a dormitory by the truck drivers who ply the desert route to and from Urumqi.

The Russians have left as well. The last diplomat from Moscow went in 1958, when China's relationship with the Soviet Union went sour. The old Russian consulate from which Petrovskj conspired for over 20 years to acquire Xinjiang for his master, the tzar, was turned into the Kashgar Number One Guest House.

The Soviet Union is no longer perceived as an imminent danger. Relations between Peking and Moscow have generally improved following the start of normalization contacts and in Kashgar nobody talks of possible sudden attacks and infiltration anymore.

On the contrary. "The border is very quiet. The Soviets have stopped sending their spies here," says Abdulla Rayim of the provincial Foreign Affairs Office. Even the vitriolic radio propaganda the Soviets used to beam at China from a transmitter in Samarkand has ceased and the clearest broadcast one can hear now on a shortwave radio in Kashgar is that of Deutsche Welle.

The border trade which had come to a complete halt for almost 20 years has picked up again: in August 1982, Kashgar Prefecture opened a frontier post to exchange goods with Pakistan; on July 1, 1983, a similar trading post was opened on the border with the Soviet Union.

"We have nothing to fear from trading with our neighbors," says the Kashgar deputy mayor, Esai Shakir. What Peking has to fear most is its own population, for now the major threat to Chinese rule over this part of the world does not come from across the borders. It comes from the difficult relationship between the minorities and the Han Chinese. Only two years ago a group of Uighur dissidents were discovered in Xinjiang, planning a province-wide uprising against Chinese rule. The slogan they were using was, "We want self-rule. We don't want to be dominated."

Recently, the *People's Daily* revealed that a "counter-revolutionary group" had been dismantled in Kashgar. The Party paper then, and officals in the city now, give no details about that group, but the classification as "counter-revolutionary" means revolt against the status quo, that is, against Chinese rule over the area.

The difficulties are shown by the figures. In Kashgar Prefecture there are 2 million Uighurs. The Han number only 360,000, but they are the ones in command. In spite of the fact that many directors, managers and chairmen the visitor is brought to meet are Uighur, only a few minutes of conversation are enough to find out that there is a Han Chinese around who is the real boss. He usually is only the deputy manager, the deputy director, but he is the one to whom the Uighur constantly turns in order to check whether he is saying the right things. He is also the one who ends up answering the most sensitive questions. This situation naturally feeds Uighur resentment against the Hans.

Small incidents risk becoming the spark of big, dangerous fires. In April 1980, the killing of a Uighur boy by a Han in Akhsu triggered a race riot that lasted two days and nights, with gangs of Uighurs attacking Han homes and ransacking Han properties. A similar incident occurred in the center of Kashgar on October 31, 1981. A group of Uighur workers wanted to dig a trench in the pavement in front of a state shop run by Hans. The initial discussion became a quarrel and a Han ended up shooting and killing one of the Uighurs with a shotgun. Thousands of Uighurs joined in. For hours the city was in chaos, and two Hans were killed. An Army unit had to be called in to quell the violence and separate the two communities.

Race relationships in Xinjiang were so bad in 1981 that Deng Xiaoping himself came on an inspection tour of the province and it was during his nine-day visit that China's strongman was confronted with the reality of the planned revolt against Chinese rule and with the open disaffection of many Uighurs, even within the provincial government.

Deng Xiaoping's visit was a turning point for Xinjiang. Having found the situation "unsteady," Deng ordered a complete reorganization of the provincial administration, removed some of the top officials including the governor, and approved a liberalization plan meant to give the Uighurs more autonomy and to restore some of their old ways of life.

Kashgar has since become the test of Deng's way of regaining the confidence and the loyalty of the local population. So far it has seemed to work.

The bazaar of Kashgar, reopened in 1981, is one of the greatest happenings of today's China: an orgy of humanity, of private entrepreneurship, a show of all the small freedoms the Uighurs have reacquired. The bazaar is open every day, but the one held on Sunday is the major event.

At dawn, endless caravans of people, carts, donkeys, horses, camels and sheep converge from all directions on the vast open space under the mud cliffs of the city. Within a few hours there are some 50,000 people buying, selling, eating, working or simply wandering around in search of a bargain. All the goods of central Asia are on display. Knives made with the famous steel of Kashgar (US$2), leather boots (US$8), embroidered skullcaps (US$3), saddles, high black velvet hats with a reddish rim of mink fur, carpets, copper ware, spices with 100 different smells. One can take away a camel for US$150, a donkey for US$40, a sheep for US$18.

There are people selling fresh mulberries, others practicing their professions in the open air: barbers shaving people's heads with big shiny razors, dentists with their foot-operated drills, shirtmakers, blacksmiths, herbalist doctors and jewelers. Pretty young girls, their eyebrows painted in black across the front, walk through the crowds. Old men with Biblical faces sit in the sun rolling cigarettes in pieces of old newspaper and waiting for fresh bread to come out of archaic, portable ovens. All of this had been stopped by the Cultural Revolution and people in Kashgar had to content themselves with what they could buy in the state-run shops.

"The reopening of the bazaar has been the most important change in the life of the city," says Deputy Mayor Esai Shafir. "Almost all the trade is now in private hands."

225

There are 3,000 full-time and 7,000 part-time merchants in Kashgar who, besides handling the local products, are able to get anything from Shanghai and Peking within 10 days. "It is an advantage for everybody, for if we had to go through the bureaucratic channel, it would take a year for the goods to reach Kashgar," says Shakir.

The "bureaucratic channel" has also been bypassed in agriculture where the People's Communes, whose establishment the Uighurs had resisted, have been completely abolished. Farmer families now cultivate with self-interest the plots of land assigned to them. Production has greatly increased. "People now feel they are masters of their own affairs," says a member of the local government, and the income of the Uighurs has gone up.

An even more important change for the local people has been the new tolerance shown by the Communist Party for their religion: Islam.

The Id Kah Mosque, in the center of the old city, has been completely refurbished after being closed and vandalized. Permission is granted for 20 people a year to go as pilgrims to Mecca. An Islamic association has been founded to train young clerics and all bans on religious activities have been lifted. In the 92 mosques recently reopened in Kashgar alone, people are free to come and go, to pray or to listen to a man reading from the Koran in the shade of the poplars, or to give a few cents to the beggars who gather in the courtyards.

The Imam of Kashgar, 80-year-old Khasim Karajin, is again the most respected community leader and is recognized as such by the local communist authorities. "The doctrine of the Communist Party is not in line with Islam," says the Imam, "but the Party in China tolerates our practice."

Tolerance, especially in the long run, may not prove to be enough because basically one ideology excludes the other. Both sides recognize this fact. "One has to choose which road to take," says a Communist Party member of the provincial government, "one cannot walk with one foot in Islam and one foot in socialism." The Imam of Kashgar says, "Allah has given man only one heart. Either you believe in this faith or in that faith. Either you believe in Islam or in communism."

This basic, general contradiction is even deeper in Xinjiang because communism is seen by the local people as the latest by-product of the Han domination and Islam has been used, even in the past, as the rallying point of the rebellious minorities to fight against Chinese rule.

One of the holiest places in Xinjiang, a place that in the past attracted pilgrims from all over the province, is a quiet compound 8 kilometers east of Kashgar.

At dawn when a pale moon is still on one side of the sky and a glorious sun rises on the other, behind a screen of trembling poplars, the green-tiled dome of the Apak Hoja Mausoleum with its four minarets is one of the most enchanting sights of central Asia. Over the rustling of the leaves moved by a gentle wind and the whispering of the water in the canals that irrigate the dry, flat land all around, one hears the litanies of people praying in front of the wooden railing that blocks access to the mausoleum and the closed doors of its oldest chapel nearby. "It is an historical monument and we keep it closed in order to protect it," says Aisan Umar, the local guide.

The mausoleum has been restored and refurbished, but it has also been transformed into a sort of museum where one has to buy tickets, and there are doors and locks that have to be opened.

Apak Hoja was a Muslim saint who used Islam to make Kashgaria into a theocratic state of which he and his family members were the rulers. He died in 1694, and for the Uighurs he is a national and religious hero. The Chinese today would prefer that the people forgot him, and forgot that this monument, a splendid example of Muslim architecture, was built for a Uighur and his descendants who ruled over Kashgar. Instead, they want the visitor to turn his attention to a small, minor tomb among the 72 which are sheltered under the dome.

The tomb is empty, but the whole mausoleum gets its name from the alleged occupant. It is known as "The Tomb of the Fragrant Concubine." The way the Chinese are rewriting this piece of history is a story in itself.

Her real name was Mamrisim and she was a beautiful Uighur girl married to a certain Hoja, ruler of Kashgaria. In 1759,

227

when Emperor Qian Long's armies entered the region, killed half a million people and re-established Chinese rule, her husband was beheaded and she was sent, as a prisoner, to the Qing court in Peking to become a concubine. Emperor Qian Long saw her and immediately fell in love with her, but she resisted all his attempts. One day, when he was away, the emperor's mother, worried about her son's suffering, ordered the girl to commit suicide. So the Fragrant Concubine strangled herself with a silk scarf at the Moon Flower Gate inside the Forbidden City.

On his return, the emperor was profoundly upset and gave instructions that her body be placed in the imperial burial ground. The tomb of the Fragrant Concubine is next to the one of Qian Long, 80 kilometers west of Peking.

Yet the Fragrant Concubine has another tomb in Kashgar and the visitor is even shown the very coffin and cart in which, according to this version, her body was sent by the emperor back to her people.

The story of the Fragrant Concubine has always been told by the Uighurs from father to son as an example of Han cruelty and deviousness. But now the guide who takes the visitor in the mausoleum says that "The love of the Chinese emperor for this Uighur girl proves the long history of unity of the races in China."

Behind the mausoleum, dozens of other graves made of mud in the shape of small huts, small domes, lie row upon row in the sun, a city of the dead in ocher color made by generations of Uighurs who have come to bury their beloved in the holy ground.

"Where is the tomb of Yakub Beg?" asks the visitor, thinking of the man who in the middle of the last century put himself at the head of yet another Muslim rebellion. He built up a modern army, constructed a network of forts to resist the armies of imperial China and, calling himself "father and hero," tried to make Kashgaria into an independent state based on Islam, until he died of poison in 1877.

"His tomb used to be here," says the Uighur caretaker of the mausoleum, pointing his finger at an unmarked point in the ground over which we walked. "There were too many tombs here and we wanted to plant some trees, so in 1978 the marker for Yakub Beg was removed, but his bones are still there, 2 meters deep." A Han official comes forward with a different explanation. "Yakub Beg was separatist. He played an awful historical role and people want to forget him."

Slowly they might indeed forget, for books on the history of Xinjiang before communist rule are not available; children in schools are taught nothing about it, and only at the university are students "allowed to discuss the negative role of bad elements like Yakub Beg," says Wu Dongyao, a Han official.

Unlike the Cultural Revolution and the attempt to force the minorities into a quick and often violent assimilation, the new policy seems to count on a slow and long-term process. Deng Xiaoping's way is to give the minorities more freedoms and let them choose willingly the path of assimilation.

In Kashgar today there are Uighur and Han schools and the Uighur family who decides to send a child to a Chinese school is obviously giving him a chance of a better education and later a better job. Yet this is still a difficult decision to make, for the dividing line between the two communities is very deep.

At the Sunday bazaar, among the colorful crowds of people who buy, eat, discuss, bargain and enjoy themselves, one does not see a single Chinese face. The smells, the dirt, the confusion of the bazaar are too much for the Hans. They prefer to do their shopping in the drab but orderly state-run supermarket which in Kashgar, as in the rest of China, is called "the shop of the 100 products," and where one can find the same thermos, the same spittoon, the same soap and cloth one finds in Shanghai or Guangzhou.

"They don't like what we like...they don't like us," comments a young Uighur who insists on saying "I speak Chinese but I am not Chinese." Whenever one talks to Uighurs without the presence of a Han, the conversation turns immediately to the Chinese. "They don't like sheep meat...they don't dance...they don't know how to sing... they...they." That "they" is the measure of the distance that still separates two peoples who are supposed to live together.

229

In fact they don't.

Kashgar is practically two cities and the crossroad between Liberation Road and People's Road is the dividing point: south of it live the Hans in their brick compounds, north of it live the Uighurs in their mud houses. There are a few "model" places where families of the two races live next to each other, but the division is there as well.

The Kashgar Grains Bureau, which is in charge of feeding the population of the city, has 1,500 employees who, according to the local guide, "coexist in peace and harmony." Yet, among the Han and Uighur families who live in a common compound, there has not been a single mixed marriage in over 30 years. The Hans do not speak Uighur, the Uighurs do not speak Han and "the common language is the language of socialism," explains Deputy Director Li Wukui with a touch of humor.

Underlying the difficult race relationship lies the fact that the Uighurs consider the Hans foreigners who have come to live in their land and that the Han, apart from some good cadres who mix with the Uighurs and have adapted themselves to local customs and habits, despise anything local. For the average Han, the Uighurs are an uncivilized, primitive people, and it is not uncommon to see a Han instinctively brushing himself off after having been touched accidentally by a Uighur on the street.

This Han sense of superiority toward the minorities is not new. Two centuries ago, after the Chinese armies had recovered Kashgar and had sent to Peking the head of the local rebel ruler together with his young widow, the Fragrant Concubine, Emperor Qian Long had large stone steles erected in this region inscribed with his imperial edict. "Hear you people...for generations you have behaved like thieves. The mighty have oppressed the weak, the many have oppressed the few...but the great Qing dynasty has been established...and this has been done by heaven." At that time, Chinese rule indeed brought order to Kashgar, and today Chinese rule, with Deng Xiaoping's reform policy, may bring prosperity to this city that seems to have been long forgotten.

Since 1949, when the Chinese communists arrived, not

much has changed in Kashgar. No major factory or industrial complex has been built, the city streets are still unpaved, peasants on the outskirts still do not have electricity and the promised railway that should have connected Kashgar with Urumqi and with Peking is still at Korla, 800 kilometers away. Other Chinese cities were tunneled to prepare them against an eventual Soviet attack; in Kashgar, so near to the Soviet border, no tunnels were dug. The Chinese probably thought that Kashgar was so vulnerable that they did not want to waste money and counted on the nearby desert as a natural defense against Soviet tanks.

Now, in view of the new international situation, the relaxation of tension with the Soviet Union, the reopening of the border, the revitalization of private trade, Kashgar is one of the foci of the plan to develop Xinjiang and exploit its resources. This will provide the Uighurs with an opportunity to get into the mainstream of Chinese life, but will also spell their slow weakening as a different race with a different culture. This is a fate faced by many of China's minorities.

The problem is in these simple figures: the minorities represent only 6.7 percent of the total Chinese population, but they live in 60 percent of the national territory. Moreover these very territories inhabited by the minorities are among the richest in China and have some of the largest untapped resources of the country.

Xinjiang has deposits of oil, coal, aluminum, manganese, uranium, nickel and gold. With the growing population pressure in the hinterland of China, it is logical that Peking should transfer masses of people to the underpopulated, unexploited minority areas.

Xinjiang, a region as big as half of India, is the most favorable choice. Unlike Tibet where altitude makes the resettlement of people from the plains very difficult, Xinjiang offers attractive climatic conditions for the Hans. It is certainly not by chance that recently, talking to a group of foreign journalists, Chinese Communist Party Secretary Hu Yaobang mentioned Xinjiang as one of the three areas of the world with great potential for development. The others are the Sahara region and the Amazon basin. Hu Yaobang said that Xinjiang could easily absorb 200 million people.

Today Xinjiang has only 14 million inhabitants of which 6.0 million are Uighur, 5.3 million are Han and 2.7 belong to other minorities. Since 1949, Peking has been sending Han settlers into Xinjiang. Recently this policy has been speeded up with the re-establishment of the Production and Construction Corps, a paramilitary force of demobilized troops, peasants, educated youth and technicians, sent to take part in major infrastructural projects and in opening virgin land. So far these masses of Han immigrants, in order to avoid excessive resentment among the minorities, have been kept away from the cities and areas traditionally inhabited by the Uighurs.

Some 40 kilometers east of Kashgar, already into the Takla Makan, is Ha No Yi, the House of the King, one of the famous cities buried by the desert after being abandoned with the decline of the Silk Road. One thousand years ago, 80,000 people lived here. Now one sees only a few stumps of the old walls sticking out of the ground, and handfuls of broken pieces of pottery surfacing in the sand.

"At the beginning of this century foreigners took away all the art treasure," says an official of the Kashgar administration. "This is what is left." What is left is now being taken away by the Hans. From behind the dunes one hears the noise of a bulldozer scraping the ground and loading piles and piles of earth into a big truck. "They use it as fertilizer. The best comes from where the stables used to be," says a young worker who observes the scene. "A few days ago a lot of bones and other things came out, but the peasants kept only the objects made of metal. Some were of gold."

The truck with its load of earth and traces of the old city disappears into the desert. Faraway in the haze of the heat, one sees the profiles of the barracks where the settlers live. Around them are the fields they reconquered from the sand which need to be manured. There are 60,000 Han immigrants living in the area. More and more will come and, although the liberal policies of Deng Xiaoping allow the minorities to have as many children as they like while the Hans are under the same one-child restriction as in the rest of the country, the

Uighurs are bound to be slowly outnumbered.

Since the presence of the new settlers means not only stronger dominance by the Han, but also progress and economic development in the region as well, the Uighurs will find it more and more difficult to resist assimilation.

Like other minorities trapped geographically between two powerful nations, the Uighurs have little choice. The idea of an independent Uighur state is out of the question, as is the idea of an independent Tibet. The Uighurs of Kashgar could theoretically cross the border and go to join the Uighurs living in the Soviet Union, as 60,000 Kazakhs from Xinjiang did in 1962. However, though they would have better living conditions, they would only trade one form of dominance for another.

The most likely choice is to join the Hans in the modernization of China and to prosper with them, becoming more and more like them. Some Uighur cadres have already renounced Islam and studied in the Party schools. More will come out of the crowds of Uighur boys and girls who, in their modern school uniforms and waving the red flag of the Communist Youth League, march together with Chinese children in front of the Id Kah Mosque every public holiday under the saddened eyes of old Uighur men and some veiled women.

The seven local cinemas are showing, in Chinese, the same movies as in the rest of China. The local TV station, which broadcasts, with a five-day delay, the national and international news from Peking, has only Chinese programs except for a news summary in Uighur on the weekend.

Kashgar itself is showing more and more the signs of that sinicization which has brought some progress as well. The new buildings of the town administration are in the usual socialist-Chinese style of the rest of the country. At the entrance of some schools, water gushes out of piles of stones as in the Suzhou gardens. On an island in the middle of a pleasant lake on the outskirts of the city, a small pagoda is about to be built. It will add just another bit of "Chinese flavor," as a young Uighur puts it, to the Kashgar mud skyline already dominated by the huge granite statue of Mao Zedong.

16

Kill a Chicken and Warn the Monkeys

The mass executions

A bullet in the back of the head is usually enough. If not, the policeman waits a few seconds and fires a second shot. This time into the heart of the condemned.

From the technical point of view, executions in China have been modernized. The victims are no longer sliced into 1,000 pieces before being beheaded as used to be the custom, yet most of the ritual has remained as in old times. A big crowd gathers in the main square, or in the sports stadium. The accused, hands tied behind their backs, their heads shaven, their eyes to the ground, are brought into the center of the arena, each with a poster hanging from his neck describing his "crime against the people." The public prosecutor makes his short speech. The judges listen to it, the crowds look on stunned, somebody shouts.

The "trial" does not last long. The accused are numerous and nobody has much time to waste. The sentence has been decided in advance anyway, and it is usually death.

The sentenced are packed into the back of an open truck and are carted around town to the beat of gongs and drums. This parade lasts quite a while, sometimes even hours, because everybody must have a chance to see and be frightened. A banner along the flank of the truck announces "we are protecting the lives and property of the people."

Once at the execution ground — in Peking this is an open field near the Marco Polo Bridge — the condemned are lined up and made to kneel. The executioner, wearing the uniform of the Public Security Bureau, goes by them, one by one, and fires at each with his pistol.

White posters with black print and the names of the condemned crossed out in red appear at market places announcing that the executions have taken place. Clusters of people gathered in front of them read in silence the five or six lines dedicated to each case.

The campaign started in September 1983. A new penal code had hardly come into effect when the Standing Committee of the National People's Congress (the Chinese parliament) approved special legislation abrogating some of the provisions of the new law and lifting restrictions on sentencing people to death.

Under the new regulations, the time to instruct a case is reduced to three days, the accused is not notified in advance of the charges against him, and the sentence no longer needs the approval of the supreme court to be carried out. "Nowadays they can arrest you on Tuesday and execute you on Saturday," says a Peking youngster.

In addition to the 21 crimes which according to the penal code could bring a death sentence, seven more have been added...with retroactive effect. They include kidnapping, robbery and the "sale of women and children."

The Party press has given great prominence to this campaign against crime. In the first three months alone, 700,000 people were arrested. The population was encouraged to cooperate and the results were "excellent." The police received 440,000 spontaneous denunciations, mostly from peasants accusing their neighbors.

The number of people executed has been kept secret, but the estimates for the first three months are between 4,000 and 10,000. Popular reaction has been generally positive. "It was time that we got rid of a few rotten eggs, the town is cleaner without those bastards, now we can have some peace," are the most common comments one hears from the people.

The reasons for this consensus are obvious. During the past several years, with the launching of Deng's reforms, criminality has been constantly on the increase. In the evening people were afraid to go out and many crimes were going unpunished. According to official statistics, from 1980 to 1983 there were 40,000 murders in the whole of China, but the police were only able to catch 4,000 suspects.

The present wave of arrests and executions reassures the people that something is being done and — even more important — it pushes away from Deng Xiaoping the charge that criminality is a direct consequence of his liberalization policy and that he has done nothing to fight it.

"It had to happen to him too...," the people say. According to one of the rumors circulating in Peking, Deng Xiaoping decided on the anti-crime campaign after his car was ambushed and stopped on the way to the sea resort of Beidaihe. One of his bodyguards was killed, and he was really furious. According to another version, the anti-crime campaign started after the daughter of a vice-minister was assaulted in a Peking public toilet and wrote a letter to the Party announcing her determination to commit suicide in the middle of Tiananmen Square unless the culprit who had bitten her breast and buttocks was executed. He was indeed shot.

Crime has always existed in China. Even when Maoist authorities were swearing to foreign visitors that there were neither criminals nor prisons in the country and that people had nothing to fear, it was enough to glance at the bicycles and see that, though none of them had a light, all had big locks.

What is new is the sudden increase in the number of crimes (between 1978 and 1980 the rate has gone up by 60 percent) and the surfacing of phenomena such as corruption (particularly among officials) which had been considered eradicated. Police, much feared in the past, were accused of inefficiency. Frequent cases of high officials who had managed to protect their children or their relatives involved in major scandals caused the Party to lose prestige. Hence the need to show harshness and impartiality.

In October 1983, the nephew of the national hero Marshal Zhu De, together with three accomplices, all children of high cadres, were brought to trial in Tianjin and sentenced to death for robbery and rape. It is said that Zhu De's widow, grandmother of the accused and president of the Chinese Womens' Union, personally went to see Deng Xiaoping to beg him for mercy, but her request was turned down.

Though this and similar episodes are meant to demonstrate that "everybody is equal before the law," the anti-crime campaign and the way it is being conducted have only demonstrated that China is far from being a country ruled by law.

There is very little respect for legalities in the way people are arrested, tried and then sent to their graves with a bullet in the back of the head.

An internal Party document says that the campaign was launched with a slogan from Deng Xiaoping, "Arrest 100 and execute one." As if the campaign to execute people was like a campaign to plant trees, each province, each county and each city was given quotas for arresting and for executing people. In some places the local authorities, short of real criminals, ended up arresting the village fool and accusing him of rape just to meet the quota.

Even the Chinese Law Society has expressed doubt about the campaign, saying that the mass executions "are undermining the legal system which has just been established." Others have called it a "feudal form of revenge." The fact that most of the people executed are youngsters has led some people to think that this is a revenge by the old generation against the young for what they were made to suffer during the Cultural Revolution.

There is no doubt that the anti-crime campaign has been an opportunity, particularly in the countryside, to settle old accounts and for the police to take control of the population again. Respect for the law is not even seen as an issue by the people in power in China.

In most cases the punishment is not commensurate with the crime. Yang Wu was an 18-year-old worker in the Shijiazhuang Number Two Cotton Mill near Peking. In July he met a girl older than himself and became her lover. After a quarrel, she went to the police and accused him of raping her. Yang Wu was arrested and sentenced to eight years in jail. According to a witness at the trial, when the judge passed the sentence Yang Wu said, "I don't accept this." The judge told him he could appeal, but Yang said that would not help. The only thing he could do would be to wait eight years and then take revenge by killing the girl.

The court then reopened the case and concluded that "Yang Wu is a dangerous element and that he ought to be killed immediately." He was, and the poster announcing his execution only said, "...in the summer he stopped a woman on the street and a few days later he raped her."

Another interesting episode of the anti-crime campaign happened in Hangzhou. The local police wanted to arrest some prostitutes, but were not sure how to recognize prostitutes from other women. Here is how it was done. One evening in a crowded cinema of Hangzhou in the middle of a performance, the lights went on and the loudspeakers announced that all men should leave the auditorium. The men did so. Then the loudspeaker said "all the women wearing trousers out." So they left too. The women wearing skirts were then put up against a wall and asked to lift up their skirts. Those who had no underwear were all arrested for prostitution. "The system proved to be a very effective way to catch hidden prostitutes," wrote the local paper.

According to the posters in various parts of the country, a large number of the people being executed are youngsters (some under 20 years of age) who were known to be unemployed and have a petty crime record.

Chinese authorities refuse any suggestion that among the thousands of people executed in the course of the anti-crime campaign, there might be people who were arrested for political reasons. Yet the Dalai Lama from his exile in India denounced the execution in Lhasa of five Tibetans who according to him were sentenced only for being "dissidents" and for urging independence for Tibet.

A man was executed in Tianjin for having distributed leaflets in a main square of the city. The poster announcing his execution said that he was "the leader of a reactionary secret society making propaganda against the socialist system."

Undoubtedly, the campaign has to do more with politics than with the law. The fact that Deng launched the campaign against criminals at the same time as he announced a major purge within the Party suggests that the execution of a few thousand young people, whether criminals or not, was also a last warning to those who still dared oppose from the "left" his liberalization policies.

The Chinese, who have an appropriate proverb for every occasion, now quote one that says, "Kill a chicken to warn the monkeys."

17

The Chinese Are Not Yet Accustomed to Living Without an Emperor

The campaign against western influence

At the corner of Wangfujing Street and the Avenue of Eternal Peace, just across from the Peking Hotel, the huge solemn face of Mao Zedong looms over the endless stream of bicycles and cars. Further south, at the Crossroad of the Pearls, another larger-than-life, intense, younger Mao is portrayed on a wall directing a major battle of the Long March. These are posters for the two new films released for the 90th anniversary of the Great Helmsman's birthday, but to the ordinary Chinese in the street the message is not lost: Mao is back in fashion again.

After having been the unnamed but real defendant in the trial of the Gang of Four, after being blamed for the mistakes of the Cultural Revolution in a major Party document, with all his portraits removed from all the public buildings of China (except from the main gate of the Forbidden City); and after having become almost a non-person with his mausoleum closed most of the time, his name never mentioned, his anniversaries forgotten, Mao is suddenly talked about again.

His birthday was marked by special celebrations, including the release of those two films (one, simply called *Mao Zedong*, is a selection of newsreels about his life; the other is a feature film called *The Four Crossings of the River*), his birthplace has been restored and the local museum reopened. Mao's thought was the theme of an eight-day seminar held in Nanning, and his military theories have been praised in the official press. Many of Mao's writings (including those that were popular during the sixties and were included in the "little red book") are again on the list of required reading for Communist Party members, and a nationwide campaign against "spiritual pollution" was launched with some of the same overtones (anti-intellectualism) and some of the same targets (bourgeois values and western influences) typical of Mao's Cultural Revolution.

A revival of Maoism? "Not at all. Rather, a revision of Maoism," says a western observer. "It is Deng Xiaoping now telling China what Mao really said, and using it for his own purposes." After eight years in power Deng's purposes are quite simple:
— to consolidate his hold on the Party and the country;
— to prepare for a smooth succession for the two men he has chosen to follow him at the top, Hu Yaobang in the Party and Zhao Ziyang in the government.

The experience of the past eight years has shown Deng that these goals cannot be achieved without maintaining a continuity, keeping a link between the past and the future, and this link can only be Mao.

The road of de-Maoization, which Deng attempted for a while, has proved full of uncertainties and dangers. To open up one dogma to discussion automatically invites the questioning of all dogmas. To look for the reasons of some errors would have necessarily led to the uncovering of other errors. If Mao was responsible for the Cultural Revolution and its misdeeds, then he was equally responsible for the Great Leap Forward and the Anti-Rightist Campaign, with all their madness and injustice.

What would be left of the much-praised New China which was inaugurated in 1949, if all that had been undertaken since 1957 was now to be considered, in one way or the other, a "mistake?" What would be salvaged of the "farsighted and always correct line of the Communist Party?" Furthermore, if the past was so full of "mistakes," how could one assure the people that the present and particularly the future would be different?

To deprive the peasants of Mao, whom for three decades they had adored as the one who had liberated them, was to take enormous risks. After all, Mao was and cannot but remain the founder of the People's Republic of China, the glue that keeps New China together.

It is for this reason that Deng stopped the de-Maoization,

and now presents himself not as the one who destroys, but as the one who continues and enriches Maoism.

Without falling into the trap of a new personality cult, as Hua Guofeng had done (changing even his hair style so as to look like Mao), Deng allows his public image to recall and hint at Mao. In Shanghai, a poster was printed in which Deng towers over crowds of soldiers and technicians exactly as Mao did in the posters of the Cultural Revolution. All the country's newspapers carried a picture of Deng swimming in the ocean exactly like the famous one of Mao swimming across the Yangtze River.

"China is not yet accustomed to living without an emperor," says a Chinese writer. Deng is now filling the vacuum left by Mao. He is the new emperor, and as the emperors of the past with their predecessors, Deng now writes with his own calligraphy the commemorative plaque for Mao's birthplace.

Like Mao he has published his selected works, a book which is now the gospel for China's future. Forty million copies have been printed and distributed. What he writes is the denial of Maoism, yet he lets himself be praised at the ideological seminars as "a man with a profound understanding of Marxism–Leninism and Mao Zedong-thought, who has made an outstanding contribution in upholding and enriching Mao Zedong-thought." Liao Gailong, one of the top Party thinkers, has gone on record as saying that the "upholding and enriching of Mao's thought" is Deng's major contribution to communist ideology. Thus he and nobody else (please forget Hua Guofeng!) is the real successor of Mao.

Which Mao? Naturally the Mao that suits Deng Xiaoping, the Mao of the fifties and not of the Cultural Revolution (the recent film about Mao's life has not a single shot of the Great Helmsman reviewing the Red Guards), the Mao who in 1957 told all Party members they should learn materialist dialectics from Deng, and who again in 1975 said Deng was "a very rare talented person, very strong in ideology" (both episodes are recalled in an article in *Ban Yue Tan* magazine).

By projecting a revised Mao and casting himself as Mao's ideological upholder and enricher, Deng Xiaoping parries attacks from the left and takes the major weapon from the hands of his potential opponents on that side of the political spectrum.

In today's China, the left may be decapitated, but it still exists. The orthodox Maoists have lost their potential rallying points at the top of the Party with Jiang Qing in jail, Yeh Jianying dying, and Hua Guofeng in the hospital most of the time, yet many of them are still in the Party structure at middle and lower levels. There they can obstruct Deng's policies. They can slow down reforms, and they remain potential protagonists of an eventual radical comeback.

On his right, Deng has another kind of enemy which must be dealt with as well. So against the one he launched the Rectification Campaign and against the other the Spiritual Pollution Campaign. The two campaigns proceed at the same time, step by step, because the former are happy with what Deng does to the latter and he can hope to leave a Dengist China when he dies. "Deng is now stronger than Mao ever was at the height of his power," says an American sinologist. While the campaign against the left is a purge of people ("we have to identify the elements who persist in obstructing and damaging the Party," writes the *People's Daily*), the campaign against the right is more a purge of ideas. The excuse is an appeal for higher morality.

"We must fight all that is obscene, barbarian, vulgar and reactionary," declaims Deng Liqun, head of the Party propaganda apparatus and a great crusader in this new battle.

Some obscenity is rather obvious. A girl in Shanghai gave a roll of film to a photo shop to be developed and was arrested. In the darkroom some of the shots of the girl with her boyfriend turned out to be indecent. A singer in a Guangzhou hotel was stopped in the middle of her show, fined and sent home. Her tight skirt showed too much of her legs. A group of youngsters in Xian were jailed because they organized exclusive porno shows using a video cassette recorder, charging 20 yuan for entrance tickets. Yet also "obscene" was a young writer who maintained that art is a means of personal expression, "obscene" was a student who said that a real democracy cannot be a one-party system, "obscene" were some intellectuals who found Sartre more interesting than Marx.

The police in Sichuan found that some 1,000 books in the local library were "vulgar" and confiscated them. The authorities in Hubei found that six of the 21 regular publications born after the fall of the Gang of Four were of "low quality" and must be banned.

Spiritual Pollution is a disease which can affect anyone and can manifest itself in surprising forms. In Tibet this pest has not been stopped by "lofty mountains and the great rivers;" it has appeared as a resurrection of superstition and religion. In Ningxia it has shown up in some advertisements publicizing foreign goods; in Henan it was revealed by the fact that some people "frenziedly advocate Jean-Paul Sartre's existentialism and even think that Sartre is more brilliant than Marx," as Henan radio reported.

Even athletes, especially those "who have come into contact with the international community and the decadent ideology and the capitalist mode of life," have shown signs of spiritual pollution.

According to the official press, the literary and artistic circles of the country have been hit hardest by the spreading disease. Even science fiction has come under attack because "robots and outer space creatures have been utilized to cast doubt on Party policies and socialism" (the conclusion of a conference held in Shanghai on the subject).

In the wake of the campaign against spiritual pollution, a visiting Portuguese ballet company was asked to change portions of their show considered "too modernistic," employees of Peking Municipality had to cut their mustaches, a barber was praised for having refused to give perms to men, while scores of young people have been put through re-education for wearing clothes considered too eccentric.

"When I get dressed in the morning I always wonder whether I am going to be called 'polluted' by my leaders," says a young Peking salesgirl.

The campaign even produced casualties at the higher echelons of communist society. So far, two top editors of the *People's Daily*, one a close associate of Deng and one of his regular bridge partners, the other responsible for ideological work in the Party paper, have lost their jobs. The writer Bai Hua, famous for his works criticizing Mao, has come under attack for "representing a political line that runs contrary to socialism." A prominent Party leader, watchdog of artists and writers, has been forced to make public self-criticism for having said that there is alienation even under socialism.

Pornography, long hair, robots, religion, Freud, etc., etc. But what is it that Deng Xiaoping really wants?

"Deng has opened the window to let fresh air in and now he wants to get rid of the flies that have come with it," jokes an American observer.

In reality what worries Deng and potentially threatens the rule of the Communist Party in China is more than the "flies" that have come in with the opening of the country to western goods, western technology, western tourists and habits and a few new ideas. It is a fact that the Party with all its campaigns and counter-campaigns, with total Maoism first and attempted de-Maoization later, feels that its legitimacy for ruling the country is being challenged.

Some time ago this problem was called a crisis of confidence and was blamed on the Cultural Revolution and the confusion created by the radicals. Now it is called spiritual pollution and is blamed on the bad influence of the west which the open door policy has allowed into the country.

Basically the danger is the same. The danger is that the Communist Party has lost the prestige it used to enjoy, that it no longer commands the respect of the people, that communism in itself is seen by more and more people as a lofty, unattainable dream.

In the eyes of old revolutionaries such as Deng Xiaoping, today's Chinese society is far from what it was immediately after Liberation and up to the early sixties. In that golden age just a few decades ago, people were sincerely dedicated to the reconstruction of the country. They were ready to make all kinds of sacrifices for the motherland and for the revolution.

Today the People's Liberation Army no longer has a huge number of volunteers from whom to choose its recruits, and the Party itself has difficulty getting the best people into its ranks. It has to be careful of the many people who want to join out of sheer opportunism. Young people are disaffected, society seems to have lost its former cohesiveness. Crime has spread, the divorce rate is increasing and the Party itself has been affected by the general disillusionment. Thirty percent of the economic criminals convicted in the recent campaign were Party members on the take. Superstitions, forcibly suppressed for three decades, have surfaced again among the masses, and religion seems to have a new appeal even among young people who have been bred and educated in socialist schools. Some intellectuals have started to study these facts. Some have spoken of alienation.

On the centennial anniversary of Marx's death, Zhou Yang, president of the Writers and Artists Federation, wrote in the *People's Daily* that humanism and communism must be compatible, that often Marxism forgets the value of the human being and that, although socialist society has advantages over the capitalist ones, "even socialism is affected by alienation." Better recognize the fact and face it, said Zhou Yang.

The article provoked a storm. The central propaganda department of the Party directed other periodicals not to reprint it. The "theory of human nature" and the idea that "man is the starting point of Marxism" were attacked as the causes of all the "bad literature" where, as the popular theoretical paper *Guang Ming Daily* put it, one reads about "free democracy, individual emancipation, individual struggle, anarchism, nihilism and negative world-weariness."

After eight months, Zhou Yang was forced to withdraw what he had said. "I was not modest and cautious enough. It was particularly improper for me to have stubbornly adhered to my views after some comrades had voiced different opinions...," he said in self-criticism. Other intellectuals followed. The faculty of philosophy at Fudan University in Shanghai confessed to having propagated "ideas inconsistent with some basic principles of Marxism," and the Party committee of the faculty committed itself publicly to building "in the minds of teachers and students a great wall to resist spiritual pollution."

Bai Hua, author of the banned film *Bitter Love* (in which the protagonist makes the now famous comment, "I love the motherland, but does the motherland love me?''), was attacked as "unsocialist" and "unpatriotic" in the *Press Digest Magazine.* The woman writer Ding Ling, who has now become a staunch defender of Party orthodoxy but has not taken up her pen to write a good novel for the last 20 years, took it up to condemn artists who felt that "the less control the Party has over culture the better." For her that was heresy. The Party must have control over all literary production.

The old tactics of having one intellectual accuse another, one writer attack another, have started to surface again. "Some people have tried to shake off the Party leadership by saying that literature and art should be developed freely, like a runaway horse," said a Party boss in Anhui Province during a rally to denounce spiritual pollution. In his words, spiritual pollution means "to spread decadent ideas of the bourgeoisie and other exploiting classes and to fan distrust of socialism, communism and the Communist Party leadership."

Even workers are affected by this spiritual pollution. The *Workers' Daily* pointed out how dangerous this trend is. "Workers pay respect to capitalist countries," it says, "because they develop quickly and their standards of living are higher than those in socialist countries."

The *People's Daily* blamed pollution coming from the west for "the national inferiority complex" from which China is at the moment allegedly suffering.

In reply, Peking launched an "international education campaign" to counter the "blind faith in foreign things" spreading among young people, which has caused Chinese people "to look down on people from poor countries and to behave disgracefully in their contact with foreigners."

The pledge used by the Communist Youth League for its members says: "I pledge to love the country, the Chinese Communist Party, the socialist system...to be hardworking, thrifty...to practice birth control, to keep weddings and funerals simple and not to act humbly in front of foreigners."

That is what it is all about. With Mao's death and the coup d'etat against the so-called Gang of Four, Deng Xiaoping had "to give the people some respite," as the saying went, in order to make himself popular. He had to loosen some controls and allow for a certain freedom of expression (Democracy Wall and Peking Spring), which helped him inasmuch as it attacked the ultra-leftists.

This loosening of control, however, unleashed doubts and second thoughts within the Communist Party itself, and threatened the very survival of the Party as the leading body in the country.

This is why writers wanting to deal with human problems, university professors discussing existentialism, or students wanting a multi-party democracy are now as "obscene" as the porno video cassette smugglers or the girl who has her picture taken in an intimate situation with her fiancé. The responsibility for all this lies, in a manner of speaking, with the western influence which the open door policy allowed to enter China.

After a few weeks of verbal violence, however, the anti-pollution campaign, which was about to throw the country into a new form of terror strongly reminiscent of the Cultural Revolution, was hushed up and set aside.

But the fact that it was launched and that the country's top leaders approved of it shows that the witch hunt mentality still exists, and that the mechanism of repression is still there, ready to be reactivated at any time.

Deng cannot renounce the policy of opening up to the outside world, for this is the only chance he has to win the struggle of modernization and raise the people's living standards. Yet, from time to time he will have to squash the "flies" of free thinking and of westernization that come with it.

The campaign against spiritual pollution was nothing but a warning for all leaders in the new Forbidden City to heed.

Prime Minister Zhao Ziyang, who loves to wear western clothes and is known to take along a number of good suits and some 20 different ties when he goes on state visits abroad, is careful enough to don, once in a while, the classic Mao jacket at Party conferences.

18

...And Now Let's Start with Your Re-education

My expulsion from the People's Republic of China

"**C**onfess, confess your crimes and the People's government will treat you leniently. If you hide anything, the punishment will be very severe.... Confess! It is for your own good. Think about your future. Confess!"

Five Chinese policemen in blue uniforms are staring at me and the metallic voice of the interrogator reaches my ear, hour after hour, as from a distance.

"Confess! We know your crimes. The masses have been watching you for a long time," says the second interrogator.

I think of books I read long ago: *Prisoner of Mao*, by Jean Pasqualini, the Frenchman who spent seven years in Chinese jails; *Hostage in Peking*, by Anthony Grey, the British journalist who was kept for 26 months in solitary confinement. But this is not the past, this is not China of the Gang of Four. It is now, 1984. And it is not them, the others, it is me. Inwardly I smile at the thought of me, now, in Peking, *Hostage of Deng Xiaoping*?

"What crimes?" I ask.

"You know your crimes and you had better confess them in time. If you confess, we can help you. We are policemen of the People's Republic of China and it is our duty to help you with your re-education. Speak up. Don't beat about the bush. Confess!"

It all started on February 1, on my way out of China bound for Macao and Hong Kong. At the border post of Gongbei, the customs officials searched me from top to bottom and took away my talisman, a small Buddha which my wife had given me in 1975 after I had been captured and then released by the Khmer Rouge in Cambodia.

That small figure had crossed the border in both directions many times. I was given a receipt and was told to go and get it back in Peking.

A week later I flew back to Peking. At the airport all my bags were again thoroughly searched. The procedure lasted a long time and I now realize that that slowness was just an excuse to have all other passengers leave so that nobody would witness what was going to follow.

As I finally walked toward the exit, a policeman stopped me. "Are you Deng Tiannuo?" (my Chinese name is composed of a first character like the one of Deng Xiaoping, and two more meaning "promise from heaven").

"Yes, I am."

"Please follow me," he says.

We go to the first floor of the airport building, into a small room where I am asked to sit in an armchair. Two policemen take up position in front of me and watch me.

"Can I make a telephone call?" I ask. The answer: there is no telephone.

One hour goes by before a tall, bony officer with thick glasses over a crooked nose enters the room, slowly takes out of his pocket a small piece of paper (I notice at the bottom of it the big red seal of an official document) and prepares to read it. My automatic reaction is to go for a notebook and a pen. "Put that away! This is not the time to take notes!" he shouts.

"I am a journalist," I say.

"What journalist?" he laughs. "You are a criminal. Sit down." He holds the paper with both hands and, as if it were a proclamation of war, he recites, "Deng Tiannuo... in the name of the People's government, according to article 38 of the Code of Penal Procedure of the People's Republic of China, I declare you detained for interrogation. I am instructed to take you to the Peking Public Security Bureau. From now on you have to follow my orders."

He shows me the warrant, he points with his finger at the signature of the Peking commander of public security and asks me to countersign it. I refuse: "First I must call either the Italian or the German embassy."

I am told I am prohibited from all contacts with the outside world and that if I insist on not signing the document

I only aggravate my situation. For that I shall be more severely punished. Still I refuse. Half a dozen policemen accompany me. We walk by the empty taxi stand where there are various telephones and I try to reach one. A strong hand drags me away.

Squeezed between two policemen on the back seat of a black Mercedes with drawn curtains, I am taken to Peking and the long silent ride along the ghostly streets of the city at night excites thoughts and nightmares.

I have been in China for four years now and I have heard many horror stories about prisoners of the dreaded Public Security Police, stories of people who for minor infractions or none at all disappear for two or more years into some labor camp, without having even seen a judge or a courtroom.

Disappear. Disappear. This word constantly rings in my mind. Nobody has seen me. Nobody knows I have been detained.

Before reaching Tiananmen Square, the car turns north into Bei Shi Zi Street and enters the courtyard of what used to be the residence of a princely family and is now the headquarters of the Public Security Bureau/Foreigners Section. In the reception room with carpet, armchairs and the usual oil painting of the Great Wall, some cups of tea are on the table, but none for me.

Policemen come and go. Some just come in to have a look at the foreigner. They whisper disquieting secrets into each other's ears and go away.

What can they accuse me of? I know that some of my articles about China have created problems with the government: my story about Tibet had "angered many officials," said a former government spokesman. Last year, after *Der Spiegel* published a series of articles about the destruction of Peking, the information department of the Foreign Ministry had called me in and, "in the name of the German masses who had protested against such a distortion of the Chinese reality," I was reprimanded and warned. I now know that some officials never believed that the article by my children about their experiences in a Chinese school had been written without my help. I know that at the end of last year the Foreign Ministry, because of my writing, had considered not renewing my visa as a resident correspondent. Yet, after an open and very friendly conversation at the Foreign Ministry, on January 17 the matter was clarified and my visa renewed for another year.

So, how can the same authorities mount something against me just two weeks afterwards? Or perhaps it is not the same authorities, but rather the Ministry for Public Security which, unhappy about the decision of the Foreign Ministry, is trying to get me out of China by its own methods? The usual struggle between moderates and radicals?

A group of policemen enters the room and takes up position in front of me. A young man places some sheets of paper on the table and gets ready to write. Next to my bony interrogator another one sits down with an unsmiling round face. The bony one: "What is your name?"

"You can read it yourself," and I give him my passport.

"What is your Chinese name?"

I hand him my Chinese journalist identity card and both documents disappear into the black plastic purse that he keeps caressing as if it contained all his secret weapons against me. Indeed. Soon another small sheet of paper with a red seal, like the first one, comes out of the purse: a second warrant, this one for "the search of Deng Tiannuo and the search of his residence."

Again I am asked to sign. Again I refuse. But while the paper lies in front of me, I notice that the date on it is January 20, three days after my visa had been renewed. It looks indeed like a move of the police against the decision of the Foreign Ministry.

A young strong policeman comes up to me and frisks me all over. The contents of my pockets are spread on the table, that of my suitcase and two bags all over the floor. Every paper is checked. Everything written in Chinese, including some addresses of Chinese people, is put aside.

At 1:45 a.m. on February 9, sandwiched again between two policemen in the back seat of the Mercedes, I am driven into the diplomatic compound where I live. On the way there the bony interrogator turns toward me from the front seat of the car and says, "so far your detention has been kept secret and we don't want to give it any publicity. We think of your reputation; we don't want you to lose your job. Now we shall go into your apartment and we shall do it quietly. We do not want to attract attention, we do not want to wake up your neighbors. We count on your cooperation.''

I, on the contrary, count on the hope that somebody will see me. But when we arrive in front of the main door of the house where I live there is not a single soul in sight, the courtyard is quiet and all the windows black, with the exception of two on the highest floor. But who lives there?

Again I ask to call the embassy from the telephone which in every lift is used by the attendant to inform the Public Security Bureau whenever a Chinese visitor enters a foreigner's flat. As an answer I am grabbed under my arms and pushed toward the door. Behind me, among the many policemen, some of whom are stepping out of the cars that have followed ours with big black plastic suitcases, I see a TV team and two photographers getting ready with their flashes. I think of a trap, of a frame-up in which kilos of heroin could suddenly be found under my bed, and I do what I have been planning to do all along. "Help...Help...I am Terzani...I am a journalist...Help!" I yell at the top of my voice.

All the policemen jump on me. One tries to close my mouth and his hand gets between my teeth...one tries to grab me between the legs, many hands grab my hair and twist my head. I feel a couple of blows on my shoulder, but I keep screaming. Called in by the interrogator, the lift attendants of my block and the one next to mine come to reinforce the police. So do the three employees of the post office doing their night shift. All of them together try to push me back into the car, but I manage to shut its door. But soon I am overpowered and a few seconds later I am pushed inside the Mercedes that speeds away, back to the police headquarters.

What I did not know at that point was that a western diplomat and his wife had been awakened by my screams, had gone to a window, had recognized my gray hair in the middle of the confusion of black shadows, and were already calling the Italian Embassy. Since the cars were not marked and the men in padded winter coats could not be recognized from afar as Chinese policemen, the first report was that I had been "beaten up and kidnapped by an unknown group of people."

Back at police headquarters, the bony interrogator was mad with rage. "You are a savage. Do you think you can scare us with your screams? We are the People's Public Security Police and we are afraid of nobody. We are afraid of nothing. We have all the means to make you do what we want. We could have used electric sticks, but we did not think it would be necessary."

When, one hour later, we leave again, I see policemen fixing truncheons to their belts. Two new strong men, assigned to control me, do not take any chances and immobilize me by twisting the fingers of both my hands.

When we step out of the car, a heavy padded coat is thrown over my head. My screams are muffled and like a parcel I am carried into my apartment. The first ones to enter are the photographers and the TV team who set up their flashes. The flat is flooded with light and I become the unwilling actor of a most absurd show.

The policemen push me around the house, force me to stand in front of my library, to sit in one of the armchairs, then at my writing desk. The search lasts from 3:00 a.m. to 6:15 a.m. More than 20 people move around the apartment. Not a single object is left unturned. Drawers are emptied, books are opened, photos, dossiers, address books (one filled with the names of all the people I know in China) are examined. Lamps are dismantled and looked at from the inside, and I am taken here and there to be filmed in front of the evidence of "my crimes," which slowly pile up on the dining table.

When the inventory is made, 64 items are listed, besides 16 family photos and pictures of artistic objects and statues that I had taken in Chinese museums. In three big bags the whole loot is carried away. Among it: a poster of Mao Zedong and Hua Guofeng, printed in China in 1980, on which I had recently pinned a small crucifix which I had bought as a souvenir in the Buddhist temple of Shaolin in Henan Province; a postcard with the reproduction of the Mona Lisa, whose face had been substituted by that of Mao (the postcard had been sent to me by a European colleague); seven buttons in soapstone; a newly made incense burner; a few small valueless bronze Buddhas which I had on a house altar; three small old bronze figures from my writing desk; a poster of a Tibetan tanka; a wooden turtle from Thailand; a silver box from Laos; a stone rubbing from Cambodia; two Chinese vases; a lock; three cricket cages (I asked whether the crickets, which had continued to chirp peacefully during the whole operation, could be saved from confiscation, and this request was granted); and a water color painting done by my children for my 43rd birthday depicting me as "Emperor Deng Tiannuo," flanked by the first ideograms Folco and Saskia had learnt to write in their Chinese school — "Long Live the Communist Party of China."

When we returned to police headquarters, Peking was coming to life. The first joggers were running along the streets and I thought of the old man teaching taijiquan in the Park of the Sun. This morning I would miss his lesson.

Interrogation goes on, hour after hour. The bony interrogator and the round-faced one take turns. I continue to refuse any cooperation. Once in a while I am given "time to reflect."

In these pauses some "friendly" policemen come in. One talks to me in French, another one in English, one in Spanish, one in German. They all give me some "personal" advice. "Confess. Sign the documents...It is better for you." Then again come the "tough" interrogators with their threats and insinuations. "There is no point in resisting...we know everything...we have been told by...."

One knows that this is a trick as old as the police, yet one cannot avoid reviewing mentally one's friends and thinking that potentially they could all be traitors. I think of the Chinese address book found in my desk and I figure out how many of those people could be blackmailed into testifying against me, into accusing me of the most terrible crimes.

The world is far away. I look through the window at the branches of a tree against the gray sky of Peking and I imagine all the Chinese I know soon being interrogated like me.

Suddenly I feel as they must feel. I feel as a Chinese must feel in front of the police: desperate, with no ground to stand on, no law to quote, no rights to invoke, left just with the possibility to confess and to deliver himself into the hands of his "savior."

Finally as a Chinese. This thought, oddly, makes me happy. Foreigners in China rarely get near the Chinese, for they are confined behind the walls that have been built purposely to keep them separated. The foreigners live in special western-style apartments, eat in special restaurants, travel in special train compartments and stay in special hotels, always guided, chaperoned, by special Chinese whose job is that of the "barbarian handler."

As foreigners, we live in China as if on a merry-go-round that keeps us away from the realities of local life. Each time we try to step down, in order to have a normal relationship with a normal Chinese, each time we go to his house or for a walk with him, the invisible wall comes up.

Protected by privileges, we foreigners have no real opportunity to experience what a Chinese dreams or fears. But here is my chance. All of a sudden a small window has been opened for me on an important aspect of Chinese life: the relationship of the citizen with the People's police; the relationship of the common man with the established power. I have been swallowed inside the belly of the whale and I am finally able to get near that heart of darkness which is so much part of life.in this country.

After 19 hours of detention, I am finally brought in front of two Italian diplomats who look worriedly at my torn coat. Only now my charges are formally being announced:
— Slander of Chairman Mao and the Communist Party of China (a "counter-revolutionary act," says one of the interrogators at one point). Evidence: the poster of Mao with the crucifix; the postcard of Mona Lisa; and the painting of my children.
— Acquiring privately and possessing "important Chinese cultural relics." Evidence: the sundry things found in my flat which, like many other foreigners, I bought mainly at bird and cricket markets.
— Transporting "national treasures" out of the country. Evidence: the small Buddha that my wife had given me

as a talisman nine years earlier.

The choice I am given is simple: either I sign the two warrants, the inventory of the search, the protocols of the interrogations and I write a "confession," or I shall be arrested and transferred to a Chinese prison.

I have already started to feel like a Chinese and I find it quite easy to decide to behave like a Chinese. In many years in China I have learned that here bending is a virtue and stubbornness a crime. So I sign the documents and draft a statement. The discussion over its text lasts a while. The security official wants to call it my "confession;" I want to call it my "statement." We agree on my "mistake." Its main point:

"I, the undersigned Tiziano Terzani, known in China as Deng Tiannuo, declare that I was indeed in the possession of a few Chinese antiquities acquired privately. I understand that certain items found in my house are considered offensive by the Chinese people. I am sorry for these mistakes and I apologize for them."

At 6 p.m. on February 9, I am released, but my status is that of a "suspect under house arrest." My passport is kept by the police and I am told not to leave the Peking area but to remain at the disposal of the Public Security Bureau for further interrogation. I return to my ransacked flat.

The next day I am summoned for interrogation in the afternoon. Same room, same policemen.

"And now we start with your re-education," announces the bony interrogator, while another one is taking notes. "Your attitude has changed after the first few hours; you have made some progress and we will help you to make more. Now tell us everything, tell us about your thoughts. Don't hide anything from us."

Various laws and regulations are read to me, with a crescendo of punishments my crimes could entail, from a fine of a few yuan, to 10 years and even life imprisonment. There is no sense in arguing and I apologize for what, in their words, I had done wrong.

"Your attitude has improved," the bony interrogator tells me with a complacent smile. With my "constant progress" comes constant rewards. During the first night I was not given anything to drink and, when a young policeman had tried to offer me one of his cigarettes, it was snatched from my hand and he was expelled from the room, never to be seen again.

During the second session of re-education I am offered boiled water ("white tea" as the Chinese call it); at the third session, a steaming cup of real tea is put in front of me.

During the interrogation I continue to behave like a Chinese, but realize that in this way I lose my European background. The German ambassador, Mr Guenther Schoedel, who had returned from Bonn on March 13 and was fully informed, waits for three days before he gets in touch with me.

There are comic moments.

"Why did you put that inscription, 'Long Live the Communist Party of China,' in your bathroom?" asks the bony interrogator.

"It was not just an inscription. It was a cartoon of myself drawn by my children...," I explain. "I could not throw it away and did not want it in the other rooms."

"But your apartment is big, very big...," says the bony interrogator. "Why did you choose the bathroom? You must have had special intentions to put that inscription in the bathroom."

Again I explain, again he insists, hour after hour, "Why the bathroom, why the bathroom?"

There are still moments of tension.

"Where did you buy that Tibetan tanka we found in your home?"

"It is not a tanka, it is a poster of a tanka, printed in London. Look here, it says so on the back: 'Printed in London.' I bought it at the Victoria and Albert Museum for one or two pounds."

"You are a liar. Don't beat about the bush. Tell the truth. You bought it in Lhasa. When were you in Lhasa?"

"I was in Lhasa in September 1980, but I did not buy the poster there."

"You are lying and you know it!" My interrogator is not a fool, so why does he act in this way? Often in China the things one sees are but the shadows of things, and what to us looks like reality is in fact theater. It is likely, therefore, that the bony interrogator shouts and accuses me of slandering Mao or of buying a tanka in Tibet, while what he really means, what he is after, is something totally different. But what?

During all these days of interrogation and re-education, I feel, even at home, under constant surveillance. All my movements are monitored and strange happenings occur: one girl "student" whom I have never met asks me over the phone whether she can borrow a book from me; a man wants to change some money; twice a team of "workers" comes to my door wanting to repair a leaking tap — which is not leaking ("We have been notified...," says their leader).

The investigation into my case is obviously not over. More charges? "You should stop dressing like a Chinese in Peking and riding a bicycle," a Chinese friend said to me some time ago. "The police may think you are a spy!"

Could I be accused of espionage?

"You must know that there are foreigners who come to our country in order to commit acts of political and economic sabotage," the bony interrogator said at one point. In China, any document which is not printed in the official press is considered a state secret and the acquisition of such documents by foreigners may be considered spying. "Mei you, mei you..." (there are none), I heard a policeman whispering to the interrogator. That is probably what they are really looking for. Even the simple translation into Chinese of articles that originally appeared in the western press, including my own, is a state secret. But I have no such secrets in my files.

The theme of espionage, however, is not taken up again during my re-education. After the third session, the interrogator gives me as homework the task of drafting my self-criticism.

"Write precisely, don't hide anything. Describe sincerely your attitude, or you will have to write it again and again," he says. I have three days to deliver my homework.

For a Chinese of today, writing a self-criticism is quite a common affair. I have heard that students returning from two or three years in western universities have to spend up to six months writing essays about what they have seen, what they have done, what they have thought and felt while abroad.

Mao once described self-criticism as "a peculiarity of the Chinese Communist Party, something like dog meat; only after eating it can one realize how good it tastes."

Self-criticism probably is for a Chinese what the confession is for a Catholic: the only way to redemption. So I write 20 pages and entitle them *China and Me*. They deal with my long-standing relationship with this country, my early sympathy for Mao Zedong. I repeat how, like all other foreigners in China, I have bought small Chinese curios and how the little Buddha taken from me at the border post of Gongbei was acquired in 1975, and how, together with other artistic objects from other Asian countries, it came to Peking in 1980, when there was no law that obliged foreigners to declare the antiques they brought into the country.

When I turn in my homework, I realize the bony one has some new worries. "We have been told that the Italian embassy mentioned that you were beaten during the search of your apartment. Now you must write a statement saying that this is not true." This I refuse to do. I am then given two days to "reflect."

"It is our duty, as policemen, to help you in your re-education," says the interrogator. "But what you have written is not a self-criticism, it is a self-defence."

I must write the whole thing again. Besides, I am now confronted with another accusation. On the night of the search of my flat I obstructed the course of justice and damaged the black Mercedes. "We have pictures of the damage."

I write another five pages in which I explain again how each of the confiscated items had been bought, how much I had paid and what receipts I still have for which items. This time the interrogator is happy, but he gets angry when he realizes that his European pupil persists in not delivering a statement on the matter of the beating.

Then he finds a Chinese way out. He gives a long speech, which is registered into the protocol. Deng Tiannuo attempted to escape and, being "three times stronger than any of them," he had to be restrained with the use of some force.

"Where would I have escaped to?" I ask. "But you must at least admit that I could have thought that you wanted to escape,'' says the bony one. That I cannot deny him.

On February 17, both interrogators come into the room and I am told that they are now going to write a report for their leaders on my "progress," and that I have to wait for the decision. The typical Chinese solution for all problems, a compromise, seems to be at hand.

Days and weeks go by in uncertainty and I don't hear anything. Without a passport and without the possibility of defending myself publicly — that, they told me, would simply worsen my situation — I wait. On the morning of March 2 the telephone rings. "This is the Public Security Bureau. Come at 3 p.m. We shall tell you the decision about your case."

While I wait in the courtyard of the old palace with its red columns and gray roofs, I wish the little window that has been opened for me on the inside life of China will soon be shut again. Same room. Same policemen. Displayed on the three tables are the 64 objects seized in my flat.

"You can take notes," says the bony interrogator before he starts to read out. The main point: "According to articles 24, 27 and 28 of the Cultural Protection Law of the People's Republic of China, Deng Tiannuo has committed crimes. According to article 137 of the Criminal Code of the People's Republic of China, 'anyone who steals or exports valuable cultural relics shall be sentenced to no less than three and no more than 10 years of detention. A fine may be concurrently imposed. In grave cases the accused may be sentenced to life imprisonment.'

"We could have handled the case of Deng Tiannuo through normal legal procedure, but in consideration of good Sino-Italian, Sino-German relations, in consideration of the progress made by Deng Tiannuo in his re-education and his awareness of his crimes, we have decided to treat him with leniency." That means: confiscation of 25 "objects" and a fine of 2,000 yuan.

The final point: "Deng Tiannuo is no longer suited to live in China." The interrogator: "The evidence is in front of you. They are priceless objects of scientific, historical and cultural significance and symbols of our long history and culture." Among them is the tanka poster printed in London.

260

The insult to Mao is no longer mentioned. "For this crime we have forgiven you because you have very well repented," said the policeman. "We also pardoned you for the crime of 'obstructing the course of justice' due to the progress of your re-education."

"What does it mean that I am no longer suited to live in China?"

"It is easy to understand. It means you must leave China as soon as possible," says the bony interrogator. Then he continues to read from his piece of paper. "I want to give you some personal advice. When you are out of China, don't try to play tricks and distort the facts because you will bear all responsibility for the consequences. We have had similar cases in the past, but we managed to deal with them. So much for today."

The next day I pay the 2,000 yuan and am given a receipt for the money. For the objects that have been confiscated, there is no receipt.

The Italian embassy asks for a list of the incriminating objects and a copy of the verdict. Both are refused. The German ambassador, Mr Guenther Schoedel, goes to the Foreign Ministry and asks to be shown the evidence of my crimes. He gets a refusal. The reason: "This would be an intolerable interference into the internal affairs of the Chinese Public Security Police."

I have not smuggled out of China any cultural or artistic treasure, nor have I confessed that I have done so in any of the documents that I have signed. I have admitted only to having bought objects which, to my knowledge of the law, it was legal to buy. Yet, now I am a criminal in China. What finesse!

In my articles, I had constantly criticized the communists for having destroyed China's old culture. Now I am described as a robber of that culture!

On March 3, I get my passport back so that I can purchase a plane ticket bound for Hong Kong. My press card I have to return to the information department of the Foreign Ministry.

On March 5, at dawn, I drive to the airport. I have left my

261

Chinese clothes at home. Once again I wear a tie. All forms I fill in in English, no longer in Chinese as I used to do, and I sign my name as "Terzani."

Deng Tiannuo no longer exists.

Index

267

269